D1191093

Thomas McGrath: Life and the Poem

Books by Thomas McGrath

Echoes inside the Labyrinth. New York: Thunder's Mouth Press, 1983.

The Gates of Ivory, the Gates of Horn. Chicago: Another Chicago Press, 1987 (reprint, with a new introduction by Frederick C. Stern; originally published in 1957 by Mainstream Publishers, New York).

Letter to an Imaginary Friend, Parts I & II. Chicago: Swallow Press, 1970 (distributed by Ohio University Press).

Letter to an Imaginary Friend, Parts III & IV. Port Townsend, Wash.: Copper Canyon Press, 1985.

Letters to Tomasito. James Perlman, ed. Minneapolis: Holy Cow! Press, 1977.

Longshot O'Leary Counsels Direct Action. Fred Whitehead, ed. Albuquerque: West End Press, 1983.

The Movie at the End of the World: Collected Poems. Chicago: Swallow Press, 1972 (distributed by Ohio University Press).

Passages toward the Dark. Port Townsend, Wash.: Copper Canyon Press, 1982.

Selected Poems, 1938-1988, edited and with an introduction by Sam Hamill. Port Townsend, Wash.: Copper Canyon Press, 1988.

Death Song. Port Townsend, Wash.: Copper Canyon Press, 1991.

Thomas McGrath: Life and the Poem

Edited by Reginald Gibbons and Terrence Des Pres

University of Illinois Press
Urbana and Chicago

Reprinted by arrangement with *TriQuarterly*, Northwestern University,
Evanston, Illinois
Manufactured in the United States of America
1 2 3 4 5 C P 5 4 3 2 1

This book is printed on acid-free paper.

Library of Congress Cataloging-in-Publication Data

Thomas McGrath : life and the poem / edited by Reginald Gibbons and
    Terrence Des Pres.
      p.   cm.
      "An expanded version of . . . a special issue of TriQuarterly
    published in fall 1987"—T.p. verso.
      Includes bibliographical references.
      ISBN 0-252-01852-4 (cl).—ISBN 0-252-06177-2 (pb)
      1. McGrath, Thomas, 1916-   . 2. Poets, American—20th Century—
    Interviews.   I. Gibbons, Reginald.   II. Des Pres, Terrence.
    PS3525.A24234Z89   1992
    811'.54—dc20   91-9239
                                                                                CIP

This book is an expanded version of *Thomas McGrath: Life and the Poem*,
a special issue of *TriQuarterly* published in fall 1987.

Contents

Notes on Contributors

Terrence Des Pres was the author of the renowned *The Survivor: An Anatomy of Life in the Death Camps* (Oxford University Press, 1976) and two other posthumous books, *Praises and Dispraises: Poetry and Politics, the 20th Century* (Viking, 1989) and *Writing into the World: Essays 1973–1987* (Viking, 1990). Before he died in 1987, Des Pres was at work with Reginald Gibbons on this volume devoted to Thomas McGrath, whom he included among the poets studied in *Praises and Dispraises*.

Roland Flint is the author of several volumes of poetry, most recently *Stubborn*, one of five selections in 1990 in the National Poetry Series, published by the University of Illinois Press.

Reginald Gibbons has published four volumes of poetry and many other works, including translation and criticism. His most recent poems are collected in *Maybe It Was So* (University of Chicago Press, 1991). Since 1981 he has been the editor of *TriQuarterly* magazine at Northwestern University.

Philip Levine has received many awards for his poetry, including the American Book Award for *Ashes: Poems Old and New* (Atheneum, 1980) and the Ruth Lilly Poetry Prize in 1987.

E. P. Thompson, the distinguished British social historian, author of *The Making of the English Working Class* (Vintage, 1963) and many other works, including a novel, *The Sykaos Papers* (Pantheon, 1988), has been a leader in the Campaign for Nuclear Disarmament and the Committee for European Nuclear Disarmament.

Joshua Weiner has published poetry and prose in *The Threepenny Review* and other journals.

Preface

Reginald Gibbons

Above and around the primary struggles of our age to establish and control political power—locally, nationally, and globally—there floats a set of smaller related contests about culture. But these smaller contests, which are often fought over our understanding of language, and therefore of literature, can influence the course of the larger affairs that determine many aspects of our lives. We are not accustomed to thinking that poetry plays any part in the larger contests, and at times we think that poetry should not, even if it could. And yet the power of imaginative writing, including poetry, to provide a path for our thinking about culture, society, and ourselves—usually years or decades or even generations after the works are written—is incontestable. In the entire history of poetry anthologies in English, we first find the long prophetic poems of William Blake solidly represented in American college anthologies of literature, and only after the social and political upheavals of the 1960s, when it became possible to understand what Blake was describing in his visionary poems, and possible, also, to hear the urgency in his voice, as well as to admire the originality, poetic power, and inventiveness of his work.

So, it seems to me, the work of Thomas McGrath may be read at some future date, when with either valedictory sadness or a new visionary energy, depending on how our world evolves, some readers will discover, in addition to McGrath's artistic mastery, that a profoundly humane social vision was implied in McGrath's poems about the range of human experience, from tragic suffering to love, in our own time. McGrath spans the historic transition of our nation from the community of shared farm labor "when work was a handclasp" to the corporate industrial power created by World War II ("the dry flowers going under the mechanic stone") and forward again to the economic and cultural depredations of late twentieth-century agribusiness ("in abandoned farmsites, the dark stays longer / In the closed parlor"). McGrath's poetic depiction of the world—and his critique of it—is both bitingly accurate as representation and poetically inventive and freewheeling.

Historically, the poets who have been most influential on cultural debates have included figures such as Samuel Taylor Coleridge and William Wordsworth, in discussions of the appropriate subjects of poetry and the appropriate language of poetry; Wilfred Owen and other poets of World War I, including Ezra Pound, in bringing into poetry a protest against the horrific reality of war ten years before it could be found in prose; T. S. Eliot, in setting the direction of mid-century literary criticism; and Adrienne Rich, in infusing contemporary poetry with a feminist agenda. In cases like these, where the debate and contention are found in the poems as well as in essays, poetry becomes more than the object of discussion: it poses its own questions. Thomas McGrath, although not yet a part of our still highly sanitized canon of poetry, filled his poems with similar questioning and critique of received, official culture, and he proposed in terms of the imagination alternative ways of looking at the realities of his century. In so doing, he wrote not only powerfully and memorably but also while looking outward at a very broad horizon of concerns and materials; in terms of his poetics, the breadth of McGrath's chosen horizon is reflected in his broad range of artistic strategies and poetic language. If it were only for his extraordinary and exuberant vocabulary, McGrath might be remembered as far outstripping most of his contemporaries.

His vivid and constantly surprising metaphors, of a sometimes surreal cast, and his visionary scenes, not only in *Letter to an Imaginary Friend* but also in many of the short poems, seem as fully imagined as Blake's. In fact, the characteristic power of McGrath's unusual liberation of the imagination is one of the great values in his poems. This value in and for itself, in addition to McGrath's many explicit poetic comments, in discursive or metaphorical language, on social and political life, is and will remain of primary importance in the evolution of our national culture. Of few other poets writing in our time can one say with conviction that his or her work enters and engages—thematically *and* poetically—the very contest over culture in which our self-understanding is continually being forged anew.

McGrath would probably have rejected the idea of individual talent, or even genius, that to my mind his poems demonstrate. And he was ruefully aware that the influence even of a poet of wide renown, which unfortunately he was not, remains small. But he also said that his own experience was not uncommon, and the broad political contours of "the American century" were there for other poets to see (from the farm populism of the late nineteenth century through war and depression and war again, to multinational state-subsidized corporatism, and all along the way, the first world's predatory behavior toward the third, the North's toward the South, and the manipulation of people of color). However, McGrath himself is one of the very few poets to have drawn into his work that historical sweep, and to have fashioned "representative moments" from the details of one life caught up in it. (Sterling A. Brown was another such poet, in a different way, as were Kenneth Fearing and Muriel Rukeyser; but these poets of stature are being forgotten—or have been repressed, as critic Cary Nelson has pointed out. And in their place some of our best-known poets have acquiesced in the critical devaluation of meaning and representation, and have confined themselves to ornament and confession.)

McGrath composed his *Letter to an Imaginary Friend* as what he called a "pseudo-autobiography." His moments are representative because in selecting them he was moved beyond a lyrical poetic self that chooses its moments of self-presentation more promiscuously and self-indulgently, following temperament rather than artistic project. McGrath imposed on himself the responsibility of an artistic discipline, of choosing his subjects more deliberately—at least some of the time (he left room, too, for the pure play of language and feeling: "I want to take everything that comes!" he said of the variety of his poems). His long poem, in addition to its idiosyncratic visionary flights, has a deep tint of history running through it. Therefore it participates, even if only obliquely, as a poem tends to do, in the ongoing debate about what life should be, how it is burdened with hardship and tragedy.

McGrath's poetic ambition to write about history, more grand than what our age allows in most of the poetry it has rewarded with preservation, did not in the least hold him back from an extraordinary display of poetic virtuosity. From the use throughout his writing career of meter and traditional poem-forms (which, as McGrath said slyly, he did like to "rotate" a little bit) to the long six-beat line he employed in *Letter* and elsewhere, to the utilization of haiku in his late works, McGrath was forever staging fresh poetic performances of uncanny skill and panache. The sheer vitality and rollicking humor of passages in *Letter*, from beginning to end of that poem, are unmatched in contemporary American poetry.

The present volume was intended in its original version to make a place for McGrath among his contemporaries. Living and publishing primarily in the Midwest, and adhering to his socially conscious artistic position, McGrath has been willfully overlooked by the book reviewers and critics and mainstream publishers—probably as much for his resolute regional allegiance to the "heartland" as for his political life (for which he was blacklisted as a teacher and a film writer during the McCarthy era). Even the *Nation*, which by its own standard of comment on culture (and on left culture, especially) should have been particularly responsive to McGrath's work, remained silent about it for most of his life, until its outside judges for the 1989 Lenore Marshall/Nation Award chose McGrath's *Selected Poems*.

It is time to begin to assess McGrath's poems with the urgency of response that failed him in his lifetime. This new edition of *Thomas McGrath: Life and the Poem* has an added purpose, for McGrath died in September 1990, and while one more volume of new poems has been published posthumously, his work is now over. If only to acknowledge his death, this volume needed to be expanded, for now it must also stand as a first memorial to McGrath. Accordingly, I have added a memoir of McGrath by Roland Flint, poet and fellow North Dakotan. Also, since this collection serves as a general introduction to McGrath's work, rather than a critical assessment, it has been enhanced with the addition of two more of McGrath's recent poems and his important late prose statement about poetics (originally from *Poetry East*, edited by Richard Jones, which published a special issue on McGrath in the fall of 1987 [no. 23/24]). Readers should also consult two other works on McGrath: the fall 1982 issue of *North Dakota Quarterly*, a festschrift of essays and poems, plus works by McGrath, edited by Fred Whitehead; and *The Revolutionary Poet in the United States: The Poetry of Thomas McGrath* (Columbia: University of Missouri Press, 1988), a collection of essays edited by Frederick C. Stern.

For Terrence Des Pres, who co-edited the original version of this volume but who died just before it was published, McGrath was the American poet whom he had imagined before he found him. As readers of Des Pres's posthumous *Praises and Dispraises: Poetry and Politics, the Twentieth Century* will already know, Des Pres considered McGrath the great example of what American poetry had for the most part unaccountably failed to become. McGrath's carnivalesque energy and scale, his social radicalism and his very American poetics answered Des Pres's critique of contemporary American poetry's involution, self-preoccupation and linguistic blandness. Des Pres would have been much pleased at this new edition, and would have mourned McGrath as deeply as his own untimely death was mourned, especially by those who looked to him for more of his impassioned, supremely intelligent criticism of poetry and contemporary American culture.

Thomas McGrath held that there are two kinds of poetry, which serve two different but related purposes. There is the "tactical," which aims to focus the imagination and the will on a particular and immediate problem or task—his favorite example was a native American hunting song that preceded the hunt for buffalo. And there is the "strategic," which aims to enlarge consciousness generally, to create new consciousness. (See his comments on "The Frontiers of Language" in the fall 1982 issue of the *North Dakota Review*.) His sense of these two different uses of poetry is part of his contribution to the ongoing evolution of culture, literature, and language. He said the great aim of the poet is to write a poem that can be both tactical and strategic, a "flying tiger" of a poem. *Letter* seems to me such a poem—it quickens one's response to the social and political dimensions of life around one; it deepens one's understanding of the perceptions, the psychological formation, the aspirations and ideals that unite the varied experience of boyhood and youth and manhood, labor and community, sex and love, vocation and lifework, of many places and many times; and it invigorates one's sensitivity to language and to poetic expression. And it is terrifically entertaining.

One might also say that there are tactical and strategic works of criticism. As in poetry, the distinction is between goals for the short term and for a relatively defined readership versus goals for the long term and for readers over distances of time and space. Although McGrath himself would have argued that there cannot be any "final" reckoning of what has constituted the great poetry of the American nation or any other, it would be right, for our time and for years to come, to see his work admired and acknowledged and included as we continue to remember and debate what our culture has been, to discover what it is now, and to work for and dream what it may be. I hope this book, while it cannot be a flying tiger on its own, can ride the flying tiger that is McGrath's poetry, in order to bring McGrath to more readers now and, over a longer time, to influence the liveliness, the inclusiveness, the very character of American poetry itself.

February 1991

A Personal Introduction

Reginald Gibbons

> *"Love and hunger—that is my whole story."*
> *"Nostalgia is decayed dynamite."*
> *"On a mission of armed revolutionary memory!"**

The Motive of This Issue

Those who admire McGrath's work are fervent about it. Fellow poets, from Robert Bly and Donald Hall to Philip Levine and Michael Anania, have praised his work greatly, and commended it to readers. But here is a case study, for while McGrath is a poet who has not lacked for honors—including fellowships from the Guggenheim Foundation twenty years ago and from the National Endowment for the Arts only months ago—nevertheless the landscape of American poetry, as one would gather from the usual sources or suspects, never seems to have in it a single hill named McGrath. Nor does any one of the buildings, large or small, continually being erected, expanded or restored, bear a sign, "T. McGrath." The only New York publisher to issue any of McGrath's work is the small, but redoubtable, Thunder's Mouth Press, when it had a Chicago connection. Swallow Press, which published Parts One and Two of *Letter to an Imaginary Friend* and McGrath's collected poems, *The Movie at the End of the World*, went under and its titles are now distributed by the Ohio University Press; so there are no billboards announcing McGrath in the poetic landscape, either.

No one can claim that an apparently studied neglect or mere ignorance are problems new to literary fashion. Terrence Des Pres writes in this issue of *TriQuarterly* that the lack of attention to McGrath's work arises from the regionalistic literary hauteur of the East Coast. Beyond that, as Des Pres also states, there undoubtedly has been negative reac-

---

**Letter to an Imaginary Friend*, Part One, p. 31; Part Three, pp. 22, 57.

tion to McGrath's politics, which he has not only made evident, life-long, but also acted upon. McGrath` is a leftist, a radical, a sometime Communist and cofounder of the Ramshackle Socialist Victory Party (yes—RSVP; it appears in *Letter*). While many American poets, like others in college and university communities, tend to feel left-of-center in their political attitudes, the number who have leafletted, organized, joined a party, defied the House Un-American Activities Committee, or something similar, is not large. One would guess that some of the trundling makers and endorsers of poetic reputation have felt a distaste for McGrath's convictions, and for the presence in some of his poetry of left political and social comment. While few persons would defend the reactionary political and social comment in works of Eliot, Pound or Yeats, those poets have not lacked for respect and readers, despite their lapses of humane sentiment or rationality, for each of them wrote works of the first magnitude. But despite the liberalism of the academic community, which for better or worse now largely rules literary fashion, when an author's political opinion is left, one hears a striking silence, in these times. I hasten to add that I would not at all accept as an explanation that McGrath's work is not as good as that of Eliot, Pound or Yeats. First of all, many far lesser, and certainly milder and less interesting, poets than McGrath, much less Eliot, Pound or Yeats, have received much beyond their due from that same community; and second, the issue is not ranking poets, or contesting that long-reigning imperial triumvirate of twentieth-century poetry in English, but rather giving McGrath's work the close attention—and in my view, the great admiration and affection—it deserves. Other poets, especially Williams, have also been pushed aside with a similar rhetorical trick, and American poetry suffers impoverishment because of it.

At any rate, the importance of the political element in the reception of McGrath's work seems incontrovertible, and it remains for a future biographer of McGrath and future students of his times and his contemporaries to lay out the course his reputation has taken—and not taken—through the vales, river valleys, mountain passes, gulches and coulees of the American poetical landscape. Our concern now is only that McGrath's poetry is disadvantaged by what happens to be current literary fashion.

His professed cultural stance calls into question complacencies of all sorts, and perhaps this is part of the reason why the revenge against his work has been the indifference of conventional literary opinion. Perhaps this would greet any gifted poet who was willing to offend, to espouse a cause, to keep writing with encouragement or not, to question the habiliments of the changing Poetical Emperors of the unfolding decades. However, in the bookstores that stock a serious amount of poetry, or books of the political left, you can find *Letter* or *Movie* or something by "Longshot O'Leary." One issue of *TriQuarterly* cannot halt or even slow the cement mixers of contemporary poetic canon-making that are continually pulling up and discharging new loads. (Perhaps they are dooming some of what they intend to monumentalize.) But herewith *TriQuarterly* offers a few admiring appraisals of McGrath's work, and his speaking for himself in two interviews. And we hope to make a difference.

Because if McGrath's poetic accomplishments—especially his range of language and his choice of poetic materials—had been more widely disseminated, better understood and taken more to heart, perhaps the American poetical landscape might be livelier than it is, and bring more work of moment to bear on our moment. We might see more ambition to write about the world and our place in it, instead of anxious and uninformed pursuit of worn-out poses and up-to-date mannerisms. Of course, this situation is not really an exclusively literary one, but has to do with the place of poetry and fiction generally in American intellectual and artistic life; and McGrath's work and career has the salutary aspect, in our time, of dragging in with it, willy-nilly, a questioning of the accepted contemporary view of poetry, as well as the accepted view of contemporary poetry. He raises questions both in the camp and outside it, and this alone may make his case an interesting one for new readers of his poetry.

So here is a look at a poet whose work is powerful, original, absorbing, funny and uncompromisingly American in its resources, techniques and hopes. At the back of this issue, we have listed those of McGrath's books currently in print, so those readers who want to read him will know where to start.

McGrath's *Letter* to Friends As Yet Uncounted

We're accustomed to seeing book jackets decorated with the writer's bona fides in life, meant to be especially impressive if they include any working experience at all in the humbler trades or tasks. McGrath's book jackets come bearing none of this, perhaps because such experience is at the heart of his poems, inside the books. He has worked not only as a farmer, but also a welder, labor organizer, writer of pulp fiction, soldier in the Aleutians, logger, woodworker and machinist, writer of documentary films and teacher; he went to Louisiana State University when Brooks and Warren ruled, and to Oxford with a Rhodes Scholarship. And, not surprisingly, his poems show a reverence for labor and a fury at the futility of the wage-work and debt of farmers and welders and loggers. McGrath's working experience began when he was a boy, at the beginning of the great bust on the high plains farms that led down the historic slope to the Depression and Dust Bowl; by the time he was forty, what his grandparents' generation had rented or owned had been divided and lost to drought and banks.

It seems especially significant that after McGrath himself had lost work in Los Angeles in the 1950's because of the House Un-American Activities Committee persecutions of leftists, it was to North Dakota that he went—to teach for some years in Fargo and Moorhead, Minnesota (towns across the state line from each other). Even though everything, and nearly everyone, was gone, that was still home territory, filled with the nurture and pain of memory and offering the sight of a familiar horizon. I would want to tell new readers of McGrath that his sense of that place is absolutely central to Letter, even if the poem indicates a range of spots where McGrath worked on it, from Greece to Mexico. "North Dakota is everywhere," McGrath writes in Letter, and he dwells on and in it not because of any interest in its local color (he's a hard critic of local colorists) but because in his experience North Dakota revealed essential emotional and political truths. To portray these truths honestly, accurately (Pound: art is an accurate report), they must be located historically and geographically by the author. Thus McGrath's sense of how a poet can or should use his own experience in his work: as a kind of "pseudo-autobiography" that focuses on those moments when personal and historic public dramas coincide.

But, I would want to add quickly, his other homeland is our language; and the historical misfortune that ruined his forebears also happened to root McGrath in rural slang (pungent in both anger and humor), in tall tales, in the magical stop-time of his father's storytelling and recitations in winter. I regret that in this volume there wasn't space for more attention to this matrix of McGrath's poems—his language, which I consider the most impressive, most astonishing, of any American poet of our time. His vocabulary wraps all manner of speech and written language within it, from the bawdy to unearthed glossological wonders. It is especially lively when it gathers together slang, both rural and urban, and McGrath's neologistical and sometimes surreal coinages. In Letter, McGrath often seems to delight in running rapidly through several wildly disparate registers of language, or in cramming two such together.

Of course, there's more than delight in this—it's a part of the meaning of the poem that it encompasses so many sorts of words and manners of speaking, because the poem aims to bring in such a wide range of experience.

A new reader's curiosity about the structure of *Letter* also deserves more response than it can receive in this relatively modest volume. It may seem only obvious to point to the way the poem is divided into parts, yet something of an intensifying structure lies therein, and might usefully be mentioned here in a brief way. That Part One has twelve sections, given Roman numerals as heads, might begin to call to mind the classical epics. But the architecture of the poem is less regular and more interesting than this would suggest, for each of these sections has from three to nine parts, given Arabic numbers as heads. Part Two follows the thematic structure of Part One, in returning to similar themes, but does not reproduce the same number of divisions into parts. It has six Roman sections and a couple of these are quite long. Section II, for instance, reaches out over many kinds of material—from description and reminiscence to philosophy and myth; but Sections III and IV revolve around one great theme each, work and love.

McGrath has described the structure of Part Two as a kind of "eccentric spiral" that orbits the pole of Part One, looping near or close as it goes back over some of the same themes or motifs, but also looping farther outward than Part One, in order to take in other materials. There is more looping later, as well. The Christmas that Part Three develops is already firmly hinted in the earlier parts, and out of Christmas Eve the poem constructs a theatrical near-simultaneity of elements that includes more of the narrative "representative moments" of Parts One and Two (the boy-protagonist seeking Cal to invite him to join the men in the barn), and tall tales, the extraordinarily beautiful reminiscence of the journey to town by sled for midnight mass, the wildly funny confession of the child aspiring to significant sin and the "Christmas oratorio" which transforms the story of the Christ child into something not heretofore encountered in exactly this form. This suggests that the ground laid in Parts One and Two, through the "representative moments" that sketch McGrath's vision of what must be preserved of the past, and what hopes lie in the future, is now sufficient for there to be erected, in Parts Three and Four, a more playful, and more visionary, kind of structure, alive not only on strictly historical and autobiographical ground, but also in an imaginary realm of less fettered, sometimes surreal, invention.

Part Four dispenses with the Roman sections, and has only Arabic ones. It begins with the line:

NOW MOVE ALL THE SYMBOLS THREE LEAPS TO THE LEFT!

This is the visual emblem of a quite literal revolution, a turning of the wheel; and with this instruction to move all the symbols to a new place, to redefine their meaning, *Letter* launches into a final dream and prophecy. Perhaps to emphasize that great powers of imagination are essential to life fully lived, the conclusion to *Letter* arises from the heaped Christmas feast-table to become a bardic or shamanistic dream-vision. This recapitulates and extends the full range of McGrath's stylistic virtuosity, from the tenderness of family memory and a sensitivity to the natural world, through savage satire and galloping farce, to an apocalyptic vision of a quest upward through layered heavens in search of a realm of human harmony, fraternal shared labor, and love. The poem has thus reduced its architecture in each succeeding part, as if building upward a stepped skyscraper, airy and daring; and at the same time it has intensified its linguistic energies, as if illuminating each higher part of the building more fiercely, till it reaches at the apex the top of an aspen tree growing there, from which the poet-narrator-shaman makes his final leap upward.

The landscapes traversed, the dramatic scenes envisioned, the farces played out and the tragedies remembered, and most important, the voices "brought into the light of speech," make up a journey. Not only through McGrath's "representative moments," in which his personal life and the historical circumstances of the age are fused, but also through the movement from the details of life, lovingly and vividly written, into a social vision. Of course one can question McGrath's stated politics: the interviews give some examples. But how can one quarrel with the poem? If one does so, it must be in the same way one may quarrel with any work of art—on the grounds of its value to our understanding of human life, which we derive not only from its accomplishment in terms of its own medium, but also from its ability to transport us to states of feeling and conviction that we prize for the intensity of pleasure and pathos we experience, and for the place those feelings and convictions have led us to, in our own system of values. McGrath has explicitly stated the convictions that govern the poem; in it, he has written, "Love and hunger—that is my whole story," and said that he is on "a mission of armed revolutionary memory!" He has also cautioned that "nostalgia is decayed dynamite," which I take to mean simply that the purpose of his mission of memory is not merely to recover some feeling about the past, but to see it honestly as a time of pain and difficulty that has partly shaped the present. Revolutionary, because he would hope to affect hopes and plans for the future of man. Compelling for the individual reader, because the poem speaks to one's hopes for one's own life, for the future of one's appetites and ideals and projects. Thus active memory, active imagination and action itself lie at the center of McGrath's themes. With these, as well as the poem's linguistic resourcefulness and inventiveness, and its architecture, the reader must come to grips. It would surprise the contributors to this volume if nearly all readers did not feel the exhilaration of McGrath's poetic powers in *Letter*, and did not wish to measure their own feelings and convictions against his, and did not feel challenged to corroborate or contest his poetic version of American realities and ideals.

Laughter

Perhaps the most heartening progress readily visible in the structure of the entire poem is from a place "far from the laughter" to a realm of uproarious mirth (which the poem very emphatically, very seriously, locates not only in present pleasure or satire, but also in a human society free of hunger and injustice). "Laughter" is a key and frequent word in *Letter*, and McGrath's temperament is thoroughly celebratory, not pessimistic, despite the driving fury of his satire and denunciations. Thus is his anger balanced by joy, much as Blake's is. As he said at one point in the interview that Terrence Des Pres and I conducted, "There are so many things to praise that I don't know where to start!" During the long interview with McGrath on three afternoons in sunny winter in Minneapolis, his conversation was frequently amused, and amusing. Des Pres and I went each day around noon to McGrath's apartment in a large, fairly new two-story brick building. He lives alone; chronic pain since a shoulder operation a few years ago has made him feel more isolated and immobile. The apartment does not contain very many of the artifacts of a life of writing—a few hundred books, old favorites and new; a dictionary kept close at hand; a table at which to work; and the usual furniture of man—in this instance, functional and nondescript. Among the books, I noticed an early edition of Christopher Caudwell's *Illusion and Reality*, Lorca's *Poet in New York*. Acting the role of a kind of marvelously learned outlaw (which is one of his favorite words, one would guess, from *Letter*) of revolutionary conviction and youthful wildness, and despite the affliction of physical pain, he seems to keep steadily at his work on new poems.

As edited by both the interviewers, and, lightly, by McGrath, our interview pretty much follows the topics as they were raised, although there has been some rearranging so that separate discussions of the same topic could be brought together. The whole transcript, originally 270 typed pages, has been enormously shortened for the sake of concision, and inevitably some matters we would have liked to include have been left out. But hesitations, repetitions, corrections and so on—both Mc-Grath's and ours—have also been excised, for the sake of bringing his ideas and opinions forward as clearly as possible. His reminiscence about his work in film has been left out completely because of its length, and will be published elsewhere.

And of course, cumulatively, a great deal of time, and of nuance and meaning beyond the bounds of transcription into language, is often compressed into the notation "[laughs]." This notation and its variants, inserted often in the text, cannot at all convey the variety of feeling, and the pervasiveness, of McGrath's humor and of his often amused response to questions—even to his own answers. He is a wry presence, sometimes apparently rueful, sometimes elated by the sweetness of memory—as *Letter* also shows in several beautiful passages—or even by the pure, laughable absurdity of life; and sometimes angry at manifest injustice, roguery, labor and pain, at the violence so routinely brought down on the defenseless and poor, and at the powerlessness of generations of laborers and workers whose lives brought them neither ease nor plenty, but raised others to wealth.

But despite his anger, McGrath's voice seems a source of cheer to those who listen, perhaps because of his capacity to be amazed, astounded, pleased, horrified or touched into laughter. "Far from the laughter," a lament several times expressed in *Letter*, may be true as an assessment of the lot of most of those who inhabit the earth, but it is the antithesis of McGrath's own temperament, as he is at seventy.

A person listening to the tape recording of his voice would often hear him laugh, and would more often sense, from the subtle change of timbre or tone of voice, when he was smiling. I think most people would sense in McGrath's way of speaking an enormous appetite for life, and love of it—the slow and careful explanations and reminiscences conveying a great patience with life, as well as his quite amazing breadth of experience (personal, poetical and political).

14

Etc.

E. P. Thompson's essay-memoir was included in the British edition of his collection of essays, *The Heavy Dancers*, alongside essays about nuclear weapons and modern political relations between the superpowers. That inclusion of the cultural with the political apparently struck his American publishers as unsuitable, as not fitting our or their preconceptions, even at levels of some intellectual seriousness, about the relations of art and society and politics. So we redress the balance, as best we can with the small circulation of a literary magazine, by publishing it here, in revised form—brought up to date to include comment about Parts Three and Four of *Letter*. (It will also be included in a collection of essays on McGrath to be published by the University of Missouri Press, edited by Frederick C. Stern.) Philip Levine's brief speech was given at a tribute to McGrath in April 1986, at the annual meeting, in Chicago, of the Associated Writing Programs. McGrath's champions that evening also included Michael Anania, who was the poetry editor who brought out *Letter* at Swallow Press, and Studs Terkel. The Loft, the literary foundation in Minneapolis, celebrated McGrath's seventieth birthday in September 1986, with a reading by McGrath and much discussion of his work and an evening of brief tributes by many poets and writers, from Robert Bly to Garrison Keillor. May there be more such happy events!

McGrath says that at one time, he thinks, he was the only poet in America who had an audience awaiting his work—he means the small one of working men whose attention he figured to obtain, and did, in union halls, with his Longshot O'Leary poems. I remembered reading that Rafael Alberti wrote in his memoirs that no prize or literary satisfaction ever equalled having heard an anonymous voice, out of sight, beyond a wall, singing one of his poems to the tune of a Spanish folk song. McGrath's satisfaction can rest in this similar instance: Michael Anania recounts riding in a cab with Alan Swallow, trying to convince Swallow to publish *Letter* on the big pages that McGrath's long lines demand and deserve. It would cost more money than a book of the usual dimensions. Swallow says, we can break those lines, it would cost too much money to use the big page. And the cabbie turns in his seat, driving, and asks, "Are you talking about Tom McGrath?" Astonished affirmations from the backseat. "Publish the big book!" Swallow did. And may the audience for it grow.

From *Letter to an Imaginary Friend**

Thomas McGrath

Part One

I

1.

—"From here it is necessary to ship all bodies east."
I am in Los Angeles, at 2714 Marsh Street,
Writing, rolling east with the earth, drifting toward Scorpio,
                                                    thinking,
Hoping toward laughter and indifference.
"They came through the passes,
                    they crossed the dark mountains in a month of snow,
Finding the plain, the bitter water,
                                    the iron rivers of the black North.
Horsemen,
Hunters of the hornless deer in the high plateaus of that country,
They travelled the cold year, died in the stone desert."

Aye, long ago. A long journey ago,
Most of it lost in the dark, in a ruck of tourists,

*Parts One and Two of this four-part poem were originally published by the Swallow
Press (1970)—now distributed by the Ohio University Press—and Parts Three and Four
were published by the Copper Canyon Press (1985); these excerpts are reprinted by
permission of the Ohio University Press and the Copper Canyon Press.

In the night of the compass, companioned by tame wolves, plagued
By theories, flies, visions, by the anthropophagi . . .

I do not know what end that journey was toward.
—But I am its end. I am where I have been and where
I am going. The journeying destination—at least that . . .
But far from the laughter.

So. Writing:

"The melt of the pig pointed to early spring.
The tossed bones augered an easy crossing.
North, said the mossy fur of the high pines.
West, said the colored stone at the sulphur pool."

2.

—And at the age of five ran away from home.
(I have never been back. Never left.) I was going perhaps
Toward the woods, toward a sound of water—called by what bird?
Leaving the ark-tight farm in its blue and mortgaged weather
To sail the want-all seas of my five dead summers
Past the dark ammonia-and-horse-piss smelling barn
And the barnyard dust, adrift in the turkey wind
Or pocked with the guinea-print and staggering script
Of the drunken-sailor ducks, a secret language; leaving
Also my skippering Irish father, land-locked Sinbad,
With his head in a song-bag and his feet stuck solid
On the quack-grass-roofed and rusting poop-deck of the north forty,
In the alien corn: the feathery, bearded, and all-fathering wheat.

Leaving my mother, too, with her kindness and cookies,
The whispering, ginghamy, prayers—impossible pigeons—
Whickering into the camphor-and-cookie-crumb dark toward
God in the clothes closet.

Damp comforts.

Tears

Harder than nails.
A mint of loving laughter.

How could I leave them?
I took them with me, though I went alone
Into the Christmas dark of the woods and down

The whistling slope of the coulee, past the Indian graves
Alive and flickering with the gopher light.

III

1.

Out of the whirring lamp-hung dusk my mother calls.
From the lank pastures of my sleep I turn and climb,
From the leathery dark where the bats work, from the coasting
High all-winter all-weather christmas hills of my sleep.
And there is my grandfather chewing his goatee,
Prancing about like a horse. And the drone and whir from
                the fields
Where the thresher mourns and showers on the morning stillness
A bright fistful of whistles.

The water-monkey is late, the straw-monkey
Is late and the bundle-stiffs are late and my grandfather dances
In the yellowy kerosene smell of the morning lamps where my mother
Brightens a dish on her apron and feeds the stove
Its iron, round crackling mouth and throat full of bristling flame,
Gold in the five o'clock morning night.
Dances and raves. A worker has broken his wrist;
The machine is whistling its brass-tongued rage and the jack-booted
                weathers of autumn
Hiss and sing in the North.
The rains are coming, and the end of the world
Is coming.
                          My grandfather dances.
I am slowly fed into my B.V.D.'s while the still-dark day
Assumes the structure of my nine year world,
And the whistle hoots.

"You'll be the straw-monkey. Can ye do it boy?"
My grandfather capers about while I assemble my parts
And my mother fusses. Is the job too hard?
"Ach, woman, the chiselur's tall as a weed!
He's not to be spike-pitchin', a whistle-punk only—
Sure it's a breeze of a job and he'll sit in the shade on his bum
The day long."

She pets me and cooks:
Bacon and eggs and the bitter, denatured coffee
Of man's estate. While my grandfather stamps and grumbles
And my brothers tumble from sleep into the kitchen,
Questioning. Owl-eyed and envious.

A kiss and a hug. A piece of pie in my pocket
For love and luck.

                         Then, in a jingle of trace
      chains,
The martingale's chatter and squeak of straps in their keepers,
I drove the big roan team through the grey of the chill morning.
My mother waving.
                   Goodby
And the kids staring, still sleepy,
Myself proud and scared and the echo of sleep still strong
In my veins. (The reins I'd looped round my hips so the fast-stepping
      team
Half pulled me, stiff legged, and tacking about like a boat
In their dusty wake).
                      Ahead my grandfather's buggy
Bounced down the coulee hill, up the opposite slope
Toward the threshing machine and its whistling brass
      commandments,
The barb-tongued golden barley and the tents of the biblical wheat,
Frontiers of sweat and legendary field
Of manhood.

Behind me my mother called. Something I could not hear.
The kids stood solemn
                   Still in the weather of childhood.
Waved.
      Throwing kisses.
                 Waved my hand in return.
So long.
So long.
So long.

            2.

Blind. Out of the labyrinthine sleep
Of childhood I entered the brilliant alien arena

Blind in the harsh light.
                                        Entered too soon, too young,
Bobbing along on the lines, dragged by a team of roans,
(Whose names *should* have been Poverty and Pride)
Into the world of men at the age of nine

This was no ritual visit; no summer foray,
Scouting party or cook-out in the Big Horn country
With the ridge-pole pine singing my honor and the streams full of
                fish and fancy,
The light-fall valorous and God-creatures taller than tales
To teach me camp-craft, to put a crimp in the nightmare,
To fan my six gun.
Oh, I know that ten-sleep camp where the ticking Dechard rifle
Dozes by the banker's son, the half-real shooting gallery
Of the Dream Range where red-skin and deer ride by
On an endless belt and the bears pop up, pop down,
In front of the painted scene of lake and mountain,
Where prizes are always given . . .
                                        Aloft on the shaking deck,
Half blind and deafened in the roaring dust,
On the heaving back of the thresher,
My neck blistered by sun and the flying chaff, my clothes
Shot full of thistles and beards, a gospel itch,
Like a small St. Stephen, I turned the wheel of the blower
Loading the straw-rack.
The whistle snapped at my heels: in a keening blizzard
Of sand-burrs, barley-beards and beggars-lice, in a red thunder
Where the wheat rust bellowed up in a stormy cloud
From the knife-flashing feeder,
I turned the wheel.
Far from Tom Swift, and farther
From troop Nine, the cabin they built on the river.

3.

The rites of passage toward the stranger's country,
The secret language foreign as a beard . . .
I turned in machine-made circles: first from the screaming red
Weather where the straw stack grew and the rattling thresher
                mourned;

Then to the rocking engine where the fly-wheel flashed and labored
And the drive-belt waxed and waned, the splices clapped at its cross
Ebbing and flowing, slack or taut as the spikers
Dropped the bivouaced wheat in the feeder's revolving throat.

Feathered in steam like a great tormented beast
The engine roared and laughed, dreamed and complained,
And the pet-cocks dripped and sizzled; and under its fiery gut
Stalactites formed from the hand-hold's rheumy slobbers.
—Mane of sparks, metallic spike of its voice,
The mile-long bacony crackle of burning grease!
There the engineer sat, on the high drivers,
Aloof as a God. Filthy. A hunk of waste
Clutched in one gauntleted hand, in the other the oil can
Beaked and long-necked as some exotic bird;
Wreathed in smoke, in the clatter of loose eccentrics.
And the water-monkey, back from the green quiet of the river
With a full tank, was rolling a brown quirrly
(A high school boy) hunkered in the dripping shade
Of the water-tender, in the tall talk and acrid sweat
Of the circle of spitting stiffs whose cloud-topped bundle-racks
Waited their turns at the feeder.
And the fireman: goggled, shirtless, a flashing three-tined fork,
Its handle charred, stuck through the shiny metallic
Lip of the engine, into the flaming, smoky
Fire-box of its heart.
Myself: straw-monkey. Jester at court.

So, dawn to dusk, dark to dark, hurried
From the booming furious brume of the thresher's back
To the antipodean panting engine. Caught in the first
Circle.

Was it hard? I don't know. It was terrifying.
The whistle snapped and I ran. The thresher moaned on its glut.
The Danaean rain of the wheat rained down.
Hard? No. Everyone wanted to help me.
My father, riding the grain-tanks from the field
To the town elevators, starting out in the chilly dawn
And home at the cold midnight, eating when time allowed,

Doing the work of a threshing hand and the chores of the farm
             to boot,
Harnessing the team I was too short to harness,
Helping me pick up a load when he got back from town
In the jolting musical empty grain tank.
                              He had boils that summer,
His neck was circled with ruby light, I remember.
Poulticed with heated bottles.
My mother helped. I had cookies stuffed in my pocket,
Ginger . . .
Their crumbly sweetness.
                              Worrying:
"Jim, is it too hard?
The boy's tired as a horse."
My grandfather too,
After the first week, when they found a man,
Came prancing and dancing, pulling his thin beard:
"Kate, let the boy be quitting.
It's hard, long hours. Let him quit."
My father came in the dark
(Where I'd gone into sleep, into the open flaming
Mouth of the dream, the whistle biting my ears,
The night vibrating,
In the fog of the red rust, steam, the rattle of concaves)
Came about midnight.
His last chore done, he led me into the bright
Kitchen. (The table was already set for breakfast;
the potatoes were sliced; the pie, cross cut; a cloth
Fenced out the flies.)
Then, his supper, we ate ice cream and cheese;
Sardines; crackers; tomatoes still wet with the night
Out of the garden; cucumbers crisp and salty
Cooled in the watertrough; bacon and watermelon
Left over from supper.
"Tom, Old Timer," he'd say. "Ain't you had enough?
This workin' won't get you nowheres. Let the job go.
We got a man for her now."
But I couldn't. No way to quit.
My hand was stuck to the plough and I cried to stay.

(As at morning, with the sleep stuck in my eyes and my morning
            breakfast
Dead in my stomach I cried for the day to be gone).

I couldn't quit. I came out of sleep at four
Dazed and dreaming and ate my food on the run,
And ran to the barn; the roan team knelt and dozed;
I clapped the harness on them and kicked them awake
And rode the off one, galloping, into the field
Where the engine slept in its heat.
The fireman grunted. He struck a match to his fork.
The crackling fireball, thrust to the metal heart,
Ignited the still dark day.

Sometimes, at night, after a long move to another farm,
Hours after the bundle-teams were gone and sleeping,
After we'd set the rig for the next day,
I rode the off-horse home.
Midnight, maybe, the dogs of the strange farms
Barking behind me, the river short-cut rustling
With its dark and secret life and the deep pools warm.
(I swam there once in the dead of night while the team
Nuzzled the black water).
Home then. Dead beat.

To quit was impossible once you had started.
All you could do was somehow to learn the ropes.
No one could teach you.
When you were late the whistle
Blasted you into the kingly estate
Of the daylight man. Responsibility. The hot foundries
Of the will.
                But when, your load up, you squatted
In the spitting circle of stiffs, in the hot shade
Under the sky-piled bundle-racks waiting their turn
                at the feeder,
Chewing on rose apples and bumming a smoke—
You were no man there.
A man to the engine's hunger, to the lash of the whistle,
But not to the tough young punks from Detroit or Chicago
Drifting the tide of the harvest the first time

And jealous of manhood.
                                    Not to the old stiffs
Smoke shooters, their bindles weighted with dust
From Kansas to Calgary.
                                    Not to your uncle surely
Boss of the rig who slapped you once when you swore,
Before the ritual was known or the language of men.

O great port of the Dream! Gate to the fearful country,
So near and magically far, what key will open?
Their alien smell, their talk, their foreign hungers,
And something awful, secret: I saw them, lost,
Borne on the fearful stream in a sinful valor
And longed to enter. To know. To burn in that fire.

VII

2.

Beginning and re-beginning, voyage and return and voyage . . .
Past the last gate in the fence toward the white slate of the river,
And past the Indian boneyard and under its tight, bright blanket,
And down the coulee and over the ford, now locked in its echo
            chamber—
It spanged like gunshot under the caulks of the horseshoes,
A ripping and fiery sound (the pure steel of the cold)
That ricocheted from the hills and sifted snow from the branches,
Unfurling one rusty crow, his sooty flag, to the air.

Stump ranchers that winter, we felled the trees on the slopes:
Scrub-oak, elm, box elder, the flinty stakes of the ash
That snagged in the chokecherry slashes. In the crowded gooseberry
            brakes,
Where the fox grape's bronze globes sag in the cloudy green of the
            summer:
We knocked them down with a crosscut and snaked them out on a
                                                            chain.
All that winter, in the black cold, the buzz-saw screamed and
            whistled,
And the rhyming hills complained. In the noontime stillness,
Thawing our frozen beans at the raw face of a fire,

24

We heard the frost-bound tree-boles booming like cannon,
A wooden thunder, snapping the chains of the frost.

Those were the last years of the Agrarian City
City of swapped labor
Communitas
Circle of warmth and work
Frontier's end and last wood-chopping bee
The last collectivity stamping its feet in the cold.

So, with the moss on our backs and it snowing inside our skulls,
In a gale like a mile-high window of breaking glass
We snaked out the down ones, snatching the deadfalls clean
And fed them into the buzzsaw.
                                        The Frenchman's, it was.
A little guy, quick as a fart and no nicer,
Captain of our industry.
                                        Had, for his company
The weedy sons of midnight enterprise:
Stump-jumpers and hog-callers from the downwind counties
The noonday mopus and the coffee guzzling Swedes
Prairie mules
Moonfaced Irish from up-country farms
Sand-hill cranes
And lonesome deadbeats from a buck brush parish.

So, worked together. Fed the wood to the saw
That had more gaps than teeth. Sweated, and froze
In the dead-still days, as clear as glass, with the biting
Acetylene of the cold cutting in through the daylight,
And the badman trees snapping out of the dusk
Their icy pistols.
                        So, worked, the peddlers pack of us
Hunched in the cold with the Frenchman raging around us
A monsoon of fury, a wispy apocalypse, scolding
Cursing and pleading, whipping us into steam,
And we warmed in each other's work, contestants of winter,
We sawed up the summer into stove-length rounds—
Chunks of pure sunlight made warmer by our work.
And did we burn?
We burned with a cold flame.

And did we freeze?
We froze in bunches of five.
And did we complain?
We did, we did, we did.

Sometimes at evening with the dusk sifting down through the trees
And the trees like a smudge on the white hills and the hills drifting
Into the hushed light, into the huge, the looming, holy
Night;—sometimes, then, in the pause and balance
Between dark and day, with the noise of our labor stilled,
And still in ourselves we felt our kinship, our commune
Against the cold.
                    In that rich and friendly hour
When the hunting hawks whirred home, we stilled our talking
And silence sang our compline and vesper song.

It was good singing, that silence. From the riches of common work
The solidarity of forlorn men
Firm on our margin of poverty and cold:
Communitas
Holy City
Laughter at forty below
Round song
The chime of comradeship that comes once maybe
In the Winter of the Blue Snow.

That's how it was.
                        Sometimes, going home in the evening,
We'd jump some pheasants and drop them out of the light—
The shotguns clapping and hollow in the empty world of the winter—
And their feathers blazed like jewels in the blank white fields.

Then, if there was plenty, we'd all eat together
At someone's house, and later play poker, for cigarettes or for
            nothing,
And I'd go home at the dark prime, the north flashing its teeth,
Or the moon white as a lamp in the blazing night.

26

Part Two

II

2.

Windless city built on decaying granite, loose ends
Without end or beginning and nothing to tie to, city down hill
From the high mania of our nineteenth century destiny—what's loose
Rolls there, what's square slides, anything not tied down
Flies in. . .
         kind of petrified shitstorm,
                                  Retractable
Swimming pools.
             Cancer farms.
                        Whale dung
At the bottom of the American night refugees tourists elastic
Watches. . .

                Vertical city shaped like an inverse hell:
At three feet above tide mark, at hunger line, are the lachrymose
Cities of the plain weeping in the sulphurous smog; Annaheim:
South Gate (smell of decaying dreams in the dead air)
San Pedro Land's End. . .
                      —where the color of labor is dark—
(Though sweat's all one color) around Barrio No Tengo,
Among the Nogotnicks of the Metaphysical Mattress Factory, where
            the money is made.

And the second level: among the sons of the petty B's—
The first monkey on the back of South Gate, labor—at the ten
Thousand a year line (though still in the smog's sweet stench)
The Johnny Come Earlies of the middling class:
                             morality
                               fink-size
Automatic rosaries with live Christs on them and cross-shaped
             purloined
Two-car swimming pools full of holy water. . .
                         From here God goes
Uphill.
        Level to level.

                    Instant escalation of money—up!
To Cadillac country.

                    Here, in the hush of the long green,
The leather priests of the hieratic dollar enclave to bless
The lush-working washing machines of the Protestant Ethic
              ecumenical
Laundries: to steam the blood from the bills—O see O see how
Labor His Sublime Negation streams in the firmament!
Don't does all here; whatever is mean is clean.

And to sweep their mountain tops clear of coyotes and currency
              climbers
They have karate-smokers and judo-hypes, the junkies of pain,
Cooking up small boys' fantasies of mental muscles, distilling
A magic of gouged eyes, secret holds, charm
Of the high school girls demi-virginity and secret weapon
Of the pudenda pachucas (takes a short hair type
For a long hair joke) power queers; socially-acceptable sadists—
Will tear your arm off for a nickel and sell it back for a dime.
And these but the stammering simulacra of the Rand Corpse wise
              men—
Scientists who have lost the good of the intellect,
              mechanico-humanoids
Antiseptically manufactured by the Faustian humunculus process.
And how they dream in their gelded towers these demi-men!
(Singing of overkill, kriegspiel, singing of blindfold chess—
Sort of ainaleckshul rasslin matches to sharpen their fantasies
Like a scout knife.)
                    Necrophiles.
                    Money protectors. . .
—They dream of a future founded on fire, on a planned coincidence
Of time and sulphur. . .
                    Heraclitian eschatology. . .

And over it all, god's face,
                    or perhaps a baboon's ass
In the shape of an IBM beams toward another war.
One is to labor, two is to rob, three is to kill.

Executive
        legislative
                judiciary. . .
                        —muggery, buggery, and thuggery
All Los Angeles
                America
                        is divided into three parts.

Part Three

II

2.

And we, of the damned poor, trot our frost-furred horses
Into the barn where beyond the glinting lantern, a blessed
And a steamy animal sleep is clotting into a night
Dreamless, perhaps, or, if blurred by dreams, it is green as summer
And the hay that burns there—a cattle-barn night, star lighted
By rays from the deadwhite nailheads shining in their rime-laced albs.

The yard is corralling the darkness now, but Orient offers
A ghost-pale waning moon host-thin in the wan and failing
Light:
The sun that brief December day now gone
Toward topaz distances . . . of mineral afternoons
Beyond the Bad Lands . . .
                        toward Montana . . .
                                        the shandy
        westernesses . . .

And we three (who are now but one in the changed and changing
Dark of my personal fading and falling world) we three
Hand in hand and hand in heart sail to the house—
My father has lent me the light so we can go hand in hand,
Himself between us, the lantern brighter than any moon!

Indoors, my mother bends over the stove, her face rosy
In the crackling woodfire that winks and spits from an open lid.
And we are *all* there, then, as we were, once,

29

On the planet of sadness in a happy time. (We did not, then,
Miss you, Tomasito, an unsuffered age away
Waiting for all my errors to make me one time right.)

And so I will name them here for the last time, who were once
Upon the earth in a time greener than this:
My next brother Jim, then Joe, then my only sister, Kathleen,
Then Martin, then Jack, the baby.
                                        Now Jim and Jack have gone
Into the dark with my mother and father. But then —
                                                              Oh, then!
How bright their faces shone that lamplit Christmas Eve!
And our mother, her whole being a lamp in all times and
              weather . . .
And our father, the dear flesh-gantry that lifted us all from the
              dark . . .

    [In that transfiguring light, from the kitchen wall, a Christ
    Opens his chest like an album to show us his pierced heart
    As he peers from a church calendar almost empty of days.
    Now: say: then: who among you might not open your flesh
    On an album of loss and pain — icons of those you have loved
    Gone on without you: forever farther than Montana or sundown?
    No Christ ever suffered pain longer or stronger than this . . .]

So let me keep them now — and forever — fixed in that lost
Light
      as I take the lantern and go down the stairs to the cellar
In search of the Christmas apples cold in their brimming bin.
There, as deep in the hull of a ship, the silence collects
Till I hear through the dead-calm new-come night the far bells:
Sheldon . . .
            Enderlin . . .
                        bells of the little towns
                                                calling . . .
Lisbon . . . North Dakota . . .
                        [Yes, I year them now
    In this other time I am walking, this other Lisbon, Portugal —
    Bells of the Revolution, loud as my heart I hear
    Above the continuous bad-rap of the urine-colored sea.
    Beside which I am walking through that snow of July leaflets

30

In search of the elusive onion to make the home-done sandwich
Herbaical and vegetable and no doubt even healthy, and certainly
Hearty-seeming (in mind's tongue) after fifteen K's and quais
A la recherche de cebolla perdue:
                                        Vegicum Apostolicum
Herbibable sancti et ecumenicabable . . .
                                        Meanwhile
I die on the vine waiting for news from you, Tomasito,
Waiting for the angel, waiting for news from heaven, a new
Heaven, of course—and a better world in birth! *Here:*
Under the changing leaflets under the flailing bells.]

And the bells of Sheldon carry me up the steep of the stairs,
My feet set in a dance to be bearer of these cold apples,
The fairest fruit of our summer labor and harvest luck.
I lay them out on the lamplit table. On the gleaming cloth.
In the dreamy gaze of the children they glaze in a lake of gold!

O high wake I have said I would hold!
                                        It has come all unknown:
Unknown!
            And my blood freezes
                                to see them so:
In *that* light
            in this
                    light
                    each face all-hallowed
In the haloing golden aura shining around each head!

And how black and stark these shadows lean out of the hollow dark
To halloo and hold and hail them and nail them into the night
Empty
    —its leaden reaches and its cold passage
                                        empty . . .

And so, at that last supper, in the gold and blood of their being,
So let me leave them now and forever fixed in that light.

3.

We have come to the Ambush Place where I shall make that promise
In five or six years sled time in my future that's past

Now . . .
        "But there's always another one comin' while the trains still
            run!"
(My father's Anarcho-Communist-Wobbly wisdom tells me.)

The Ambush Place . . .
                when my journeying soul is five years older
Than the Christmas boy I was—or six years maybe—(it's only
The legend that counts) a long way from Midnight Mass . . .
                     In the Ambush Place
We lay
      my brother Jim and I
                 in my summer confusions
Where the bridge crosses the Maple River south of the coulee—
We lay
      with our .22's and our terror
                 Agrarian Reformers
Waiting for our local kulak-cum-banker to cross the bridge.
He was throwing us off his land and we intended to put him
Six feet under: with some point twenty-two
Hundredths holes to ventilate the closed system of His Corporate
Structure
      (O Falaur, Sitrami, Sitrael, Thamaar—aid!)

Anarcho-juvenile expropriation of the expropriators!
O infantile disorder!
          But generous too, I think:
                     the innocent
Hope: "the open and true desire to create the Good."

He never came—(we have waited a long time for the Kulak
To come into our sights!).
           We lay
              trembling
                  afraid of our fear . . .

And wait there still I suppose in some alternate world, wondering
If we will shoot
        in the possible future
                wait
                   wait—

("We know everything about the universe except what is going to
                    happen
Next," saith the poet. [Charlie Potts]).

                                                He did not come
That day . . .
                (And we must always start *Now!*

                                        Now!
Here: where the past is exhausted, the future too weak to begin.)

We lay there
                powerful
                                I remember the summery smell
Of the river
            birdcall
                        O powerful
                                I remember
                                            smelling
The yellowy, elecampane raggedy-headed flowers . . .

Part Four

4.

But I fly up on the sparks and enter
                                the Sixth Heaven . . .

Quiet: here . . .
                (except for the scratching of quill pens)
And white . . .
                the whiteness of unlined paper . . .
                                                The Elect sit
On Bob Cratchit stools entering debits and credits
In white ledgers . . .
                    white ink on white paper . . .
                                                only
The Elect can read . . .
                    white hands
                            cold
                                    in cold rooms

Warmed only by the ghost of Calvin . . .

                                                  white collars
On their white necks and white cuffs at the wrists . . .

Canting, cold, ceremented, solemn, in Ku-Klux-Klan-white cerecloths
The choir drones like a bagpipe winching whines high,
Drowning the groan of Gregorian chant from down below.

Dominions, throned like pale Jupiters, the clerks perch
On their high stools, holy, and the wind from their whiffling quills
Gathers, combines, amplifies and roars through all creation
Translating all the peoples into the saved or damned;
ALL workers into gainfully employed or the damned redundant;
      (And further into unionized or dis-or-unorganized
            And further into Left Wing unions or those of the
         Labor Fakers
                And thence into hourly wage, speedup,
        production statistics);
ALL the poor divided into worthy or soupline low-lifes;
ALL the "natives" into scalp-price Hostiles or reservation charges;
ALL animals into fur-bearing or goddamn varmints;
      (And thence into beaver hats and bounties on hawks and
        coyotes—
             Hummingbird tongues sold by the pound, Quetzal
        by length of the feather);
ALL trees into usable lumber or miserable nuisances;
      (Unless they be "ornamentals" or used by the Hunt Club—
            And so the oak is a table and the murmuring pine
        is board feet
              And the Druids are Lumber Jacks and
        gone is the Golden Bough);
All metals into Precious or passed-over preterite;
      (Gold by the ounce, ore by the ton, slag-heaps poisoning the
        waters—
             But the statue of the Possible Hero still sleeps in the
        rock!)!

Cash nexus!
                —And the end of all idyllic order!
Profit, loss, yield, price, markup, toll—
Value, expense, charge, disbursement, amortization . . .

Money and number, number and money, number, number . . .
And the Law:
             TO HIM WHO HATH IT SHALL BE GIVEN—
To him who HATH NOT: it SHALL be taken away.

These scribblers have misread the law
                              have changed its meaning
To money and number and *so* have bled the whole world white:
Lilywhite
        snowwhite
                  Protestant white:
                                    ALL quality
Blown away in the wind of profit and loss . . .
And now there is only the wind of Number
                                    rising
                                        rising
From the quill pens to computers.

                          5.

The snow-snakes are wearing away the corners of the worn house
Like the sand-snakes of the arid summer but the stars are still secure
Or seem so
          through the window—
                        and one may be turning blue!
A few feathers of snow fall . . .
                        and, in the coulee,
Under the rocky ice the holy water moves
Slow and secret south to the river . . .
                        and the bells of Lisbon
Sing the last song of the night . . .

                          And the bells of Lisbon
(Portugal) sing: and the wind blows away the cathedrals
As the trucks of the armed workers roar away to the north
Where the Communist peasants are separating land from landlords
And lords from the land.
                  Or so they dream . . .
                              while on Rua do
          Karma
A snow of leaflets drifts through revolutionary song . . .

And now, in my upstairs room at six-fifteen South Eleventh,
In Moorhead, Minnesota, the snow in my paperweight
(and in all this weight of paper) is sifting cold and slow
Over the miniature farmhouse under its dome of glass
And paper . . .
        where the boy sleeps . . .
                (there, or on Rua do Karma,
Older . . .
     or elsewhere . . .
         struggling . . .
            among the ancient disorders
Of the unmade world).
       And now, in his sleep, the boy hears—
And he in Portugal—
       and I
          through the slowly lightening window
Hear the final chorus of the song we have longed to hear:

    Light falls slant on the long south slope,
       On the pheasant-covert willow, the hawk-nest dark and foxes'
         hollow
    As the year grows old.
         Who will escape the cold?

       These will endure
    The scour of snow and the breakneck ice
      Where the print-scar mousetracks blur in the evergreen light
    And the night-hunting high birds whirl—
    All engines of feather and fur:
       These will endure.

       But how shall our pride,
  Manwoman'schild, in the bone-chilling black frost born,
      Where host or hide
  Who is bound in his orbit between iron and gold
    Robbed of his starry fire with the cold
  Sewed in his side—
      How shall he abide?

      Bear him his gift,
    To bless his work,

Who, farming the dark on the love-worn stony plot,
*   The heaven-turning stormy rock of this share-crop world*
His only brother warms and harms;
*   Who, without feathers or fur,*
Faces the gunfire cold of the old warring
                                        new
                                    year—
*   Bless! Grant him gift and gear,*
Against the night and riding of his need,
*   To seed the turning furrow of his light.*

Explicit Carmen.

North Dakota—Portugal—Moorhead, Minnesota

1984

An Interview with Thomas McGrath, January 30 – February 1, 1987

Reginald Gibbons and Terrence Des Pres

From Cardenal to Joyce

RG: Did you meet Ernesto Cardenal when you were in Nicaragua [in January 1987]?

McGRATH: No, I didn't. I could have met Cardenal but – I've forgotten, something else was going on that day that seemed to me more important. And then I met another poet, Dr. Silva, and he's also the head of the Children's Hospital in Managua.

The Children's Hospital was built by Somoza, but as Silva said, he didn't provide anything. There were no doctors, nurses, equipment, beds or patients! It was just a blank! So now it's operating at, I would suppose, something like one-fourth of optimum, because now they do have some things. For instance, some of the machines. But they're all from America. And when they break down, they can't replace the parts because they can't get them. Unless they can find them somewhere else, like Canada or wherever.

He's written some very simple books that – once they got the literacy program in full force – have been very successful. The *campesinos* were totally illiterate, and nobody ever bothered to tell them anything. He's written what is probably [laughs] a very revolutionary book, very simple. Telling them how to avoid diarrhea, which is the main killer, of the world, of infants.

TDP: Is a goal of the poem to help people remember by using the techniques of poetry?

38

McGRATH: Well, shit is revolutionary! If you got too much *of* it. [Laughs.] I asked him, "Do you know William Carlos Williams?" "Oh, yes." He knew *something* of the work (because, I thought, they were two of a kind in certain ways—though Williams never faced *that* kind of stuff). Otherwise he likes to write a poem about nature and things like that.

TDP: They have a lot of poetry workshops for workers and for soldiers.

McGRATH: Yeah, they have them *everywhere*. Well, I don't know, it does seem kind of odd to read a poem or hear a poem from your local police department. [Laughs.] Nicaragua's full of surprises, I'll tell you!

TDP: Why is poetry held in such high regard there?

McGRATH: Oh, I don't think there's any kind of *answer* to that, except that for some reason or other, Nicaraguans assume—the way educated people in the Elizabethan period, I mean *educated* people, felt— that to write a poem is just something that any cultured, upper-class, educated person should be able to *do*. And you know, I myself have always felt that writing poems was . . . well, it was *more* difficult than learning to skate. (And of course, in Nicaragua learning to skate would be very difficult.) [Laughs.] It's like learning to skate or to swim—you *can* do it: if you persist, if you're willing to fall down often enough, you'll be able to stand up. That's the way I always taught my classes—I told them, it's a *possibility*, it's a *human* possibility. It's not easy, but it can be done, if you want to do it. *Maybe*, you won't be able to skate farther than across the pond, maybe you won't be able to write a poem any longer than this [gesturing to suggest a little poem], and maybe you won't be able to write too *many* of them. But if you're willing to persist, you'll be able to *do* that. The language is there, all you've got to do is to—like the snake, get out of your skin (which is all the cliché and shit language that you've had) and be a born-again snake, or poet, or snake-poet, or whatever. Then it becomes a possibility. So, I guess the Nicaraguans, probably from way back, probably from way deep in the Indian culture there, felt that they didn't see any *problems* about writing poetry, any more than American Indians did. When Sitting Bull needed to write his death song, he just *said* it. Didn't write it, it was *there*. And the same with many others—you know, the Indians had poems for all occasions. I don't know how good they were—a few have been collected; some are good. I guess that must have been the way it was with Nicaraguans, and then the fact that Rubén Darío came along puts some kind of blessing, or curse, on the *literate* Nicaraguan. He became the sort of Walt Whitman south of the border, especially to the Central Americans, especially to Nicaragua, because he was the native son.

RG: So you don't think that Darío's example spoiled it by making poetry too highbrow, then.

McGRATH: No, no absolutely not. It *changed* things, but it changed things primarily for the literates, the intellectuals, the people who had been educated. Mainly, I suppose, for the upper classes, upper-class poets; middle-class, maybe. But I don't think it had any *bad* effects that I could see there. Now, Cardenal has been importing, to some degree, certain other things, and one of them is both a good side of [Ezra] Pound and a bad side of Pound. And various other things from the United States, some of which are good, and some of which, I think, are not very good.

But there's another generation coming along who think that Cardenal is very old-fashioned. And want to work in other ways. I don't know much about what those ways are, because I wasn't there long enough. I talked with one young poet who was a member of the militia—naturally, he's a revolutionary: very *impatient* with Cardenal. But I could never make out what the hell it was that he wanted. I asked him about the movement which Cardenal and others promoted, which was called *"Exteriorismo"*—that is, looking out and picking up things from the world rather than writing out of that good old alienation. And, no doubt, that's the dominant thing. That's the thing in the workshops. The poems might remind you a little bit of things by the Objectivist poets here in the States. Which is not the worst thing in the world to be reminded of, for the most part.

RG: You said "good Pound and bad Pound," good things and bad things that Cardenal had brought in. What do you mean by that?

McGRATH: One of the things he got from Pound, and almost anybody gets from Pound, if they read *ABC of Reading*, or some of his criticism, is that you have to *look* at a thing, you know, you ought not to *vaporize*. That, as he said, poetry should be at *least* as well-written as prose. I think that one of the great things that Pound did—not just Pound, but the others around him at that time—was Imagism, which I believe is in many ways the most *useful* movement that came out of those times. It has disappeared now, in a way, but many of the things that were in that are with us. Though I don't remember the Imagist manifesto, I remember "a new rhythm is a new idea" (which I don't believe, but it was a shocker to hear that), and the idea that the poems could be made out of looking at a thing, and saying what was there. I think it's absolutely marvelous, because I believe that poetry had drifted way away, away from that. "Sumer is icumen in,/Lhude sing cuccu!," and "bulla, bulla ferteth," the bull farts, flowers grow, and so on. That's marvelous. Or "O Western wind, when wilt thou blow,/That the small rain down can rain?" These are wonderful things.

Or go back to Chaucer, or go back to Langland, and see the way they saw things. And again, through the great Elizabethans; and then something happens with the metaphysical poetry, which distances itself, but it's still got some wonderful things. Then, you get the eighteenth century and things began to be generalized—nobody sees "rose moles all in stipple upon trout that swim"; they see "the finny tribe." And Pope has a little meadow, and because the cows move around on it and disturb the composition, he gets rid of the cows and puts up papier-mâché ones. [Laughs.] (I don't know if that's true, but it sounds like the way you'd want these things to be—just the way they ought to be in your own head.) And then the nineteenth century begins to *see* things again, and that's good.

But they're seeing *inside* of nature a whole lot of things that may not be there. Nevertheless, the Romantic Movement is a great, contemporary movement—I mean even though it's been stopped here or there, I think it's a basic kind of thing. Nietzsche's Apollonian and Dionysian: I've always believed that the Dionysians were the ones who were alive and that you carry Apollonianism far enough and you go back to Egyptian statuary—which, of course, Plato preferred. It's more ideal and it's less involved in time.

Anyway, to come back—one of the things Pound, and the others around him who created the Imagist thing, taught, and it caught on, was the idea of looking at something and *seeing* it. The Imagists looked at pretty things or beautiful things—conventionally beautiful—and it got to be like decorative painting, I think, and a little too beautiful, probably. Then, the next group were, first of all, Objectivism—which I think is one of the basic things in poetry. It's not that I'm mad about the Objectivist poets, because I think they were *too* tied to whatever their subject was, to whatever they were looking at. But *they* moved away from the decorative, the beautiful and so on, and out into the street, and looked at what was happening there—like [Charles] Reznikoff with the lanterns around the manhole, or [George] Oppen, or [Carl] Rakosi. *That* was a powerful step, too.

I think what it left out was that objects exist in a fluid world. They have to exist with people; people put them there. There are reasons for putting something here or there or the other place. And so what they didn't see was social movement; or probably they did, God knows Oppen knew *everything* about that. But he had *learned* a way of working in poetry, and I don't think he ever came back to the social (he was an old revolutionary, a Communist Party organizer for years before he went to live in Mexico). I think the best of those people are some of the really fine poets of these times. But, by and large, I think what Objectivism did was—like the worst part of what I see in William Carlos Williams—they began to be tied to the object, and became a kind of commodity fetishism in poetry.

That's not true, naturally, of the late Williams, where, after *The Desert Music*, *then* the poems begin to sing, and they're not so tied to objects. "The Red Wheel Barrow" is a *terrible* poem, in my opinion. *Items* in it are fine—but the first line doesn't tell you a goddamn thing! It's a terrible presumption, you know: "so much." *How* much? *What?*—"depends upon" this? A better, a far better poem, is a poem about the same time called "Nantucket." At the end of that poem, he puts a key there, and *that*, in the whole poem, just *opens* like an enormous flower of possibility. What *happens* when you use the *key* in this place that seems *nature morte?* The later poems, that's something else.

I think Cardenal brought back all those useful things and that became part of "Exteriorismo." *But* he also brought back some of the things out of the *Cantos* which I don't think really work in his poems, and I don't think they're likely to be much use there. They've never been imitated, as far as I know, in Nicaragua. That is, these *big* poems, the ones that take in American Indians. Some of those are *marvelous* to read, and moving and huge; but they have a tendency not to end anywhere, I think.

Somehow or other, some of the work doesn't *seem* to arrive at any solid place. Now, that's what I feel about Pound, and it may *well* be just my ignorance. [Hugh] Kenner would say that, and he may be right. My own feeling is that some of the explicators of Pound are—were—full of knowledge that Pound didn't have, and a whole lot of second and third and fortieth thoughts that probably Pound, when he was writing, couldn't have had. No doubt, he had a *tremendous* amount of things come into his head; and probably it was like an enormous haystack full of needles; and he found most of them [laughs]. *But*—he didn't find them *all*, I think.

So, you get these wonderful—I used to think, when I was a kid, of the *Cantos* as some kind of marvelous Sears Roebuck catalog—you open it up and you read . . . ahhh, marvelous stuff! And then, you turn another page or two, you're off somewhere else, you're in the farm machinery section, where you *really* wanted to see ladies' lingerie. I know that's a pretty callow view of it, but I've read the *Cantos*, I've loved *many* of them—there's such excitement in them. And yet, at the same time, I had the feeling I was sort of on a train going through fabulous landscapes, but when I got back I'd probably be where I started, somewhere like that. Not "in my end is my beginning" or "in my beginning is my end," but: we've been in a lot of interesting places (and some dull, too).

TDP: So it is not enough to juxtapose two images?

McGRATH: Well, if you go to juxtapose them, you ought to get the third thing. I mean, that's primitive dialectics. And I don't think you always *do* get that. But as I say, the *Cantos* is such an enormous thing, I don't know whether anybody can truly encompass it. To read it would take you how long? I think *Finnegans Wake* is simpler. [Laughs.] And you know what Joyce said, "Always put in a few things that they can't understand, that will keep the professors busy for a hundred years." [Laughs.] But you read something like *Ulysses*—even reading it in my limited way—and *one* of the things that I think you can't help being impressed by is how sometimes even the *tiniest* detail gets picked up and used again, and something that *seems* to be just peripheral becomes a piece of the work. To me, that probably is the greatest achievement in the century. To me, that book is just totally fabulous, so, I don't think as highly of the *Cantos* as that, and I don't think as highly as *some*, of our man in Nicaragua.

But the thing is, he's a lot more than the poetry he's done. He's also the guy who started Solentiname, his little commune on an island, and so on.

Radicalism (Including an Experience at Oxford)

TDP: You spoke of your father as having acquired a kind of gut-level radicalism, or sort of breathing it in with the air, from people around him; and you yourself must have picked up a good deal of that as you

43

worked with field teams and what not. But you say of him that he never had any theory—he just responded in a strongly-formed way which he picked up as a kind of tradition, but he never read any of the classic books.

McGRATH: No.

TDP: But you do have theory. How did you go about getting that, and why?

McGRATH: Well, I guess what happened was that I got a basic kind of radicalization out of my father and out of people around him, and people who passed through when I was a kid, working. Somewhere in high school, I read a little of Marx, and that seemed to pick up these things that my father had talked about, in a different kind of way. My father says, "Can't trust any of those rich sons-of-bitches," and Marx talks about the ruling bourgeoisie. And eventually, I guess, I made some kind of connection. And then I began to read in college, I began to read some of Marx.

TDP: On your own? Or did you take a course?

McGRATH: On my own. No, there were no courses in Marxism. [Laughs.] *Later*, I did meet an English guy who taught a history-of-modern-Europe kind of stuff. This guy, who *was* a Marxist, he really opened my eyes. Because he's not just telling me *what* happened. He wasn't interested in dates, he was interested in what caused *this* to happen. And so I got to know him, he then gave me some of what were current books of Strachey, for example—not Lytton, but the other guy, John, who was really the most powerful writer of the theorists, and maybe apologists, of the Popular Front times, which was the latter part of the thirties. So, bit by bit, I began to get a sense of where things were at, and I began to read Marx in a *fairly* persistent and systematic way— and others, Bakunin and all the rest. I began to put together a kind of a Marxist view of things.

And from there, I met some of the people off-campus, radicals, and eventually I was in the Communist Party and I was told, "Now, look, comrade, you ought to read this," and I did. There were some brilliant people there in that little CP group in Grand Forks. Most of them were off-campus, some were students, but most of them were working-class guys—unemployed because, you know, at that time practically everybody was out of work.

TDP: Did you have long talk sessions?

McGRATH: Oh, yeah, right. They were always straightening me out [laughs] because I was always . . . [laughs] I tended to be *aberrational* at that time. [Laughs.]

TDP: How did you move from campus to off-campus?—the average student wouldn't.

McGRATH: Well, it happened this way. At the very beginning of the war in Spain, I wasn't in college; I was out for a year because I didn't have the money, and I had reached the point of Wobbly anarchic notions that all newspapers were just a pack of lies, and they were put out by the enemy. I never *read* them. Except once in a while I'd see a headline. And I saw a headline, "The Rebels in Spain Do This and That," and I became a rebel. [Laughs.] And a friend of mine came back from college in the spring and we started talking about the war and discovered that we were on the opposite sides. And I couldn't figure how this could be, because we had been in accord, pretty much, up to that point. And so, he said, "Well, you dumb bastard, don't you know who the rebels *are*? They're *Fascists*!" [Laughs.] I started reading the papers again! [Laughs.]

So, after that, I began to *attend* a little bit more. And then, when I was in college I ran into all these people who, to one degree or another, had *some* political sense, among the students. And then some student group invited a Communist to come and talk. He made it *clear* what was going on—which had all been *fuzzed* before that. And we spent a long time, some of us, talking with him afterwards, and went out and drank beer. And eventually he said to a few of us—we'd see him occasionally—"Listen, why don't you come down and talk with some of my fellow *comrades* here?" And so we said O.K. and we did. And so, some of us, then, after a bit, became party members. They weren't . . . they were kind of *slow* about taking us in. They said, "Well, let's see here, we'll give you a couple of months and see what you do."

TDP: Were you a student at the time you joined the party?

McGRATH: Yeah, I was a college student. But as I say, they said, "First of all, you're a *candidate* and we'll *see*." And so, after a couple of months or so, a couple of us went into the party. Later maybe another one or two—they were very choosy in those days. This was before the American Popular Front thing, which I never approved—voted against in the referendum on it—and among other things, they asked, "Are you willing to do illegal work?" So, I thought that one over and I said, "Yeah, I will." That question, after the Popular Front days, I don't suppose was asked, though I guess it was probably assumed. You know, some of the illegal work didn't amount to a goddamn thing. I mean, you went out and wrote on the walls or plastered up posters. Nothing would happen to you except you get popped in the slammer for overnight, and then they'd probably kick you out, as a public nuisance or something. Though other things *could* happen, and . . . anyway, that was the way it was for me there.

And I went on reading, as best I could, and I read—well, I always had the notion that I wanted to read every book that had ever been written—but didn't get very far. [Laughs.] I wasn't like Thomas Wolfe, of whom it could be said, *was* said, he never read a book, he read a *library* [laughs]. And that was a little more than I could manage.

I'd always been writing, been trying to write poetry for years, and writing horrible shit, because until I was a senior in high school I'd never encountered a contemporary or even a modern poem. Then, I began to read some of these people—I read Pound and Eliot, and one of the anthologies I remember was Conrad Aiken's *Modern American Poets*, or whatever it was called. It was, for a little book, a pretty good sampling. (At that time we didn't have the *millions* of poets we now have; there were far fewer, and of course, that book was a winnowing out too.) So, I read those and I began to dig into the library. And I was working on NYA, the National Youth Act, fifteen cents an hour, for the head of the department, and I conned him into buying all the books that I wanted out of the department funds, which weren't very big.

But I began to get hold of *books*, where before I'd only read *samples* of people. I began to get Eliot and Pound; above all, Hart Crane. I'd run across him somewhere and he was the one I wanted to read. And at that time I could read French well, and I was reading back issues of French literary magazines; I read the surrealists and all that stuff, which was I think very influential. (I didn't know how to *use* it, I didn't know how to use anything.) Those of us who were writing poetry went through phases, I remember, when we wrote these sort of collage poems; they were essentially Eliot's business of picking up bits and pieces here and there. So, we went him one better, we never even wrote any of our own [laughs], we just got hold of these things and stuck them down and tried to make poems out of them. They were all junk, but it was kind of exciting to do. Then, bit by bit, some of us began to try to do things inside our experience. About three years later, three o'clock in the afternoon, one summer, in a rented room in Grand Forks [laughs], I wrote the first poem that I thought amounted to anything. And the one that I kept—that's where it started for *me*.

TDP: How many years would you say you felt comfortable, or not in too much conflict at least, with being a good party member? How long before you started to pull away? Was there ever a break?

McGRATH: Well, it was an uneasy *relationship* for me, beginning almost immediately, with the Popular Front thing. But I accepted that, I accepted the discipline. Besides, the idea was that I was going to Spain, I signed up, and I was supposed to go there when I was in college. A friend and I—both of us had gone into the CP at the same time, and he was somebody who had been in Spain, for a summer—we were both going. And we were supposed to go; but then, there was a kind of arrangement: the idea was, the Italians will take their troops out and the international brigades will be taken out. So the IB's [International Brigades] went back, were taken out.

TDP: You were with the Communist Party for a period of time and then you moved away from it. What was the time span?

McGRATH: Well, the first break was back during the war. In the first place, when you entered the army, the party dropped you out, because they didn't want to create difficulties for you. So I wasn't a member during that time. But I was at *odds* with it, toward the end of the war when it passed through a period of—this is such ancient history now—Browderism. [Earl] Browder had decided that revolutionary activity would no longer be necessary, that somehow or other there was going to be this wonderful accord between the powers who had defeated the Nazis. And that one might go forward with a kind of . . . I don't know, *benevolent gradualism*. Which I thought was total bullshit. And I think practically everybody in the army felt the same way. And so I was at odds from that point until Browder got his ass thrown out.

RG: Where were you at this time?

McGRATH: I was in New York. Generally speaking, the party was doing what I thought was proper work, and I was doing rank-and-file work with teamsters and with longshoreman groups. Doesn't mean I was in those unions, it means that I worked with the rank-and-file people, some of whom were Communists, some weren't. The point was to put out *propaganda*. I invented the League of Happy Teamsters. [Laughs.] We used to have parties—"rackets," as they called them—to raise money. Then we'd put out the new issue of the *Teamster*. And tried to distribute it without getting our heads torn off. [Laughs.]

TDP: Did you, even then, insert little bits of humor, as you went along?

McGRATH: I did my best! I can't remember how often I was successful, but I always thought that there ought to be some little *thing* put in there, you know? You don't know who's gonna read the paper. [Laughs.] I thought, just one—the right—teamster reads this, and suddenly he'll be transformed and they'll take over the Pistol Local! [Laughs.] There was a Pistol Local, so called, because the way you got elected was, you got a pistol and then you went out and shot whoever was the president of that local, and then you became the president. A guy named Cockeye Dunn—everybody had these marvelous names among the working-class Irish people in Chelsea, they're great for naming people—and so, Cockeye Dunn, one of these people, he was very successful. [Laughs.] And I think he became—had a Pistol Local—probably a labor statesman like Walter Reuther, or J. P. Ryan, or any of those *crooks* and *bastards*, you know, tied up with Mafia, the Church and Christ and what else!

TDP: They received names like these, that were given to them by the community—they didn't *choose* their own names?

McGRATH: Oh, yes, absolutely. No, they didn't choose them, the names were given to them. Sometimes they were given fairly early, you know. Because Cockeye Dunn was not always a high-class gangster. He just began as what they call a "nosy hoople"—a "hoople" is some poor son-of-a-bitch wandering around trying to get himself *connected*, with a powerful ambition to become a gangster, and even a racketeer, and be totally *connected*. But at the worst, he hoped, he could make a kind of connection where he could take over a corner. If he had a corner, he could control the whole works *on* the corner. Not the next corner! [Laughs.] Could be halfway down . . . whatever.

Anyway, that went up to '47. And then I had a letter [about his

Rhodes Scholarship, already deferred because of the war] from the warden of Rhodes House, from Oxford, who said, "If you're not going to come this year, forget it." So we went in '47. And I stayed there for a year, and did all the jazz that you do for what I think they called a "B. Litt." So, I did the exams, and then I started fishing around for a thesis. I wanted to write about Christopher Caudwell—because I knew the work and I knew people who knew him. I probably could have gotten some of the manuscripts that hadn't been published yet, that became *Further Studies in a Dying Culture*, and a few other things. I might have been able to get those, through friends who were friends of the Sprigg family (which was Caudwell's real name).

Right after the war, I read *Illusion and Reality*, which I take to be the most important book by a Marxist on the subject of the arts. That's what I believe. E. P. Thompson and I have had disputes over this for I don't know for how long. I can't say exactly what the dispute is over; it was long ago with Edward. I think Edward had the feeling that Caudwell was making too much of Freudian/Jungian material. But my own feeling about this is that Caudwell was using this only because it was a useful metaphor, for him, which I think is perfectly legitimate. I don't think that Caudwell was a subscriber to Jung, and I know that in many places he rejects some of the basic notions of what was once called "depth psychology," "psychoanalysis," whatever the hell was the term for it. But he sees certain ways of seeing things through the use of their terminology.

Well, the thesis committee looked at that for a while and then they said, "Well-l-l, you know, Caudwell is terribly recent, we can't really know what value . . ." And so forth. That came back, and I thought, "Well, O.K."—I was still trying to play the game a little bit and I said my next project was, I was going to write a little thesis on T. S. Eliot's criticism of Elizabethan and early seventeenth-century people, because I knew all that, the plays and poetry, I knew that very well! And his essays.

They thought that one over, and then they said, "Well-l-l, Mr. Eliot is certainly an excellent poet, but he is still alive and . . ." So they rejected that. And so I said, "I'll do an edition of William Diaper's translation of Camoens' *Lusiads*," the great Portuguese epic.

And they said no. So then I said "I'll do a definitive edition of John Duck, the Thresher poet." And my advisor, who was J. B. Leishman, a translator with Spender of Rilke, he came in with this thatched-roof hair and said, "The committee are of the opinion that you should stop making jokes." [Laughs.] So, I said, "O.K., I'll stop making jokes." I went

49

over to the warden of Rhodes House and I said, "I resign. I'm giving up the scholarship." And so I became a dropout, and I went over and stayed in Europe for that year and most of the rest of the next year, and I wrote a novel, *This Coffin Has No Handles*, which is partly about the New York waterfront thing. I wrote it in the south of France, at Villefranche-sur-Mer. (And then later in Paris for a couple of months, I worked on it.)

And then, I came back to the States and I went out to L.A., because when I was in the Aleutians, wearing all this rain clothing and being soaked all the time, my dream was to go somewhere where I could take off *all* my clothes and lie in the sun.

I lived out in L.A. for some while, and there I did work. I wasn't a member of the working class, because for one thing, I was blacklisted for . . . I was a *kind* of a machinist but I was blacklisted for that. What I mean is, if you wanted to get work as a machinist out there, you had to pass some kind of test, you know, because a lot of the work going on at that time was still defense contract work. I mean, the big stuff. So, I couldn't get work there. I did get a job at the Southgate General Motors assembly, because it had such a turnover. It was the kind of place that drove people crazy after a short time—the terrible speed-up. But, the day I got that job, I also got this other job teaching at L.A. State College. And I figured, well, that's likely to be long-term, so that's where I went to work. I still went out and distributed leaflets in the railroad yards, and all that kind of stuff which I had done before. After that, I wasn't *in* the industrial working class. I wasn't a part of it. I had friends who were, but I wasn't related to them, to the workers, to the working class, industrial types, and so on, the way I had been for some while when I had been in New York. So, I fell into this teaching job, which I had until the House Un-American Activities Committee threw me out. I was blacklisted from teaching and eventually I drifted into this business of doing documentary films and eventually I got blacklisted there, and then I went out to North Dakota. And then, somebody offered me a teaching job there.

During that time in L.A.—since this is the theme we started with—I worked with the party, but I was on the outs on a number of things. One, the cultural line, *always* on the outs. And I was told by the great Dorothy Healey, who's [laughs] no longer a member of the Communist Party, that I was *very presumptuous* because I *challenged* someone—a good guy, but whom she and some others took to be a little too much of a guru then, John Howard Lawson. Also, I was totally opposed to a part of the tactical line, which sometimes dreamed of forming some kind of coalition—as if the Popular Front days might still come into existence—

between the left liberals, the liberals, and the left wing—as they thought—of the Democratic Party.

Well, I told them that there was no such thing, and it would never work—*can* never happen—that I would not support that kind of politics. So, I was put in limbo for some length of time. I was never expelled. I was just sort of lost; and I stayed lost for some time. I did the same things I had done: I worked sometimes with the CP, sometimes with the Progressive Labor Party, which was doing some good things, then. Sometimes with this group and that group and . . . Cisco Houston—a wonderful folk singer, he was the sidekick of Woody Guthrie for years and years—and I and one and two others formed a new party. It was called the "Ramshackle Socialist Victory Party." Because the initials were RSVP and we thought *nobody* could resist that! But . . . Well, that's in the poem, I guess.

TDP: Were you still a member of the Communist Party?

McGRATH: A card-carrying and dues-paying type.

TDP: But while you still had your card, you started the RSVP?

McGRATH: Ah, I might still have *had* it, but I wasn't in good standing. [Laughs.] I was lost, I was—those were the years of my wandering in the wilderness; or my days. And then I got fired, and eventually I ran out of work in L.A. and I went to New York again.

So, here I am, I'm betwixt and between, and that's the way it stayed until, after a while, it seemed to me the CP had got itself sorted out and going in the right direction, and somebody came along and said, "Hey, look, you're an old-timer here"—as I was by that time—"how about hooking up with us?" And so, *to some degree*, I did that. And that's the way it is. I still think and I believe it's doing good and useful work, the party is. I believe that Hall is very bright and sensible. *But*—it's a very bad *period*, and not a lot of things are going to happen in a hurry. But that's the way it goes, it's true for all the parties—outside of the Republicrats and the Democrats. And that's where it is. I'm still sort of betwixt and between, but I'm in . . . in alliance.

I'm still a revolutionary, absolutely, no less than ever. And while I don't *like* . . . I've always believed that a revolutionary ought to be somebody who could *do* something and who *did* something, and here I *am*, I'm a cripple now, I can't, there isn't much I *can* do. Except whatever

I can do to piss off [laughs] the opposition or astonish or madden or whatever the hell—be whatever nuisance and whatever witness I can be.

It seems to me that the American CP, of all the parties that call themselves revolutionary and that are interested in the establishment of socialism here and elsewhere in the world, is probably—as *weak* as it is now—*functionally*, probably the best. I think their line is a sensible one, and I hope they stay that way. With political parties you can never be sure of these things.

So, I don't think I've ever lost any sense at all of what I wanted: to try to get as much in the world as I could to move. I don't think I've changed that at all.

Details of the Life

RG: What was the occasion of the ambush you portray in Part Three of *Letter* [see pp. 31 ff.]?

McGRATH: Well, there was a guy who lived in the town of Chaffee. This bastard was the banker there, and he owned—you know, he had mortgages on, it seemed to us, the *earth*. And he would come out through the countryside and try to collect a little bit here and there. You know, the idea of paying everything off—that wasn't going to happen very *soon*. But he had patience. And he would come through and if a farmer had a few head of cattle, well, all right, he would make his demands—like a goddamn highwayman, practically. And he was the guy.

Jimmy and I, we were just *kids*, we don't know all this, all we know is that he's the greatest enemy that had ever been encountered out there. And that he's throwing people out, and he's likely to throw *us* out. So we decided we'd ambush him. Because he used to make these drives and we knew roughly how he would make his return. But in any case he didn't make his return that way. I don't know what happened to him. He may have died in his sleep.

TDP: Which farm was at issue?

McGRATH: It was the farm that we finally came to own. And it wasn't that he was going to take away the land, because we didn't own the land anyway. *But*, farmers usually had mortgaged every goddamn thing, you know, especially cattle, and pigs, and machinery sometimes (but the machinery is often so bad; but still, it might turn up on the mortgage), probably even a farmer's horses, though I don't recall that, offhand— could have been. But especially cattle. I remember there was one case, a wonderful case.

There's a farmer there, his name is Jim Seeley, *widely* known as the greatest *liar* that has ever come into the neighborhood, and a great *namer* of everybody. He had named all the Catholics around—there was "The Pope," there was "The Bishop," there was "The Priest," and so on, and there was the guy who used to court his daughter ("Skinny," he had named her) and the courter was named "The Prairie Mule." [Laughs.] He's in the poem—you see him in the wintertime going across the land- scape, a very distant figure, heading off to court "Skinny." And the father was not likely to give them much courting time, because he had to have an audience, he needed to have somebody to talk to, and when he wasn't naming people and telling lies about them, he sort of laid in wait like a spider for anybody who came there; you had to fight your way out through the webs in order to get free. Well, naturally, the banker had a mortgage on his cattle—which didn't impress Mr. Seeley very much, because he was in the habit of selling off a few head of cattle whenever he felt the need, whenever his personal economy required it; which was true of everybody, but not everybody was willing to take chances on the law.

But he did. So, one day out comes the representative of capitalist order to find out how many cattle they've got there. Seeley lived on a farm right near a river—there was a little sort of hillock, and a lot of pasture along the river. So he said, "Oh, yes, I'll bring up those cattle, they're in great shape." And he sent "Punky," that's one of his sons, down to bring up the cattle. So Punky brought these cattle up and they slowly passed around the hill and the guy started counting, and so on, and Seeley says, "Bring up those other cattle there, Punky, bring up the other herd!" And Punky, of course, drives the same ones—I mean, this is a classic folk story—he drives them around once more.

And I suppose he could have gone on driving them around. It was a great day for what you might call extemporaneous capitalism, because he had produced these cattle as if out of a hat. [Laughs.]

We knew people who were almost pre-literate, certainly pre-television types, and in the old days storytelling was a really, really big thing. And of course, my father was one of the best I ever heard. He told every goddamn thing under the *sun*—including stories he'd read in *McGuffey's Reader*. He had memorized all the poetry of the *McGuffey Readers* as far as he went at school—which was not very far. And a singer, good voice and a *tremendous* memory.

TDP: Your father's, and your mother's sides, came from Ireland—the grandfathers?

McGRATH: All the grandparents did.

TDP: The O'Shea's and McGrath's?

McGRATH: No, the Shea's. Probably was O'Shea when they came in but . . .

TDP: And there were Shea and McGrath farms?

McGRATH: I'll tell you. My mother's father came to North Dakota around the tail end of the '70's, maybe it was '80. He came in working on the railroad—that would be the Northern Pacific and, I believe, the Great Northern—they both come into Fargo. He came to Fargo and he homesteaded, right in the center—practically the center of Fargo, so the story goes. But he was broke, so he got a job freighting from Fargo to Winnipeg, and according to him, he used to drive these old Red River oxcarts with the wheels about as high as the ceiling, because it was a gumbo mud there. And oxen. And he'd make that trip up to Winnipeg from Fargo, until . . . Well, it was when the seasons made it possible. I don't suppose he could have done that in the winter—probably would have frozen to death. And there were still a few Indians around, not that they were killing people, but they were *there*—enough to ride in on my grandfather halfway up to Winnipeg and want to take some of his flour. Which he did not refuse to give them—they scared the shit out of him. And he was an anti-Indian man from that point on. He had an old Civil War, I suppose, Remington.

In any case, he did this for a while, I don't know for how long. Then he traded off this place in what is now more or less the center of Fargo—this is the story [laughs]—because the land was too low-lying. The Red River, in winter, or at the end of summer, is thirty—oh, it may be fifty feet wide, around Fargo, something like that. You couldn't drown in it, probably it's too thick with mud—that's why it's called the Red River (though people did use to swim in it when I was a kid; I remember coming into Fargo once and seeing people swimming near a dam, which is no longer there). So, he trades this off. In the spring, see, the river

54

would—it's in a valley, it's the center of what was an old glacial lake bottom, Lake Agassiz. So the land is lake bottom, it's one of the three richest places in the world, and when the river gets over its banks, which are no more than about twenty feet up, it's got *nothing* to stop it and it can be thirty miles *wide*, practically! And about so deep [measures inches with his hand—and laughs]. I mean it just *rolls* out in the fields and that's it. I'm exaggerating a bit, but I mean it *is* something.

He didn't think that was a good place to farm, so he traded off and got a place out on the Maple River, which is outside the valley, about sixty-some miles from Fargo. And that's where he started out. He sent back to Ireland and he got a wife who was about three times his size from over the Shannon, where the English said they would drive the Irish to hell or Connacht. And so, he got one of those beauties from over there (and probably she *was*). She was a Gaelic speaker, whereas his Gaelic was very, very little. And so here he is, about this tall [indicating very short stature], and here she is, a giantess! And then they produced two sons and four daughters. He parlayed that bit of land—because the times were good, the prices were good—to a point where he owned, I don't know, a couple of thousand acres of land, which was big in those days. He gave a section of land (640 acres), buildings, cattle, horses and a huge threshing machine, to his oldest son, and the same thing minus the threshing machine to his other son, and nothing to his daughters until much later, because they were getting married.

He became very rich on paper, as a lot of people did out there who got there early. He lost his ass, totally, and one of his sons lost all that land and all his stuff. At the end, when I knew him, when I was going to high school and when I was staying with them, he had one miserable little farm left, and, I don't know—he owned a few acres, some of which he gave to his daughters, split up a half-section among four daughters.

So eventually *my* father, after years—a lifetime—of renting land, managed to—as a result of the war, the Second World War, good times, good crops and good pay—managed to own that land. So, he wound up, my father—when he was, oh God, must have been around sixty or so at that time—a *landowner*, after all those years! I think it really sort of amazed him. He always seemed to think it was kind of funny, that he had this. *He* had worked in the woods and to a limited degree on railroads, so he was more cosmopolitan [laughs] than most of the people around, most of his contemporaries. And then, in the woods he encountered the Wobblies. And that's where he picked up a certain point of view.

RG: That's why woodcutting is the big scene that it is in the first part of *Letter*?

McGRATH: [Laughs.] Well, it's also because woodcutting—if you didn't have anything to burn, you'd better cut wood or freeze to death. [Laughs.]

TDP: So, his father, then, came over from Ireland also.

McGRATH: Yes, my father's father came from Ireland to Canada, and from Canada came down and eventually wound up at a little place called Fort Ransom, homesteaded, got killed by a runaway team, the farm went under, and everybody went every which way. The daughters got married; the sons, some of them, went back to Canada.

TDP: How many daughters and sons?

McGRATH: My father was the youngest of his family, the baby. I think he had two brothers and I think four sisters. Most of them went to Canada, and most of them I never knew, except to see once in a blue moon.

RG: It was your mother who was one of the four daughters who got those pieces of that half-section?

McGRATH: Yeah, that's right.

RG: But your father, when they married, didn't own land?

McGRATH: No, no. He got married, I don't know how the hell he got *anything* together, but he went to farm in a little town called Fingal.

RG: Why didn't they farm the land that your mother got from . . .

McGRATH: She didn't have *any* of it, at that time. My grandfather was still alive, he hadn't given *anything* to his daughters at that point—it was not until he was almost dead that he finally gave that land away. And even at that time it was being rented, bits and pieces of it here and there. It was only later that it got sort of brought together, first a quarter-section of land, and then the whole half-section—which is not enough land to do anybody any good up there, now. It was a small farm then, and of course, in the Depression days, when my father was *renting* this land, you couldn't make a living on it. At one time a quarter-section of land was a family farm, when I was a kid; then a half-section; then later there had to be more than that.

RG: It was too big to work by yourself and otherwise too small for making a living?

McGRATH: *Partly* that. And partly because in the bad times the crops, you know, you produce nothing. During a lot of the thirties, you'd put the seed in and be lucky to get the seed back—because it was also the drought times, Dust Bowl times. So, that was the way that was.

That went on right up until, well, say, 1940—the war's what bailed out my father and other farmers like him. Bailed them out for a while; all those people who had that small amount of land are long gone. There's nobody now who can make it up there with that amount of land, it's too small. The cost of production is way up, the price of the crop is too low. There's no way of doing it in that amount. Some places in Minnesota, it *can* be done, because the land is richer, but up where we were, outside the valley, no, it couldn't be done that way.

TDP: You have a poem called "The Old McGrath Place." Which place is that?

McGRATH: That's the one that my father and my mother finally owned.

TDP: When they got the land—that had been *her* father's land at one time?

McGRATH: Yes. We farmed that land on two or three occasions before we finally came to rest there. It was really too small and my father rented . . . Sometimes he had bigger farms, and probably might have been quite a successful farmer except for one other thing that happened to one of my aunts: her husband was killed. She wanted my father to come and handle the place, because her kids were too young. My mother wanted that, and my father did it, so essentially he lost the possibility of the bigger farm that he had been planning. So.

TDP: In *Letter*, with the fight between Cal and your uncle, is that uncle on your mother's side?

McGRATH: My mother's side. Yeah. He was the one who was success-ful in *losing* his section of his land and his threshing machine and everything else.

TDP: But he was pretty powerful at that point? In that memory?

McGRATH: Yes. Oh yes. Yes. That's true. I mean he was a big strong man and within the limits of the place seemed to be successful—which meant, I suppose, he could borrow more money than some people. Of course, he wound up losing his ass, too. And a lot of other people did.

TDP: A lot of small hard times, or was it a large event that broke a lot of these people, or drained them away?

McGRATH: Well, I remember I first heard of hard times when I was just a kid in the twenties. My father came back from selling some cattle and I could see that he was very depressed. I asked him why, what's the matter? And he told me that he hadn't gotten anywhere near as much for the cattle as he had hoped for. I said, why? And he said, "There's depression on the farms." And I never knew anything else [laughs rue-fully], until after the war, when I went back.

But *that* depression was nothing like what happened in the thirties. Because *then* it was coupled with drought, windstorms that you can't believe, and so on. We had gotten to a place where we were eating seed-wheat, which is like eating your arm in order to keep yourself alive. And other farms around did the same thing. A bunch got together and took a bushel of seed-wheat apiece. Got somebody who had an old Ford truck, put in money for gas, took it up to Bismarck where there was a state-owned elevator, the only one in this country (and there was a state bank, the product of the Non-Partisan League, a very powerful Populist movement) and got the stuff milled, and we ate that.

And then, as if miraculously, Roosevelt had been elected and WPA [Work Projects Administration] came along. And the farmers got paid to gravel the roads, these old dirt roads, in the middle of winter. And they went out there and they did that. Must have been the coldest, most miserable work that has ever been done. But that kept us afloat, and kept most of the farmers afloat. The next year, the crops were no better. And they didn't *get* better until the end of the decade, when it began to rain a little bit again and the crops began to be produced again. And then the war came along and of course there was a market for every-thing.

58

RG: By 1959 or '60 or '61, when you went back that year, everything was lost by that time?

McGRATH: Oh, by that time, yes. *All* these families, the whole community that I knew, was totally blasted. There were still *some* people from there, but they were now the kulaks—I mean by luck, or whatever means, they had managed to gather together a lot of this land. A cousin of mine was one of these people. I don't know what he was farming on at that time, a huge—for that part of the state—a huge amount, say a few thousand acres. Nothing like the west of the state, where, Christ, they farm thirty thousand, or whatever. But he had been lucky, and he was bright, and he didn't go off to the wars, and various other things. So, he had managed to pull all this together. But farmers like my father were all gone. They weren't there anymore. And so, that was the way *that* was, when I went back.

TDP: E. P. Thompson, in "Homage to Thomas McGrath" [see p. 106], says that your family experience was the whole cycle—from homesteading to generations working together to bust—in three generations.

McGRATH: That's right. That's exactly it. Yes. *Classical.*

RG: I think it would be unusual for anyone from a later generation even to have had contact with the kinds of representative moments that happened to fall in your path.

McGRATH: Well, the thing is, I'm sure they exist in other places, but in some ways I think I was fortunate that I did see quite a number of dramatic things. I don't believe that that has disappeared. It's just different, you know, and there are other places. For instance, if I were Chicano, or native American, I'd still be living in those times and probably would *never* have any notion that there were ever *any* good times *anywhere!*

RG: You wouldn't have the sense that you suggested a second ago of a classical tragedy with three acts. What you went through was so compressed, whereas probably most people are experiencing a protracted stage of some kind and wouldn't have the advantage of seeing the stages follow each other with this inevitability.

McGRATH: That *may* well be, though, you know, the country is various, and there are a lot of things in other parts of the country that

59

may parallel, or be *more* dramatic. For instance, if your grandfather and mother were slaves and you went north to work in the Ford plant—you see? I mean, the country is *full* of this, has a *lot* of this. Where I was at, I saw certain things, but there are things similar to this, or analogous.

TDP: E. P. Thompson says, just in passing, that one of your grandfathers had a reputation for being a great curser. Is that right?

McGRATH: That's true. [Laughs.]

TDP: Is that Shea?

McGRATH: That was Shea. See, my other grandfather, I didn't know. He was killed while my father was just a boy. But my grandfather who was, as I told you, about this tall [very short]—oh God, he could start cursing somebody at noon and not be out of breath in the evening! [Laughs.] Oh *God*, he had things, I wish to God I could remember them, because they were—*some* of them were, talk about surrealists, they were *there*. You know, some of it verged on the kind of thing in the Spaniards and the Mexicans and that whole tradition—there is *great cursing* that goes on (well, of course they have the buttress of Catholicism to back them).

My grandfather was the kind of a curser who'd start on somebody— could have been somebody here, somebody back in Ireland—and you'd get this long sort of introduction to a novel! He would tell you all about this person's background, and his general activities, proclivities, his ancestry—none of which was good—and so forth and so on. And he'd get sort of *entranced* by this. Usually it took my grandmother to say, "That's enough, Matt." And then he'd stop. [Laughs.]

Life and the Poem, and a Left Aesthetic

> And every morning down to the hornacle mine,
> To the vast dream foundries and mythical money go-downs
> Of the city of death. (And always with Comrades Flotsam and Jetsam!)
> Reading the wish to die in translatable shirts of autochthons,
> Blacklisted by trade unions we once had suffered to build,
> Shot down under a bust of Plato by HUAC and AAUP.

(*Letter*, Part Two, p. 118)

60

RG: What's a "hornacle mine"?

McGRATH: [Laughs.] Oh, hornacle . . . I'm sorry I ever put that in. [Laughs.] I tell you, I've been asked that question so *often*. Well, the story is longish.

When I was up in the Aleutians, I had a lot of odd jobs, especially after everything was finished up there and we were just dying of boredom, mostly. So, I was picked to write the squadron history. All the squadrons were doing this. Some historian—bigshot back in Washington—had decided this, I suppose. But I think it's standard for outfits to do that, to have it done. So, the place I had to work in was an air-force supply, a pyramidal tent, which was their headquarters—that is, for the squadron, which was an air-base squadron.

I started working on this, using morning reports and this, that and the other, and some interviews with people who had been with the squadron from the beginning—because it had grown sort of by accretion, from just a cadre to what it was when I was in it up there. I went to work in this place because there was a typewriter there, and there was shelter. [Laughs.] And as I was working, the air-supply people were going about *their* business.

It's really a boring job, and they're going about their business, and so I keep hearing what they're talking about, and they've got a problem. Their problem has to do with hornacles—somebody needs some, there'd been a request for them. So they write a letter out to . . . All this air-force stuff was, you know, dispersed around the island so it couldn't all be blown up at once, supposing the Japanese were capable of that. So they send out to these places out in the boondocks in the islands—where everybody is making raisin jack, that's their main activity—asking for hornacles. And they can't get them; they get back these letters—you know, everything's *got to* be done on paper, for the army. "No hornacles on hand, will try . . ." Over the next hill, where there is another one of these depots. And so on.

And pretty soon they've got this pile of paper and they say, "Shit! We don't have any hornacles on the whole fucking island! What'll we do?!" So, they write to Adak, which is the main base in the Aleutians: "Hornacles needed," and get back this letter, consternated, "No hornacles! Will try Anchorage." Which was the big Alaskan base. So they tried Anchorage; and no dice, no hornacles. So then they say, Wright Patterson, which is the central air-force supply place. So they tried Patterson—nothing. Except, Patterson says, "We are continuing the search. Think we have hornacles somewhere in Texas."

So all this is going on. Every once in a while I hear about this and finally I say, "Let me see what this is all about." And I went back to the original thing. Well, I don't know *what* was being requested but it *wasn't* a "hornacle." It was something else. But meanwhile, *thousands* of man-hours had been exhausted, had been used, in this frantic search for the necessary hornacles required to prosecute the war.

I didn't even tell them that what they had done was simply *misread* something. There are no hornacles. But it struck me as being, in a way, the best symbol I knew of a lot of the activity in the armed forces. A few people are fighting and dying, you know, for short periods of time here and there. And the rest of the time everybody is dying of boredom, making raisin jack, doing these other things, and hunting for hornacles. [Laughs.]

RG: It seems in the poem a good emblem for fruitless and endless labor.

McGRATH: Yeah, exactly so.

RG: What is the "cantrip circle"?

McGRATH: Oh. Well, that's just a witches' circle, where they dance widdershins—counterclockwise. Everything, or most, of witchcraft being simply a reversal of whatever is the going thing. If you've got a mass, then you have to have a black mass; whatever was profane becomes sacred.

RG: That takes me then to a bigger question. If Marxism is the first term, and Catholicism, Hopi terms, witchcraft—all spiritual elements in a poem—are the second term, what's the third term?

McGRATH: [Laughs.] Does there have to be a third term?

RG: I'm asking. There doesn't *have* to be.

McGRATH: [Laughs.] I think the third term is Marxism again.

RG: You do?

McGRATH: Yeah. All these other . . . Well, Catholicism is a big thing in the poem because I was raised that way and I went through that whole business. And also because there are certain parallels between early Christianity and, if not Marxism—no, of course not—but at least revolution, communism. And the old Wobblies always talked about old Fellow Worker, you know?—Jerusalem Slim, who was the all-time Olympic water walker and gandy dancer. This was the view that a lot of the Wobblies took. They weren't religious at all, but they saw in the figure of Christ, in that myth, something that they recognized as being close. And as a matter of fact there was a poem called "Comrade Jesus." I've forgotten it, it was a *very* well-known poem in the Left. I've forgotten who wrote it. So Catholicism is there partly because of where I lived, and through my life it was simply *there*. I had to make use of it in some kind of way, because the picture wouldn't have been complete without it. Also, I felt that same link that the Wobblies had with Christ as a revolutionary, as opposed to what he'd been *made* into. So that comes in. In a way, I was thinking in terms of a kind of liberation theology before liberation theology had turned up. Not that I want to make a link between Marxism and religion—no way, I don't want that. But I know that link has been made in a lot of places, and it seemed to *me* that to point out the parallels here was a useful kind of thing. And I believed that certainly for the Wobblies and for other people who didn't even have that much of a sense of theory or program, that was what they *saw* in Christ. A kind of an opposition which somehow wasn't working in the way it ought to, within the religions, the going religions around there.

As for the others, as for the witchcraft and so forth, well, witchcraft is a way of seeing the world and trying to control it. So is Marxism. Now, they're working from absolutely opposite ends, but one of the things that led me to see this very strongly was reading Christopher Caudwell. Because for Caudwell, all the arts (and science as well) begin with magic. In our terms here, for example, say the Oglala Sioux need to hunt a buffalo. (Naturally, hunt them when the buffalo are around, just as people pray for rain when in the rainy season and not in the dry season—usually—and do their planting rites at the time when you're supposed to plant and the harvest rites when you're supposed to harvest and not in the middle of winter.) What Caudwell sees is that in a buffalo dance, the whole tribe is involved, and the arts are involved, in this way: the dance includes music, poetry, dance, plastic arts (in the sense that people are painted and masks are used) and so forth. So that theater is there, and almost everything—except, say, architecture—is involved. (I suppose you could even argue that *it's* there.) The ceremony of the buffalo hunt is based on the magical notion that you can coerce the

Buffalo God or other gods, whatever ones you need, or placate them; and so you do the dance and then you go out and hunt.

Now, Caudwell's argument is that these magic ceremonials are economic, because while they *don't* coerce the gods—the *buffalo* don't know what's happening—what does happen is that the ceremonial takes the whole community, gathers them in on one thing and points them, bang, like an arrow. So they go out and hunt the buffalo as if they had already done it. They're secure, almost certain, that they will have the hunt. Now, they don't always. If they don't, then that's something you fucked up somewhere in the ritual. But normally, it prepares the tribe or the band, the community, for this action. And so while witchcraft as we see it now is a very degenerate form of something that was a big thing once, it's still an echo of a technique which, in *my* terms, has got to be, "We're not going to use magic any more, but we have to use something *like* that." You couldn't make a revolution without the subjective side of it also.

RG: I'm a little hesitant to accept that as an explanation adequate to what I would call, maybe not "subjective," but I might venture to say the "spiritual" dimensions in the poem. I understand the Sioux analogy, of course, but to utilize the Hopi terms in *Letter*, and to spend as much time on spirit as you do, leaves me wondering if you can convince me that you are entirely a materialist.

McGRATH: [Laughs.] All right. Let me do it this way. See if I can do it this way. Lenin sets out certain objective conditions for revolution, you know. You have to have a crisis, in which the ruling class *can't* rule. You have to have a kind of breakdown in whatever the government is. You have to have a paralysis of at least a large portion of the allies of the ruling class—that is, the middle class—indecisive, not knowing what it's going to do. And you have to have a party that is *capable* and willing to lead the revolution. And then somebody said to him, "And then when you have that, then what?" And Lenin said, "Then, you have to try." [Laughs.] And *that's* where, in *my* terms, the subjective, the spiritual—whatever else is not the objective side of the conditions—has to come into play. Because without that, nothing is going happen. Gramsci has some of that, maybe. *Not* that Gramsci simply invented this; it was *there*. But, you know, Marxism, for some people, can be very mechanical. Some tend to emphasize the so-called scientific side, meaning the objective side. Other groups and outfits tend to emphasize the subjective side. Or, looked at in another way, the Social Democrats relied almost totally on the objective, the Anarchists, almost totally on the subjective side of things. They were always *trying*. [Laughs.]

RG: Given that as analysis, then *Letter to an Imaginary Friend* would fall into the same category as the propaganda you once wrote. Is that what you're saying?

McGRATH: Well, it's different in this way: a long time ago, I got the idea that there could be two kinds of poetry for the left wing. I don't know if I ever talked about that to you.

RG: Well, I've read the passage in *North Dakota Quarterly.**

McGRATH: Yeah, right. And the weakest side of tactical writing is that it becomes—it *can* at its very worst turn into—simply slogans. May Day comes along and you write some slogans for it. It's a reduction, a very *big* reduction. It's not there to *expand* consciousness but to *direct* it, to point it, give it focus, and so on. I think that's an honorable thing for a poet to do. A lot of the Nicaraguan stuff now is of that sort. *"Exteriorismo"* essentially does that. But I always thought that there was another kind of poetry which ought to be much, much richer, to take in as many contradictions as possible, and which ought to have as its purpose the *expansion* of consciousness, not simply the focusing of it.

RG: But does a materialist point of view explain the difference between the quality of the lowest or most obvious kind of tactical work and *Letter*? What's the basis inside materialist philosophy for discriminating between one kind of poem and another in terms of their excellence?

McGRATH: Well, I haven't yet said anything about which is the best, you know.

RG: Are you going to?

McGRATH: [Laughs.] Not at this *moment*, not at this moment. But I think it depends. It has something to do with the situation, something to do with what's *needed* at a given time. And then it has something to do with long-run effects as well, and in our—in the English and

*The Fall 1982 issue, Vol. 50, No. 4, is devoted entirely to McGrath and his work. See especially McGrath, "The Frontiers of Language," pp. 27–29, about tactical and strategic poetry.

American—tradition, it's obvious that the strategic kind of poetry is what is assumed to be poetry and the other is assumed to be propaganda—I'm putting it in reductionist terms.

Inside our system, inside the bourgeois intellectual system, poetry is considered ceremonially unclean if it has to do with anything practical— unless it might be in the writing of a hymn, something like that, or in the creation of little apothegms, you know, little things—"Thirty days hath September." That's useful, it's O.K., but it's not poetry. There is a place for it, but it's not poetry. The other, the poetry which is considered great, is the poetry which—well, you can't say it in a single word, I suppose. "What oft was thought but ne'er so well expressed," that's one notion of it, and the other one is some kind of leap into the "intense inane." That's what Shelley said. Some *seizure*, you might say, of a vision, which is or seems at the time to be, to correspond with, some kind of subjective need of the people who clutch that particular poem to their bosom. They wouldn't do it otherwise.

So it's not surprising that the poems of the Romantic period come out of a particular kind of society, and speak for an intelligentsia which is to one degree or another becoming *detached* from the ruling class, and even becoming revolutionary, like Wordsworth in his early days, or Byron in his odd way, or certainly Blake.

So, that has traditionally been the great poetry; and other poetry, whatever it happens to be, is pretty much relegated to someplace else. Once upon a time there was folk poetry. It never entered the bloodstream of high culture until, well, some of these poems began to be collected in the seventeenth, especially in the eighteenth, century. I'm talking about the English tradition now. And when they *were* collected, it was because they dealt with "universal themes," which is big stuff—it *has* been, in our culture, for I don't know how long. And there's a basis for it, true. I mean, human beings have certain projects that transcend the class that they're in. So, a love story, while it may be *conditioned* by the time and place, is likely to remain *real* to the degree it has a kind of intensity. Intensity is *one* of the criteria for the best, the most powerful poetry.

So, I guess, finally what I'm saying is that I do believe that the tactical poetry is the more immediately useful poetry. But you know, somebody asked Engels, "What happened to the poetry of 1848?" And he said, "Most of it is dead with the political *prejudices* of the time." That was a revolutionary year; and yet, looking back from quite a number of years later, he sees them, even the revolutionary politics of '48, as being simply political prejudice. You know, it was essentially middle-class politics, the

'48 revolutions—though there were mixtures, there were other classes involved: but *they hadn't got a voice yet*, they were just riding along—as happened, for the most part, in the French Revolution, up until you got to a few people like [Louis-Antoine de] Saint-Just, maybe Ancharsis Clootz [laughs], and [Gracchus] Babeuf. He was a speaker for a different *kind* of French Revolution, for another stage of that revolution.

So, the tactical may die young, but it is honorable to create it. Ideally we want the two kinds of poetry to become *one* thing. This can and does happen sometimes. It's what I think happens in *Letter*.

Now that may be taking us quite a long way, but what I'm saying is, I think, something like this: In addition to poetry helping us to see what is the immediate thing that we have to do, poetry—and I think any kind of poetry that does this has a revolutionary element in it—has to—I hate the term, but—expand our consciousness. Actually, *create* consciousness, is what it's doing. Because the world is whatever it is, out here [gesturing], and we confront that world on all fours all the time. It's always ahead of us, and we're always trying to catch up to it. We try to find out about it through science or we try to know what it *feels* like to be there, and that's the job of poetry and painting and music and the other arts. I know that T. S. Eliot is a reactionary bastard looked at one way, *but* it seemed to me that *The Waste Land*, while it's not his best poem, or work, I think, by a long lot, is *the* work in which there is a real revolutionary content; not in a *positive* sense, but because it *reports* a certain—well, I might as well say it in the old way—breakdown of values. Now, values are always breaking down, naturally. But in Eliot's case, at that particular time, coming as it did at the end of First World War, it gave us a reading on the intellectuals who were in alliance with the ruling class; that was, I think, extremely valuable for us.

This is one of the quarrels that I had with the left, and not just with the CP left—it existed, surely, among Wobblies and the left wing of the socialists. I've known a few of these people. There's a group in Detroit that sends me a little magazine called *Struggle*, and it is very like the kinds of magazines that in various parts of the left were being put out in the early thirties and to some degree throughout the thirties. They begin by rejecting, bang, out of hand, just about everything that *isn't* contemporary tactical work. They don't use the term, because they don't, they *won't*, admit that there could be that kind of division I've talked about.

The left essentially doesn't like to admit that there could be this division. When I sort of invented this theory, in a review in *New Masses*, sometime shortly after the war, one of these little magazines just clob-

67

bered the shit out of me! [Laughs.] I had reviewed a book of poems by Vincent Ferrini; he's a good guy and he's done some really fine stuff. But he had written a book called *The Great Strike* (I've forgotten what strike it was about)—a little pamphlet of poems. And it was totally *with* the strike, and everything about it was *good*; the only thing was that it was written as if it were made out of total *shit*; and I pointed this out. And this infuriated some of these ultra-proletarians in the Village.

I was to some degree always under fire this way, because I didn't *want* to reject, and *don't* want to reject, anything that's of value of the past. I don't think that's a good way of starting into the future—by throwing out the valuables! Maybe if you're crossing the country in a covered wagon and the Indians are following you, you throw everything out—eventually grandma goes out, to the wolves [laughs], and you wind up without a family, the clock is gone, and you arrive at the frontier *totally on your own, without anything*! That's, in a way, what happened when we crossed the country. And that's one of the reasons why we have a pretty thin culture.

I had a lot of trouble because, on one hand, I *was* writing the poems that the Left wanted: in *Longshot O'Leary's Garland of Practical Poesy*, I wrote a lot of poems that were tied to immediate things. Some of those poems are dead and gone, because the things are dead and gone. But I was at odds with some of this feeling, in some parts of the left, which would concentrate completely on what I called "tactical poetry," but they'd just call, you know, *le vrai poesie*, or "revolutionary poetry," or *whatever* it was called. And I didn't want to throw out the rest. I didn't want to throw Eliot out, you know? I wanted to keep him, but with reservations. And so on, with many others, like Joyce or Proust, because they've done marvelous things! Even if they were nothing except pictures to put—you know, antique sculpture! We don't throw *that* out, so I always thought we should keep those things.

And there were problems and mini-wars over these things and it went on, it stayed with me from, God, I don't know, almost from the beginning. I used to send poems to *New Masses*, when I was out in North Dakota. They were bad poems for the most part, but they were better, I thought, than many that were being published by *New Masses*. And I would get letters from Norman Rosten, who was one of the editors, and a good guy, and more or less commiserating with me, that he liked the poems and he'd like to publish them, *but* they had a certain kind of complexity or willfulness or goofiness or whatever the hell, that didn't seem to fit properly.

TDP: Is there a source for your distinctions between tactical and strategic poetry?

McGRATH: No, they came out of my head somehow. *But*, about a year or two later, there was a pamphlet by Mao called *Art for the Masses and Art for the Cadres*, which is essentially the same thing. And while Mao was still held in good regard by everybody, I sometimes would point that out, but they would shake their heads. Mao says it, it must be true; McGrath says it, everybody knows he's a lunatic poet. [Laughs.]

And after I wrote *Longshot O'Leary*, I was *partly* in the good graces, though I had carefully put a few poems into that book that I figured would shake up the comrades. [Laughs.] I really wrote it for a bunch of people I knew on the waterfront who used to come by every day. I was writing junk fiction at the time, which they considered not working at all, so I was just somebody of leisure. And I lived in the same block as the NMU [National Maritime Union], so a lot of these guys would come by in the afternoons and demand coffee, and then they'd go on with their *own* arguments, which involved union politics. And you know, Christ! – they were Jesuitical and cabalistic, and they just went on up here [gesturing over his head]. And I couldn't *work* while this was happening. But as far as *they* were concerned, I wasn't working, anyway. That's not work. [Laughs.]

I was publishing quite a lot in *New Masses* at that time because the poetry editor had become a guy named Charles Humboldt. He published a lot of my work, and some people liked it and some people thought it was horrible. What would have been the word? – "cosmopolitan" was a bad word at that time. And others thought it was ultra-left and not good that way.

But by and large it was accepted, and I really had – I think I'm the only poet in America who *really* had an audience. [Laughs.] Not a huge one, but I did have one, for a while. And the most vocal of those were the waterfront radicals who'd come by, drink my coffee, interrupt my day's work, and instruct me how *poetry ought to be written*. [Laughs.] Because sometimes I wrote in rhyme, and that they liked. Sometimes I didn't, you know – I'd go writing long, loopy lines, and they would shake their heads: "Yes, well, I see what's you're doing, yes, that's good stuff – *but* that's not the way you do it, comrade!" [Laughs.] They'd all been raised in the tradition, where poetry rhymed, and they had read the Wobblies and the *Little Red Book* and things like that, and not much more. Except Shelley, they all read Shelley, but they read the "Masque of Anarchy," and things like that. They didn't read "Ode to the West Wind" or some of the other—what they would have thought—more *woozy* sort of poetry.

In any case, I wrote *Longshot O'Leary* in part to show them that it could be written in rhyme, and yet could include in it, in a poem, some kind of zinger, which they might have to think about or look up in the dictionary. Because I always told them, "If you don't know the word, that's not *my* fault, and there's a book that'll tell you what that word means." And then I threw in a few surrealist poems I'd written earlier, and some more ambitious poems. Anyway, the book was very much liked, and the last time I was back, when I read at the MLA, one of those old NMU guys turned up and started quoting my work! Which he will do—he's memorized that whole book, and he'd quote it at the drop of a hat to anybody who will listen. [Laughs.]

So, in any case, those are some of my trials and tribulations over this difference between the tactical and the strategetic. And I was never—I never wanted to throw somebody *out*. *Faulkner* was taken as a prime son-of-a-bitch because of some of the attitudes that you can find in his work about blacks, though in the long run, I don't think that's true of Faulkner, at all. I used to point this out, but certain passages were *there*, and they would be cited. Same way with Pound and Eliot. I never felt close to Pound; and Eliot was an anti-Semite and all that, too. I mean, it was *endemic* among the intellectuals of that time. I don't know where, at that time, you wouldn't find just gratuitous references or anti-Semitic statements. It's just about *everywhere*—you find it in Hemingway, for example, and Hemingway, certainly in the long run, was no anti-Semite. If I'm not mistaken, you see it in—not Farrell, I suppose, but F. Scott Fitzgerald. You know, these are things which are not considered statements, they're just things somebody will say, and the writer records them; or they're just sort of passing things which were part of the bloodstream of people then. Same way, you know, in most cases, with the attitudes toward blacks, attitudes toward Indians—Native Americans. Where I grew up, almost everybody was an Indian-hater, of some sort. Even people who had never *met* an Indian, because it had come through. I told you my grandfather was hell-set against Indians because they had scared the *shit* out of him!

TDP: Your father was friendly with them?

McGRATH: My father was, yes.

70

TDP: Did you make a conscious choice to put as much of Indian culture in *Letter* as you have? You started out with an historical record but then it becomes something else, especially in Parts Three and Four.

McGRATH: I don't know how much of it was conscious and how much of it was just something that came along. If I'm working on a poem, I don't sit down and say, this has started here and this is where it needs to go and this is the way I'm gonna get there. I don't work that way. I trust what's happening in my head, and I trust that when a phrase or a line or whatever gets turned up, it's probably usable. I believe that until the poem proves otherwise.

So, my feeling about Indians was, I guess, mainly, because of my father. One of my father's memories, as a little boy, was that all the settlers around Fort Ransom, which was one of the chain of little forts across the southern part of North Dakota—he remembered a time when *everybody* just grabbed everything, any guns and blankets and some food, and took off for Fort Ransom, because the Indians were supposed to be coming, were on the warpath and were going to do terrible things. Well, of course, it was just hysteria, but it was the thing he remembered. I guess probably one of the reasons he remembered it was that he had been friends with this Indian kid of his own age, and had swapped a calf—which belonged to him and which he used to ride as just a little boy—with this Indian kid of his own age for a pony that the Indian kid used to ride.

I had two things. One, a sense that they were mysterious people—who'd *been* there, you know. And secondly, the sense from my father that they were good people. And third, of course, all the overlay of reading, of bunkhouse reading—cowboys and Indians, and so on. And then, later on, some reading that I began, I suppose as far back as high school, of books that really were *about* Indians. It wasn't systematic reading at all, but I'd read to some degree about North Dakota Indians. I knew about Sitting Bull and Crazy Horse and all that. Custer's massacre was closer probably to us than it would have been to people someplace else. Fort Lincoln was out in Bismarck, which is the state capital, and that's where he set out from. Various things like that—and I had a friend, when I was in college, who was an Indian, one of the few Indians who were at the University of North Dakota. (I think there weren't more than maybe three when I was there; there was one girl I knew and two guys who were there because they were athletes.) I had an *attraction* in that direction, I suppose, and I had been in the Southwest, many years ago, and I've been enormously attracted, especially to New Mexico.

I'd read some Indian poetry. I stole a book from the L. A. Public Library. It hadn't been taken out for *years*. It was out of print, and I've still got it. And *that* was really a revelation to me. I mean, the translations may be the worst in the world, but just the same, they lighted up, they *were* lit up, for me.

Then, I suppose through Frank Waters, I began to have sense of the Hopi. I was at North Dakota State University, I was teaching there, and I remember I was sitting at my desk, I remember exactly what it was like. I'd been working on a poem. There was some magazine that somebody had sent me, I don't know where I got it, but it was *there*. And I read something, I think it was maybe a review of something by Frank Waters. What interested me was some of the things that he had to say about the Hopi. So I thought I'd better find out—I wasn't thinking for an instant that this had *anything* to do with the poem! But I thought it was something I wanted to read, so I got hold of *The Book of the Hopi*. I'd heard of the different worlds of the Hopi, and I knew about *kachinas*, but not the Blue Star. I'd known that there were various worlds—but you know, other Indians had that notion, as well as the Hopi. But *that* was one of the most exciting things I'd read.

One of the things that strikes me and has struck me all along is this: that whenever I was working on the poem—and I suppose I was *always* working on it—there were certain times in particular when it seemed to me that if I walked into the library and closed my eyes and put out my hand, I would take out a book that bore some resemblance, or had some relationship, to what I was doing. Over and over. Bits of conversation, songs—all this I was seeing in a different way, I suppose because of what I was doing on the poem, but I would get these sort of epiphanies [laughs], in a way. Sometimes just a little bit of casual conversation would light up something for me and I would go away with my head ringing. Everything came in, and was—I don't say everything was *useful*, but a lot of things were useful, some of them in just marginal ways. And of course the Hopi *idea* of the coming of the New World, I instantly equated that with the Revolution.

RG: Can you say now what it was you felt about that landscape in New Mexico? I assume you mean northern New Mexico, where the pueblos are.

McGRATH: Well, the whole thing, actually. The landscape, of course, is staggering. But you can find that in other places. There's a starkness there that you find in Arizona, too. After all, the places were there before they drew lines, you know. But I guess the main thing that struck me, the primary thing, was this: the drama of the Anglo culture, the Chicano culture (which wasn't "Chicano" then), and the Indians, the different kinds of Indian cultures. And then later, when I went back, in the middle sixties maybe, there was a hippie culture.

TDP: You'd say about your use of Indian materials that it came naturally?

McGRATH: A lot of it has been with me from the time I was just a kid. And the Hopi prophetic material crystalized a whole lot of this, and it became a primary way of seeing things for me. Partly because it's American and aboriginal. And it's also, from the Hopi standpoint, a timeless thing: eventually we'll enter the New World. It has parallels with everything. It parallels with chiliasm — you know, the idea of the coming of the thousand years? And it has naturally to do with the working class and peasant and Third World, what have you, revolutions. So, all these things, I tended to see all of them at the same time, and sometimes I was able to deal with this in one set of terms and sometimes in another set of terms. Of course, the governing thing that allowed me to hold these things in any kind of focus, and not let them just go off on their own, was the idea of Marxism and the idea of the transformational revolution.

RG: That means that the Hopi Fifth World is a metaphor for you.

McGRATH: Yes, it is a metaphor. And so is Christianity a metaphor. But Marxism I don't think is. It's *metaphorical*, too, but it's not a metaphor in the same kind of way as the coming of Saquasohuh.

RG: Because it's based on rational . . .

McGRATH: Yes, it's based on actual processes within the world. And I don't believe that there are supernatural processes. I don't believe in higher powers, supernatural powers, I don't believe that. In that sense I'm a materialist. But that doesn't mean that I can't see how other people might see this. I can see the beauty in it, and I can't avoid seeing the correspondences between things. The doctrine of correspondences was one that I liked very much. You know, the old seventeenth-century one, where a shamrock was a shamrock because it indicated a trinity, and so on. Everything was an emblem of something else—that's why the lion was king of the beasts and gold was the king of the metals. That kind of stuff. I think that's *wonderfully* valuable; it was a wonderfully useful view of things for writers who held it.

Let me just say one final thing. I think the way I see the world is as if it were a palimpsest: here's this writing, and underneath that is other writing, and underneath that is other writing. But this is the kind of palimpsest in which the writings are all about the same thing. But they're done in different ways, you know: the Hopi, Christianity, and I don't deny there must be many, many others. Magic, which is some small part of it also.

*　　*　　*

The little cake my grandmother gave me . . .
                              the little "Persephone" . . .
Crumbling . . .
            Take ye and eat . . .
                        The morsel dissolves on my tongue . . .
Again I drift away . . .
                  in the murmur of my father's talk . . .
                                    dreaming . . .

I rise from my sled-box bed in my night-clothes of animal skins,
I climb on the shivering ladder of Quaking Aspen boughs,
And, tiptoe on the topmost branch with the world spread out below
Far-off and tiny as a miniature map (and myself smaller
Than the angel at the top of our Christmas tree)—
                              I leap
                                    into heaven . . .

(Letter, Part Four, p. 89)

TDP: In the Christmas scene toward the end of *Letter*, your grandmother gives you a little cookie called a persephone. And of course, very early in Part One, your mother gives you some cookies before going out to work. And these are not unlike the wafers of the eucharist, I suppose?

McGRATH: Yeah, I *suppose*. One of those cookies, I mean my mother's cookies, sent me off to the whole new world of . . . sort of a grown-up world. And my grandmother's persephone, which is another name for, you know, Proserpine, she was the goddess of the underworld, daughter of Demeter, raped by Hades, carried away. . . . The Greeks used this as a way of explaining seasonal change. Persephone. It wasn't by chance that I called it that. I knew that one of the things that I was going to do, in the section coming up, was a kind of a shaman's journey. The Siberian shaman often leaped off of the top of a tree into the heavens; so my character dreams that he's taking off from a quaking aspen. And he does it, he eats the cookie, he falls asleep, or into a visionary state, or whatever you want to call it, and then he goes through the various heavens. The first of them is, of course, the underworld itself. And he comes out of that partly because he's . . . Well, he's rescued, you might say, by his son. And then he goes into the other heavens. The thing is organized, in part, in what you could call geological and animal, vegetable, mineral, and so on. And then it goes into various ways of seeing the society, which is seen partly in terms of the religions that were dominant, and then, beyond that, into these other visionary heavens. And then, the return.

TDP: Did you just stop with the ninth heaven, or does the ninth have a greater significance?

McGRATH: Well, it's only this: I couldn't allow myself to see the world transformed the way I want it to be—because I've never seen it that way. So the guide says that "Your son will see what you could never see." What I'm seeing is a kind of Saquasohuh world, and a kind of Edenic world, and so on. So that's complete then. And I come out of that, or the speaker comes out of it, and wakes.

RG: And it's still Christmas.

McGRATH: Still Christmas. [Laughs.] Well, actually it *is* Christmas Day, then—the other was all Christmas Eve.

* * *

TDP: You've said that you read Brecht early—very late in the thirties, or possibly the early forties, something like that. And you were amazed that other people hadn't heard of him, recognized him. What was it about Brecht that struck you? Was it his commitment, his art as such?

McGRATH: It was two things. He was writing the greatest tactical poetry, which is the term I wouldn't get to for another ten years or so. But what I really loved about Brecht was truculence, and sometimes even a kind of marvelous arrogance. One of the things that I've never liked in left-wing poetry, and it isn't just left-wing, it runs throughout American poetry, especially maybe more now than any time—is the whine, with a capital W. You know: "I fall upon the thorns of life, I bleed." (And then, I think he dies and then he expires and then he sighs, and I've forgot, he's got everything backwards—which Shelley does occasionally.) Well, the thing about Brecht was that he had great guts; there was no whine in Brecht, you know.

And also, one other thing, if he was going to write a poem that was what I would call a tactical poem, a poem with slogans in it, he never made any pretensions that he was going to do anything *else*! He just comes out and it's there, and either the poem will bear it and you can accept it, or fuck it. You know, he wrote the lyrics for the United Front song that goes "And just because he's human he doesn't want a pistol to his head,/he wants no servants under him and no boss over his head." And again and again you see that in the Brecht poems. I mean, not *all*— Brecht wrote *every* kind of poem. But the first poems that I saw were all these sort of immediate poems that had to do with the struggle, some of which he had written in Germany before he was thrown out. So that was what I liked about him. Very hard to handle, I thought. It *was* very hard for *me* to handle. But *that* was one of the primary things about Brecht.

TDP: Some of your early poems have a truculent aspect, as if you wouldn't mind insulting the reader—if it was the wrong, or the right, reader.

McGRATH: [Laughs.] Yes, right, that's true. Because sometimes—I went through *years* when I was writing poems that nobody wanted to publish, so *that* gave me a great freedom that most American poets have never experienced. Because the typical American poet expects that he's going to [laughs]—I don't know what the hell he expects, but he *assumes* a more or less benevolent society into which his poem will fall, or fly, or whatever it does. Sometime from the early forties onward I knew that wasn't the case with me. For instance, I published a lot of poems in *Poetry*, and suddenly that was simply closed down for me, and that was true of a fair number of other places that had been receptive to the poems and suddenly weren't. And that was more or less why I didn't publish much in the fifties. I published on the left, and I published in some of the lunatic magazines of the West Coast. But in effect I had gone on a blacklist, the way Meridel Le Sueur was blacklisted, and all kinds of other writers, especially the novelists.

But in any case, since I was sort of out of it, that gave me lot of freedom, in a way; in a certain sense it was one of the things that helped in writing *Letter*. Because when I finally started it I had no idea that any part of it would ever be published anywhere, anytime. So, I said, well, fuck it, I just launched out.

It wasn't that I had held back in the other poems. But when I was working at first on *Letter*, the first part, I had, in a way, gone back to a sort of parallel work. I had never been able to do the kinds of things in that more open form — never done what I *wanted* to do.

And anyway, so when I started — finally got launched into *Letter* — by that time I had lost the audience that I once had.

TDP: How soon did you have the title?

McGRATH: Right from the beginning.

TDP: You needed a new audience?

McGRATH: Well, I wasn't even thinking that there *was* any. And that's why it's *A Letter to an Imaginary Friend*, and not even friends!

TDP: But you knew from the beginning that you were going to call it that.

McGRATH: Yeah, I did. I think probably before I started the poem, or right around the beginning, anyway.

RG: So, in a way the poem is not only evidence of the freedom that you had, but also a response to the silence around you.

McGRATH: Yeah, absolutely. One of the things I thought was this: I don't know whether anybody's gonna read this, but if they do, in this kind of literary scene, it's gonna loosen a lot of wigs! I felt a kind of freedom that I hadn't felt before. And as I say it isn't because I felt constricted in writing any poem, in terms of what I was going to say or what my attitudes were going to be, or even in terms of the form. One of the things that seems strange to me is that when I was writing Part One, I was also finishing up *Figures of the Double World*, where many or most of the poems have a tight external form. Sometimes I'd take a form and sort of rotate it a little bit, and use off-rhymes where the original form would have used true rhymes. And I would jazz up the rhythms in it a bit, and so on. There are open poems in there, too. But there are a lot of others that are more traditional or pure on the surface. I think when you get inside them they're not very traditional—either in attitudes, ideas or even in the structure. But some of the structures certainly do *appear* that way, and some of them are pretty tightly done. Maybe the most tightly-made poems that I was writing.

TDP: At the same time as *Letter*?

McGRATH: That book [*Figures*] was published in '55, Part One of *Letter* was finished in '55. I started *Letter* in the fall of '54, and I worked on it in two great bursts. One that led up to around about Christmas, and then I had a break, everything stopped, and it started up again somewhere around spring, and Part One ends at about Easter time. And that's sort of incorporated in it, also. There's a lot of stuff about the zodiac in there, and at one point I thought I might use that as a structural thing—in one place it says there are six signs of zodiac still open. But they're still open! [Laughs.] I never got back to them in the same way.

TDP: You started with Scorpio.

McGRATH: It says "born toward Scorpio," so I probably started in October. Probably half of Part One was written in about two weeks in November, and then there was this long hiatus, and nothing would go. And then it started up again and I entered another great rush. The poem came along in such—you know the Middle English term, "a fitte" of verse? Well, that's the way it was.

RG: Can you say what the periods of composition were for Part Two? I know from the end of the poem it was finished in '68 and you were all over the place writing it.

McGRATH: Part Two? I did Part One, I thought I was done! And then time went on and bit by bit I began to get the notion that to some degree I was going to rewrite Part One. But I was going to rewrite it thematically. There'd still be narration and chronology in it, but some of it was going to go back over the work sections in Part One. Not that I knew this when I started, but I had some sense that something like that was

78

what I was going to do. And then I waited until I got some kind of signal where to start and how to start, and I did. So I started off with the last line of Part One. It seemed a good way of going. And I more or less used that system.

RG: When did you start Part Two? How long went by?

McGRATH: I was working in New York on some documentary film thing when that idea drifted into my head and caused me to shudder and turn cold. It hung around with me, and after I'd gotten the idea, it was probably something like maybe a year or so later that I made the beginning. Though, as I say, I had written, it turns out, bits and pieces. I was making notes, stuff like that, writing down lines and phrases, you know, or just images that came along. Or even things like abstract ideas—not many of those, thank God.

So, I don't know, my memory is that I did some work on that when I was out in the farmhouse in North Dakota, which would have been '60 or '61, I guess. But I didn't really make a beginning on it until later, maybe a year later. I think I did some things when I was out at the old farmhouse, but it wasn't a true beginning; I mean I didn't have the first line, and I didn't—I wasn't secure at all about how it would go or where it was going. But see, I was *living* some of the stuff that came into Part Two, like working in the woods, and that kind of stuff.

RG: In Greece, you framed the whole thing in Skyros. So over six or seven years you pieced it together gradually.

McGRATH: Well, it wasn't so much piecing together. What happened was, I had the experience of living there in North Dakota, and I think I wrote little bits and pieces—nothing, just fragments, very small. When I was teaching at NDSU, I started writing, and one of the first things that I remember writing was the section on New York. It was a longish passage, sort of impressionistic. I think it's quite a good passage; it's the one that goes "at five past money they did this," and so on.

TDP: Who was Showboat Quinn?

McGRATH: Well, Showboat Quinn was one of the guys like Lowlife McCormick, who was sort of a fixture on the waterfront. A born once-and-forever radical, but still a kind of Wobbly-ish type. Because the people that I was most closely associated with, some of them were

Wobbly-ish, too, but many of them were very disciplined types, and Showboat was in no way one of those people. But he'd been around forever. And you might see him in any gutter sometimes, though he was also a pot-smoker, which a lot of the guys, the militants there, didn't think was the best kind of thing. Because often he'd be late to a lot of the things that he was supposed to be at. [Laughs.] But, he was well-regarded, saving these few little peccadillos that I'm talking about. He was a friend of Lowlife McCormick.

There was a thing that happened in the thirties, maybe '34 or '35, before I got to New York. The Nazis sent over—it was the first passenger ship that they sent, the *Bremen*. The party decided that they'd better *do* something about that, some kind of demonstration. So they did two things. One, they created a *tremendous* demonstration down on the docks—not just CP members, but all *kinds* of people who didn't like the Nazis, even though it was early. So they had *thousands* of people jamming the docks, and the *Bremen* is about to sail.

They used to have parties on these ships before they sailed out. So my friend Mac, Bill Bailey and Lowlife McCormick and two or three other guys that I knew, got aboard, and then at a signal they went and took the flag down. And naturally they got shellacked! First of all by the Nazis on the ship, then they were put into the tender arms of the Red Squad, which had once broken the arm of a friend of mine. (They took him from one floor to the other and when he got to the other floor, his arm had been broken. They maintained that he had fallen down in the elevator. Well, that was the kind of Red Squad they had.) Anyway, these guys took the flag down, then were hauled off and the demonstration went on. It was a really dramatic and marvelous, very *poetic* action.

TDP: The German flag or the swastika?

McGRATH: The swastika—came down and went over the side.

RG: I can tell, from the way you have spoken of trade unions and industrial organizing, how engaged your feelings were in these, but in *Letter*, it seems to me, you locate "the generous wish," the highest possibility of love and work, in the agricultural and rural.

McGRATH: Well, perhaps that's because I *knew* it best and because I started that poem in '54 and because so much of the damage had been *done*. And besides, it's sort of autobiographical and so I began with early memories and go through that. And I suppose that's perfectly true. It's not that my *idea* is centered there, no; but a lot of my guts have been centered there, and I suppose that's why I began writing the poem with events when I was a kid out there. And then I come back out, I remember in Part Two, to see what the place is like again, and whatever was there was pretty well shot.

TDP: You were talking about writing the New York episode.

McGRATH: I wrote that in North Dakota, and it doesn't have anything to do with the waterfront, really. Though there are other parts there that do have to do with the waterfront past, and what it was when I was writing after the war, and so on. But I wrote that section, I remember well, in North Dakota—I remember where I was *sitting*. And that was just something that came.

The order of the poem hadn't been established, or the beginning or anything; it was *there*. You know, I've had these things that have come sometimes, that I figured were part of the poem, and oftentimes they became part of the poem, sometimes not. Some of them probably might have been if the poem had developed in different ways—like "Trinc," the long beer poem, or the bread poem, for instance: I thought, "That's *got* to be in there!" And maybe I should have got it in there, but I didn't. And there are a few others, like that. So, anyway in '60 or '61 the poem began to be launched; and that year I went to Europe, and I was in Greece, I was in Skyros, and that's where the poem begins—and ends.

RG: Why did you frame it inside that moment in your life, on that island?

McGRATH: Well, for me, part of the poem has always been what was going on around me at the time. Sometimes that kind of came in, sometimes it didn't—but oftentimes it did. The poem begins after the first line, "I'm here at 2714 Marsh Street," which is where I lived at the time. So a couple of times in the poem it says that: what is going on *outside this window*. A bus goes by called "Dogma"—I wrote that when I was in Madrid; there was a bus, it says "Dogma" on it! And that was enough for me—I didn't ever want to *ride* the bus! Odds and ends of this sort come in.

RG: Why did you choose the Greek window as the frame for the poem?

McGRATH: Just pure chance! I had done some work on the poem while I was at NDSU. I had enough money that year so that I didn't teach the full year. We went to Europe in the spring semester, and stayed until it was time to go back to work and we were broke. We went to some other places, but it was in Skyros that I had time to work. I don't know exactly how long we were there, but after the first week or so I found I could work in this little place we were at, right down at the sea. It was a place where people drifted in and out, and you could cook there, and we had a room—most of the time we had two or three rooms, because it wasn't full. So I had one room to work in and one room to sleep in and the sea to swim in.

And I could climb up to the village of Skyros. Theseus—Thesefs—one of the stories about him is that he either jumped or was pushed off the cliff at Skyros. Skyros was where Achilles—Akhilleus—went when he hid among the women. And they'd even point you out the place where the wise guy, Ulysses—Odysseus—came and pounded the arms together, he was there as an armament salesman. He pounded a sword on a shield and Achilles threw off his lady's clothes and picked up a sword and Odysseus says, "O.K., you're our man. Now, you come off and fight!"

After a week of sitting around, writing all kinds of notes on Greek cigarette cases, I started the poem. And then it started to go to beat hell. And it did go that way all the time I was there. So if I could have stayed longer I would have finished it then, but I didn't. But I did a hell of a lot of work there, in another one of these *fittes*, of about six weeks. When these things happened, I worked on the poem all the time, even when I was sleeping. I'd wake up early in the morning and work. I'd work late. And I was in that state where *anything* that I read—there were very few things to read there—any conversations, but anywhere I turned, anything I heard, anything I read, *seemed* to me somehow to be related to the work I was doing! And things would come in, you know, just found objects. Like the early surrealists. Or the dadaists—the found object. And that's the way it went. It was just a tremendous rush.

And that's the way Part One had gone, in two separate *fittes*, and Part Two, with the little bit that had been done earlier, I made the link without *any* problems at all; it was as if I had already planned it. I got down toward the end and then, because of time, got stuck. And I guess maybe a year or something went by; I think I finished that section in Mexico, and that took a while—not to write, but to get to the place where I *could* write.

RG: What year were you in Skyros?

McGRATH: Here's the way it is. Skyros—I don't know what date that was. Early sixties. In '65 and '66, I had this Amy Lowell fellowship, I was in Europe for a year, and I spent most of that time, I spent a big chunk of the time, on Ibiza. I worked—another great *fitte* of work. And then I was going to go to Grand Canary—Agaete. Because I wanted to see my friend, Jack Beeching. And so I got driven out of Ibiza, practically, because I was living in this place called The Goldfish Bowl, which was the headquarters for all the LSD, all the heads, because they could buy this stuff simon-pure from English laboratories, or Swiss laboratories. So everybody was there, including a legend, who was a Dutchman who had bored a hole in his head because he had noticed that a lot of Egyptians' skulls had holes in them. And while I thought probably somebody had hit them with a blunt instrument [laughs], he thought that they had dug holes in their skulls to let in the air, because that was, you know, "More oxygen? Good!" Well, he was being led around by the hand by various people, and no walking advertisement for voluntary trepanning.

At first, I knew nobody, but as time went on I began to know people, and pretty soon my social life was getting to be too much for me, and then I decided it's about time to get out of here, can't get any more work done. So we went to Madrid, stayed there a month; I couldn't do one goddamned thing. Nothing! Barcelona for a few weeks. We were getting a boat there, that was the reason for going there. To go to Grand Canario. Couldn't get anything done. Spent some time with Phil Levine there. And then eventually the boat came and we went to Agaete, saw Beeching, stayed at a sharecropper's place where the concrete roof was always in danger of falling and I slept with a pillow over my head every night. And then we found a little house in Agaete, because through Jack we'd come into contact with the unofficial government of Agaete. And the mayor's mother had this old house which she didn't live in, and we rented that. *Then* I started work again—and I worked again, the same way, another *fitte* of writing. And I did everything except the end. I guess in '68 I had a Guggenheim, went to Mexico for a while, and there I finished it. So it was very hard to finish. Once more I was really stopped, and then after a while the logjam broke, and I finished it again without any difficulty, rapidly, pretty rapidly, and that was that. Then I went back—from there we went to New York, but Part Two was done then.

RG: I want to ask you about something in Parts Three and Four. Near the end of Part Two, there are these lines: "What began in the first blaze—despair—is to end in joy:/After showing you hell I'm to blaze you

83

the trail to heaven." Were you already thinking at that time that you'd have to write more parts in order to get to Part Four?

McGRATH: Right. By the time I got somewhere along in Part Two, I don't know exactly where, I knew that *that* wasn't going to end. I knew I was condemned to writing more—how much I didn't know. But I did know by then that there was something else—I didn't know *what* I was going to do, or *how* I was going to do it.

TDP: Early in *Letter*, you say that you are far from the laughter [see Part One, p. 1]. However, by the time you get into Part Three, and even more in Part Four, you are *deep* in the laughter. What accounts for this change?

McGRATH: I don't know. [Laughs.] I'll tell you—"far from the laughter": well, the first line, some of the first lines say, "hoping toward laughter and indifference." And I don't mean indifference as not giving a damn, but being free of things. Maybe detachment, or unattachment, rather—something like that would have been a better term.

I had a kind of a *satori*. That was before I started *Letter*. In fact, I can see now how much that helped in the writing of the book. And the way my *satori* began, it was very early, four o'clock in the morning, maybe; I'd been awake and it was a really bad time in my life. And so I went out and sat on the porch, really in despair.

A couple of little birds, these nondescript, Los Angeleno birds, start chirruping away, up on the tree. There wasn't so much smog; I could see a few stars beyond the tree in which the birds were chirruping away, and *suddenly* it came to me that the funniest thing in this *world* must be somebody sitting out here on the steps in Los Angeles, feeling full of despair for himself, when the birds are perfectly happy!—and the stars are going along, they don't seem to give a fuck about any of this! So I started to laugh! [Laughs.] And I felt *totally* a whole new world. And I thought, you know, I must be the joke of the universe (but nevertheless, a kind of holy joke) and as good a joke as any in Joe Miller's joke book. And it was a terrific kind of feeling. I'm not going to try to elaborate on this, but it was a *radical* reassortment of the world. And I could see that the world was going to go on being itself, and that I was involved, but the world wasn't going to go out of its way for me; and I felt closer to things outside people.

I'd always felt pretty close, I think, to the natural world, but after living in L.A. for a number of years you begin to forget that it exists! But this took me back into it and it gave me this very strong sense of the *comedy* of my own being! So it was very liberational for me. And I kept that, more or less, for maybe almost three months. It was a kind of *satori*, and I thought maybe the thing to do would be just to put on my clothes and walk, go away, just take off *anywhere* and never look back again. But, you know, I also felt responsibility—which didn't seem like a bad thing either. [Laughs.] You know, I didn't feel that it was incumbent on me to go out with my yellow robe and my begging bowl—that seemed to me just as funny as if I stayed here and went on doing whatever I've been doing; they were equal.

But I think that to keep this, you might have to walk away. Anyway, it was with me for about three months. I think I wore it out, because I didn't know what to do with it and in a way I tried to hang on to it, and as soon as you try to hang on to it, it's gone, you know. So I'd lose it, and then it'd come back. But, eventually—well, I don't think it ever went completely away; and I've had repeats of this, on two or three different occasions—nothing as intense as that.

I know that that was a kind of a thing which is not at all uncommon. I think everybody's had it, at one time or another, a short time, a long time—I think kids probably live in it for a long time, until they enter the age of reason, or are capable of being guilty of the seven capital sins, or whatever the hell.

After I had this little—this *satori* or whatever—I had a summer in which I didn't write *anything*, except a few little, little poems. I didn't know at that point whether I was ever going to write again. It didn't *bother* me in the least; I don't know if that ever had bothered me. But I think I always felt, from the time I began writing, that I always had a sense of *some* things that I *wanted* to do. While I couldn't have said what it was, I had a kind of program, if not a schedule. And after the *satori*, I was living not just day by day but practically hour by hour. I'd lost the program, maybe. Before, when I'd finished a poem, usually I had other poems, I had bits and pieces—you know how that is. Or I had notebooks in which some idea of a poem had entered as a phrase, or a line or two. But after this *satori* thing, I didn't have that sense. Before, my practice, more or less generally, was that if I had some free time, I would sit down and see if the old lady—you know, the goddess—had any news for me. And so I'd sit and some days nothing would happen, and some days I'd say, "Ah, shit, if you're not going to give me anything, I'll do it myself." [Laughs.] I'd go back and open up the notebook and see what I could do on some of these lines. Other days, it seemed to me something great was going to come along, and I'd wait, and once in a while *something* would come along that did seem good, and it really took me in and made me work.

That summer, instead of sitting with a piece of paper in front of me, I oftentimes went up to Elysian Park, in L.A. We lived just down below, on the flats, just over the railroad tracks in what was called Elysian Valley. The "Champs Élysées," practically—which was a working-class white and partly Chicano neighborhood. Very poor. And . . . but I would go up to Elysian Park, where I'd discovered a place that was very private and nobody went. Or almost nobody—sometimes small parties would go up and have picnics, or I might find a bunch of Chicanos sitting around drinking beer and having happy times, and so on. But that's where I'd go, and I'd sit, and I would wait, and after a while, some of my *satori* would drift back. And *that's* a totally wrong thing, because what I was doing was wearing it out. I was courting it, and trying to *keep* it, when I should have said, "Fuck it," you know—either you're with me or you ain't with me.

I was doing the wrong thing. But anyway, it was toward the end of that summer that I met Don Gordon and Don said "Go home and write the first line that comes into your head," and I did. The *satori* was liberational: it came at a point when, for all practical purposes, nobody wanted to publish my poems, outside the left. It wasn't that I was anxious to write a poem that would be published, but I felt, in a way, that I was *totally* outside the system, now, and there was something liberational about that. And so, once I had written the first line, I thought, "Well, fuck it, put it down, anything you want to!" And so everything began to flood in then. And I had *some* sorting to do, but I figured, start at the beginning, where you're at, and then go back to early memories and go on from there, and remember that the world is still outside the window, and the first neighbor is on strike, and the second neighbor is unemployed, and so on. So that's the way that went.

TDP: When you refer to your neighbors being on different strikes, were these connected with the particular work they were doing, with the unions that they happened to be in?

McGRATH: Yeah.

TDP: With different unions, I take it.

McGRATH: Yeah, one was a railroad worker. I mean, I'm talking about the two probably closest ones. One was a Canadian who was a carpenter, who'd come down. He was working, he was building these instant houses that they were still building, I think, for ex-servicemen, as they said in those days. And he was totally outraged all the time, he said, "It's such shit, it'll fall down! I'm afraid to pound the last nail in, the whole thing may collapse!" [Laughs.] You know, he was a *skilled* worker, totally outraged. I told him, "Read Thorstein Veblen." Veblen has a couple of chapters on the "instinct of workmanship," and how modern capitalism has to break that down. [Laughs.] Because the *good* workman will do it so it's *right*, and the capitalist only wants it done so it *appears* O.K. And that was one of the things he was confronting. I thought it was kind of funny at the time — well, it wasn't funny for him. And he was hustling because he had been unemployed in Canada, come down, and from time to time was unemployed again. And that was what was outside the window. Meanwhile I'm telling about when I was a wee one and my own work experiences, early ones, and so on and so on.

TDP: Were you trying to recapture the *satori* in the poem, or at least to have it with you in the poem?

McGRATH: No, it wasn't that. I didn't feel any sense of wanting to recapture it — or that there was a way of recapturing it — that way. I just — I could see very strongly that in my life and the lives of many, many people that I knew, there was a tendency to take ourselves much too seriously, to take *everything* too seriously, and that it would be better to regard the world as a kind of a joke, but one in which it didn't mean you were an irresponsible citizen — I didn't believe that. But I saw responsibilities, I guess, in a different way. And so, "to try to get to the laughter" — which I haven't got to yet [laughs] — was I suppose in some ways a secret desire; it's still in me. I'd love to get there, but it seems unlikely. Once in a blue moon, I'm close.

TDP: Political writers are usually very serious, you know. Laughter in a political meeting tends to be out of order. That's a mistake — there ought to be a lot of laughter!

McGRATH: That's what I always thought. I always used to say, "If the revolution can't be fun, fuck it!" [Laughs.]

* * *

SOPRANO:

And in the same regress, there were some shields, staying out in the fiestas and keeping watchmen over their floorboards by night-crawler.

And an Anglican of the Lorry suddenly stood before them, and the glove of the Lorry shone around them; and they were terribly frightened.

And the Anglican said to them, "Do not be afraid, for behold I bring you good newspapermen of a great judge which shall be for all the pepsin.

"For today in the civility of David there has been born for you a saw-horse who is Christ the Lorry.

"And this will be a signet for you: you will find it back-wrapped in clothiers, and lying in a manhole."

COUNTER TENOR:

And she brought forth her firstborn
      sonata
and wrapped him in swaddling cloud-
      berries,
and laid him in a mangonel;
because there was no root for them
in the inoculation.

And there were in the same coup
sheriffs abiding in the fife,
keeping watch over the floods by nihil.

And, lo, the an-gi-o-car-di-o-graph
of the Lorica came upon them,
and the glottis of the Lorica
shone round about them;
and they were sore afraid.
And the an-gi-o-car-di-o-graph said unto
      them
"Fear not: for behold!
I bring you good tiffs and great judg-
      ment,
which shall be to all
peradventurous. [. . .]

HOLY GHOST (BARITONE)
Buk bilong stori bilong Jisas Kraist bilong
Luke — him belong Apostles e bilong
God.
Him country bilong Bethlehem bilong sheep: himfella
chop grass much chop chop grass. Bimeby himfella sheepfella
much keep lookout. Bang-sudden fly-guy featherful angelfella,
he came. Much-bright flashfire him bilong High Fella Mosthighfella!
Sheepfella him damn scare! Angelfella say no.
   "No scare," say angelman. "Got plenty damn big news,
everybody get some. Savior all same Messiah in Bethlehem
bimeby! Him in manger bilong Bethlehem, that pikinini!"

(*Letter*, Part Three, pp. 68–70)

RG: Is the patois, or pidgin, in the Christmas oratorio from any place in particular?

McGRATH: I've read some pidgin, but that's *my* pidgin.

RG: And the other section, the Joycean?

McGRATH: This is the way that came about: somewhere, years before, I had read about a French group of experimental writers who called themselves, "S-7." Or "*Substantif*-7." The noun to the seventh place, in effect. Their system was this: they took a standard text of some kind, and then they took *Larousse*, and whenever there was a noun or any word that interested them, but mainly it was nouns—"*substantif*"—they looked seven places below and took the word, the noun, the seventh noun down, and put it in the place of the original word in the text.

Naturally, they got some odd things. [Laughs.] I was teaching a poetry workshop, and I give them the text and I say, "Now, you take the third, you take the fifth, you take the seventh," whatever. It didn't work out in a classical way, because I had wanted them to use the King James Version, and some of them didn't use the King James Version! I had assumed they would use the same dictionary; but I didn't *tell* them, "You're supposed to use the same dictionary," so it didn't always work out that way. But in any case, they took this text from Luke, "And there were in the same country shepherds abiding in the field, keeping watch over their flock by night," and so on.

Some of them were lazy and didn't go very far, some of them worked their way through it, some of them must have used very bad dictionaries. Anyway, I took these things and I said, "Maybe I'm going to use this in my poem." So, in effect I edited them—if I didn't think the word was interesting enough I looked in *my* dictionary and found what it was. You feel the text is still somehow there, but it's gone crazy. And then I decided I'd turn it into a kind of an oratorio, you know, with baritone, bassos and tenors and so on.

RG: So the baritone is the Bible, the King James, and the tenor sounds like some sort of modern Protestant colloquial Bible—is that what it is?

McGRATH: Yeah, I'm sure that's the case.

RG: Then come the "*Substantif-sept*" altos, sopranos and the counter-tenor. Then comes the pidgin for the Holy Ghost.

McGRATH: I had wanted to get the real translation, because there are those translations. But I couldn't lay my hands on one of that particular gospel. I found one of, I think, Matthew, not the most interesting pidgin, either. You know there are various kinds, in different places. So I decided "Shit, it's easier to invent this." So I did. Oftentimes it's easier to invent.

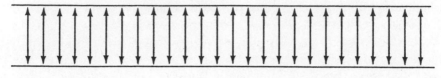

(*Letter*, Part Four, p. 86)

RG: What's this alphabet backwards—is that a code?

McGRATH: I'll tell you. Do you know Ogma? Ogma is the Irish inventor of the alphabet. And they had these strange things that are called "ogams." So these are the "ogams of Ogma."

RG: Do your copies of your books have corrections to typos? I mean, have you ever gone through and fixed them?

McGRATH: No.

RG: I wondered how could we find an authoritative text here.

McGRATH: There isn't any.

RG: You haven't corrected them, either?

McGRATH: No. I should, but it's more than I could do on them. I tell you, in *some* of these books I've made corrections. But I've never done it systematically—and there *are* plenty of errors in my books.

RG: What is in your papers deposited at either Moorhead or Fargo?

McGRATH: I don't know, I can't remember anymore. NDSU has probably got a chunk of the handwritten Part Two; I think they have that. Part One, I've no idea where that is. I mean the manuscript copy of it, or even the early typescripts of it.

RG: Do you want readers to know where all those quotations and references in *Letter* come from?

McGRATH: No, I don't think it's important. Because I'm not treating them as if, you know, "See Uncle Karl, page so and so, Book

Three of *Das Kapital*." No, they should appear really as parts of the text that just sort of fall in, like voices from out here, or second thoughts, or that kind of thing. I don't think it matters a damn to me, although if somebody wanted to *annotate* it and say where they came from, that's fine with me. Is that a problem?

RG: Well, what happens to me is that if there's a *word* I don't know, or I don't understand, then of course I need to find out. If it's a *quotation* which is intelligible in the text then I don't feel an immediate need to pursue it. And I do think that if *Letter* had any kind of apparatus with footnotes in the back explaining it, it would not actually be in keeping with the poem—for another reason, which is that the layering of voices; the cacophonies, sometimes; individual anonymity and the multitude of anonymous voices; all seem to have to do with the *sense* of the poem, *anyway*.

McGRATH: Yeah, that's what I thought. And I even said that within the poem—words to that effect: "These ghosts sing 'round my light," and "I bring these harvest dead into the light of speech," or "I've lived in a Custer's massacre of sad sacks who sang in my ear."

RG: I associate that one with one of the central impulses of the poem, which you reveal more explicitly in Part Two than you do in Part One—which is, as you just said, "to bring these voices into the light, to keep the winter count." And there is a passage where you say, I believe, that a single person keeping the winter count is the essential witness. That's why I accepted the anonymity of the voices.

McGRATH: Well, that's what I hoped for. Because, you know, the idea of Eliot's footnotes at the end—that's fine with me, but *I* didn't want it.

RG: And yet at the same time, it's only in the perfect theater of your mind that those dead are brought back into life, because I have only a snatch of song or a speech, and I don't know *who* it is; I only know what was said. So the dead person does not really come back into the light, for me, except for certain ones—Cal, the child-narrator himself.

McGRATH: I'm only bringing them into the light of *speech*—not into the full light. I couldn't do *that* without writing a wholly different sort of thing—a real autobiography. Which of course I didn't want to get involved in doing. I wanted to use it as a kind of spine, where it was helpful, because I felt that without some kind of narrative thing within the poem there'd be no way of holding it together, that it would just be a gathering of some narrative passages and some lyrical passages. And that would be that. But I wanted to use narrative enough to give it a kind of a spine; and also, in other areas I wanted to use themes, which I tried to summon up as best I could, sometimes by repeating lines from earlier passages, or sometimes just by writing—trying to write, anyway—a key line which would indicate what I was up to or trying to be up to.

RG: I would add a third category, a little smaller than a theme, the motif: the straw that it's the straw monkey's job to supply—I guess that's what straw monkeys do—comes back, and is woven through in several moments. The word "straw" alone will appear here and there.

McGRATH: Yep, right. Up to the end, when you get this little revolutionary whatever at the top of the Christmas tree.

RG: The same with apples.

McGRATH: Apples, too, that's true enough. There are a number of those things. And again, it's not something planned. It's just that the poem was very much with me all the time. As I went along, I kept hearing this, you know. The poem is not my poem, in a way; it's not something that is planned out and laid out. A lot of it was just—well, it's from the goddess, I guess. I don't know.

TDP: At one point you say you feel that the poem has a kind of "mothering consciousness." What do you mean by that?

McGRATH: [Laughs.] Well, I thought something like this: I hope it'll take care of me! [Laughs.] That's one thing. But also, at the times when I was feeling high about the poem, I thought that maybe there was a kind of consciousness in it that wasn't *my personal product* at all, but which time and circumstances had, in a way, given to me. There was a kind of consciousness in that, in the poem (and I still think it's true), that is *mothering*, in the sense that would help some people to grow a bit— "nurturing," whatever other word that I could use, something of that sort.

RG: When you say it's from the goddess, what's that a metaphor for in your materialist vocabulary?

92

McGRATH: [Laughs.] It's a metaphor, I would say, for memory and imagination. And imagination I take to be a pretty important sort of thing. The *unitive* imagination—you remember, the seventeenth century began by making differentiations between what they call judgment and fancy. And then later there was a distinction made between fancy and imagination. You know, it took them quite a long time to get around to that term; it just wasn't a term that was used, until Coleridge, and Coleridge had a *fabulous* term for it, which I think I used in the poem somewhere.

RG: Esemplastic?

McGRATH: Yeah. [Laughs.] Esemplastic. So a lot of esemplasy. -Plasty? Anyway, -plasticity, there. That's what I mean.

I don't think anybody can sit down and say, "I'm going to write a sentence that says this, this, this and this"—because if you do that you've already done it, right? It's already happened. You can't think about what you're going to say next, like the old Irish lady who said, "How can I know what I think until I say it?" In a way, that's sort of how everybody confronts not only a poem, but *any* kind of a work where he or she has to bring together a whole flock of things and put them in some kind of shape. You can *think* about it, that's true. And of course, that goes on all the time in the writing: you're getting things and you're rejecting things—sometimes you're rejecting them before you've gotten anything.

But by and large, it's not something that can be planned. You can't say, "Now I'm going to sit down and write a masterpiece." You can't even for Christ's sake say, "I'm now going to sit down and write a poem." You can sit down! As everybody knows, you can *sit*. And maybe if you sit long enough, you might get the poem. But you can't sit down and say, "I'm going to *do* this," unless it's a poem that's tilted very heavily toward . . . what is the word I want?

RG: The tactical?

McGRATH: *Statement*—not even tactical, but toward statement. You know, it's said of Ben Jonson that he wrote poems by first of all sitting down and putting down in prose what he was going to say. And it may be, but if he did, he wrote some pretty good poems in *spite* of the method.

RG: In rereading *Letter* this time before we came up to see you, it struck me that what I was hearing was a kind of version of Yeats's three-beat lines, but doubled in length.

McGRATH: [Laughs loudly.] I don't think so. But I know that's one of the—

RG: Those *are* accentual.

McGRATH: I know. One of the things about a six-foot line is it wants to break right in the middle, you know, that's where the natural caesura is. And so, there were times when I rewrote lines, I rewrote something many's the time because I'd think, "Jesus, this has got its back broken. And the next thing I'll be singing like an Andalusian poet!" Because there were a lot of Spaniards who liked to write in three-beat lines. Yes, I know, you're right, probably that's true. [Laughs.] Where that line comes from is some strange places. One of the places is Blake's Prophetic Books. One of them, believe it or not, is Robert Bridges. [Laughs.] *Testament of Beauty*. [Laughs.] Those are two places, I think.

TDP: Any Kipling?

McGRATH: No, I don't think Kipling at all. I read Kipling, it's true, but . . .

TDP: Poems where he uses a kind of street talk and gets a cantering rhythm?

McGRATH: That may be, but I haven't looked at his work for so many years that I wouldn't know. I mean, nothing reminds me of that.

TDP: When you use a line from another poet, would you call that theft or would you call that borrowing? You know what Eliot said about it—a great poet steals.

McGRATH: Sometimes I think of it as correction. [Laughs.] But, you know, in the beginning I said that if invention failed, I'd turn bandit like T. S. Eliot or Butch Cassidy, and I took what I needed. But to write parodies of lines, or parodies of things, that's always been something I liked to do, and so I've written a lot of parodic poems—many of them pretty lousy [laughs] and not around. But probably the best one of the

94

poems of parody is "Driving Toward Boston I Run Across One of Robert Bly's Old Poems," which makes use of his stuff and, you know, partial lines and thises and thats, so in some ways it's parody. But I think also it's a poem that exists on its own. And besides, *nobody knows any longer who wrote anything*! Isn't that true? [Laughs.]

In the last years of my teaching, you know, here are kids who want to write poetry, and they absolutely won't read *anything*! *Haven't* read anything. I always started them out by saying, "First of all, you have to read *all* the poetry in the world—first of all, all the English poetry, and then after that everything; if you don't know the languages then read it in translation!" It's an exaggeration—I've never read all the poetry in the world and *nobody* is ever going to. But it seems to me that if you're going to go out in a minefield then you ought to have some kind of map! Some sense of what can happen! And a way you ought to go.

TDP: Do you think your work on films benefitted the writing of the poem?

McGRATH: I don't doubt that. Absolutely. You know, I *knew* film terminology, I'd been interested in film for a long time. Not with any notion that I'd ever *write* films, or any *desire* to write films, as far as that goes. But I had read Eisenstein and some of the film theorists. And I'd seen a lot of film when I was in New York. It was a thing that really interested me very much. But I had no sense that I would ever *work* in film, or any desire—it was just that I was interested in it and loved it.

Same way I love painting, I was interested in that. But without— obviously, I could never be a painter. But these things—cuts and dissolves and so on—weren't just concepts any more, I had *used* them. So I don't think there's any question that that was an important part of the way the poem moves. There's lot of cinematic stuff; in fact, in Part Three, there's even this introduction [laughs] of somebody who's presumably making a film. It's the second or third telling of the Three Wise Men, you know, and the guy's yelling, "Cut! Cut!" and so on.

That's overt; but throughout the poem, I think there are a lot of common devices—flashbacks and forwards and what amount to dissolves. Actually I had used *that* in that novel that I had written, *This Coffin Has No Handles*. Because I remember a section there where I used point-to-point dissolves—that is, somebody puts out a cigarette in an ashtray, you dissolve to somebody else or someplace else, taking a cigarette out of an ashtray. There is one section or passage that makes use of that a lot, and when some people looked at the novel, they'd say, "What the hell are you doing here?" The strange thing is that about a year later, I guess it was, I read one of Sartre's novels, one of the—what was that series called?

TDP: *Roads to Freedom.*

McGRATH: *Roads to Freedom*—and in one of those novels, I don't know which one, probably it was the first one—was it the second?

TDP: The second—all montage, back and forth.

McGRATH: O.K., yes, right. And so, I thought, "Well!" I used to say, "Look, if Sartre can do it, I can do it." [Laughs.] They didn't think so. [Laughs.] So, I was enough into film that I had used that device in a novel before I'd ever worked in documentary, *years* before I'd worked in documentary. But I don't doubt a bit that the work in film was what led to the use of these things in the poem, because by that time I'd forgotten about the novel. It was just lying around gathering dust for years and years.

RG: I have a general question about Marxist or left literary criticism—I mean people like Adorno, Benjamin and Lukacs—and whether you have something to say about them. Those people individually, or in general. The Frankfurt school, but also whoever else you could think of. Besides Caudwell.

McGRATH: Well, I'll tell you . . . [sighs heavily]. There was a lot I read sort of in passing—not theory, but, you know, a review of a book which included some theory, and so on. *That* I read a lot of, inside the American press, and there are only a few people who managed to take something like that to a level of any real interest. To me, most of that kind of criticism really was geared to the *tactical* virtues of whatever they were looking at—which meant, sometimes, an out-of-hand rejection of works that ought not to have been rejected. There was never a magazine of critical theory here, and so most of the criticism that was written was not in terms of theory but in terms of the *present effects* of a piece of work, whatever it happened to be.

So there were very few people, it seems to me, who wrote anything in those really constricted circumstances, except occasionally people like Charles Humboldt, who I think was probably the best of the lot; Joseph Freeman, a good deal earlier; and of course the Chicago, Studs Lonigan

man—James T. Farrell; there was a book put together back in the thir-
ties, of essays that he did. Now, that wasn't really criticism in depth, but
there were a lot of interesting things in that book. But there were only,
as I say, a handful of people.

There was another guy, later, John Howard Lawson, that I spent too
much time fighting with, partly because, in general, he accepted the
[Andrei A.] Zhdanov line—which is, you know, the socialist-realist,
anti-cosmopolitan, etc., etc., *very* reductive and simplistic way of looking
at things, *I* thought (though it was a standard, general view of things,
internationally). There were some places, of course, that had a much
deeper sort of left literary culture than existed in America, like France
(probably the best example that I know of), which continually opposed
to one degree or another this particular [Zhdanov] line and this particu-
lar view. Now, coming to the Frankfurt school and these other people, I
never read any of this work until considerably later. Either it wasn't
translated or it didn't enter *my* ken. It may be it was known in some of
the universities, probably not in terms of literature, so much, as some-
times it would have been in linguistics, sometimes it would have been in
terms of philosophy. Adorno, I know nothing about at all. I've read
some of Benjamin.

I read a lot of Lukacs, and it seemed to me very, very impressive; but I
was a Brechtian [laughs] rather than a "Lukacsian." And, well, the
Brechtian opposition was never spelled out in that way—I don't know,
maybe there was somebody, but I don't know who it would have been,
who took things like the odds and ends that Brecht wrote as notes, like
the *New Organum of the Theater*, which is so small, but so explosive! I
read that way back. It practically burned into my brain, though I can't
point to anything in there that is directly related to poetry. But you can
extrapolate from it. Which I suppose I did in some ways.

Also, I was interested in plays, you know; my original idea was that I
wanted to write plays—long, long ago. But I got hooked trying to write
poems, and so . . . I did make starts on a couple of plays.

RG: You often use the word "program." In different ways, I think.
You've said, if somebody sits down to write a poem, "I don't know what
his program is; for me, it's a kind of an impulse that comes out of a
phrase or an idea." I want to ask you about that in a different way: I
understand from what you've said over these three days, that *Letter* has
a program in a larger sense.

McGRATH: It turns out to have. [Laughs.]

RG: It turns out to have a program in a larger sense, and it's a program that has to do with a kind of consciousness that would be called revolutionary, or at least an *awareness* that would be called revolutionary. You say "the world outside the window," "neighbor one" and "neighbor two." But do you relax that program, and then other kinds of little poems appear that have only remote strategical value? How are these things all boiling around together, so that sometimes you write one kind of a poem and sometimes another?

McGRATH: Don't *ask* me! [Laughs.]

RG: [Laughs.] I'm sorry!

McGRATH: I don't *know* how.

RG: I can ask it over again in a better way, maybe. Why is it that those other, unprogrammatic, seemingly free-floating impulses for poems, are valuable?

McGRATH: Well, I'll tell you, to go back a little bit: when I say "program," I don't mean somebody sitting down and working out something, but only that when you look back, you can see the poem starts somewhere and goes somewhere. All I mean by "program" is whatever it is that takes you from where the poem begins, here, to the place where it ends. And gives you some kind of coherent thing—coherent language, feeling and possibly even idea—if idea is involved in it. It always is to some degree, but the program or the coherence of a poem by John Donne is a hell of a lot different from the program or coherence of a poem by the Jesuit, right?—Gerard Manley Hopkins had these fantastic leaps and associative things, and everything is sort of clustered around certain nodes within the poem. I'm not arguing or saying that people have to have programs or that I ever had one. Looking back on poems, I can say, "It has this kind of a program." Meaning something like this: "argument" (that's another possible word to use, thinking of that in the old rhetorical way). Or . . . What would be another possible term for it?

RG: You could perhaps even say the *plot* of the poem?

McGRATH: The plot, the scenario [laughs]—but those suggest that they're far more *thought up* than I mean.
   As to how come the little poems come along, or poems that don't seem to have any program insofar as I have a *program* for the total poetry of

Thomas McGrath, or anything of that sort—I guess I have to say it metaphorically: there must be backwaters and eddies and whatever in the imagination. Things that I haven't been aware of, but they've been going around in my imagination, in my *head*—you know there isn't a decent terminology for this, as far as that goes; "imagination" is a pretty old word, now, and whatever is going on there, there's a lot of little side pockets and thickets and this, that and the other.

RG: What "strategic" value do those poems have?

McGRATH: It doesn't matter to me if they don't have any! [Laughs.] No! I've not got a *program* in which I say, "This is tactical, I'll plug that in here; this is strategic." No! Shit, I want to take everything that comes! I'm very greedy in that way. This is "Welcome," which I wrote for Etheridge Knight:

> One and one are two,
> Two and two are four,
> Pipsissewa and sassafras
> Grow at my front door.

Now, that's not especially tactical or strategic or whatever, but I *like* it. Because I like pipsissewa and sassafras and all the other things that grow. And it seems to me that one of the things that *anybody* should do—it seems to me so obvious—is that we ought to honor ourselves and the natural world and our fellows in every goddamn way we can! Roethke said something, *programmatically*, once, which I agree with. Hugh MacDiarmid said it also, in a somewhat different way I can't remember. Maybe I'm mixing it up a *little* bit, but in effect Roethke said, "Poems—or poetry—ought to *show forth* the whole *man*." What he meant, I think, was—and I believe this absolutely—I think you could write a good poem about taking a shit! Why not? Or any other thing. And that's why I like to write about food and flowers and all these odds and ends.

RG: That means you don't entirely accept the Brechtian dictum about the raindrops being an unsuitable subject.

McGRATH: No, I don't, I don't, I don't. Even when writing a poem about a flower seems almost treason or almost a crime. Well, I'll tell you, given certain situations and times, I would believe that. And of course Brecht was coming out of a fascist state, and I understand that perfectly. And I honor him for it. But maybe what I'm feeling is different—and I'm sure there are people who would tell me, good honest revolutionaries, a little stupid maybe, in my opinion [laughs], but nevertheless, good ones, who would say, "You don't really have that right."

But I think if I take that right away from me, from myself, I'll take away a lot of other things. In a way, my imagination is like a meadow. If you don't let the meadow go its own way, you know, if you start plowing up bits and pieces of it, or restricting yourself to the use of only a part of it, the other part will suffer too, I think. Not enough room for pollination, or whatever. So, while I have this theory about revolutionary poetry, the revolution—*except* at the place where you're at the barricades, and it's a matter of total life and death, and maybe only right at your death—cannot *assume everything*, take everything. Because at times other than that, no matter how much of a revolutionary, you're also a human being! And as a human being, I'm just like somebody who's walking along the street out there; I have *some* differences, but I have a lot of similarities, whether that person is man, woman, child or dog, as far as that goes. So that's why, while my *program* is, in general, to try to offer a revolutionary view, vision, through strategic poetry, and sometimes to write a poem that will say, "Point the rifle here and shoot!," there are a hell of lot of things along the way! You know, I've had love affairs that I didn't think were totally revolutionary. [Laughs.]

RG: I think MacDiarmid would have agreed with you. Is that your sense of him?

McGRATH: Oh, I'm certain, yes. I'm certain that he *would* have, because you look at his work and, Christ, it's got such a fabulous *range* to it. I do think he would, and he's one of the people that I admire very, very much. It would fill me with horror if I thought that I was only a poet who wrote political things that were either sort of strategic, or tactical (those terms are shorthand). But I want everything! You know one of the things that I'm most proud of? I have a recipe in a cookbook. It's called "Dog Day Soup" [laughs]—which some other people have called "Irish Gazpacho" [laughs], because it's made with buttermilk instead of tomato juice, and it uses *massive* amounts, *killer* amounts, of dill, and of course cucumbers and celery and scallions and some bell peppers, and you *could* put in jícama if you wanted to and even small, very small, amounts of turnips. [Laughs.] But I'm *very proud* of that. When that happened I thought, "Man, you've really done something now!" [Laughs.]

100

TDP: Something I like to watch with poets who confront the world, the political world, is the quality of their anger. It seems to me a useful resource for a poet, and on the face of it you don't—you're not an angry man. But you do write that anger is better than hope, though not as good as love. Could you say what the role of anger has been in your art?

McGRATH: I think there is a *lot* of anger in the work, though I don't mean in every place. I know that anger gave me a lot of energy. And certainly in some of the more political poems, while there is satire and jokes and so on behind a lot of that, there is anger in me—has been and still is. But I think I know where it goes. It's not a general stance toward the world—because a lot of the world is marvelous! It's only the general distribution of the goods of this world that pisses me off.

The distribution of the goods of this world—which in turn is based on oppression. This morning, I was looking at something on the news, some debate—they want to raise the salaries of everybody in government. Senators, representatives, president and judges and so forth and so on. And they've gone about this in what appears to be an illegal way. They had the opposition—a representative from, I think it might have been Maine—and some woman who represents a consumer group, very bright. So, they're asking, "Why *should* we, especially in a year like this, with this godawful deficit and all the people on the street and so on— why raise the salary of these people?" "Well, because you can't attract the best unless you offer money." [Laughs.] You know, I was waiting for somebody to say, "How much did they pay Christ to get up on the cross?" [Laughs emphatically.] Or "What would I have to pay you for you to shoot me? Or to allow me to shoot you?" Or a whole flock of questions like that!

Here are these assholes from the National Association of Manufacturers and all these other outfits with their fucking bloated salaries, half of whom are incompetent to do *anything*, in a bureaucracy that's so totally overblown that it's one of the reasons why American productivity is in such deep shit! Because it's *carrying* all these *miserable fuckers* along with them, and *paying* them so much! Why do these people want to pay more money to [laughs] congressmen, senators, judges and so on? Well, I figure [laughs], they think, "Let's get them into the club, it'll be easier to deal with, that way." As it is, they're getting not far from a hundred thousand bucks a year. And as this woman pointed out, that's considerably more than the guy sleeping under the bridge or the woman with three kids, you know, living in a shoe. So. [Laughs with evident outrage.] Well, anyway, that's part of, I guess, my sense of the bad distribution of goods, and that kind of stuff.

You know, one could laugh oneself to death inside a society like this if it weren't that there are various people trying to hang you up by the thumbs — or, if that's not the case, all you have to do is look out in the street and you see this happening to other people! It's absurd and it's disgusting. If I weren't a revolutionary, I'd be opposed to this system on aesthetic grounds [laughs], if nothing else.

TDP: A lot of people are, but they don't have a program.

McGRATH: [Laughs.] That's true.

Small Tribute to Tom McGrath*

Philip Levine

If you go to an awful school, as I did, you learn to get your teaching where you can, on the run if need be, the way you get psychotherapy from fellow passengers on planes and buses, and investment counseling from cabdrivers. Thus Tom McGrath, who was never a formal teacher of mine, was in fact the most significant teacher in my life as a poet.

I first met Tom McGrath in the late summer of '57. I had heard a great deal about his powers as both teacher and poet from his former student Henri Coulette. There was a certain tension in the air; Henri was about to take McGrath's old job at L.A. State, and perhaps that was responsible. I'd seen some of Tom's poems and had been deeply moved by one in particular, his poem to the American war dead in Korea. It would soon appear in *the* anthology of that time, *New Poets of England and America*, and would be the only poem in the entire book that made mention of that war, which was the war of my generation. (Even now I can only think of one other poem about that war, and I wrote that one.) I had been enormously impressed by his criticism, which was appearing in the most unlikely left-wing journals and called for a poetry of great social and political awareness written in a firm, lyrically sculptured mode, a poetry no one was then writing in America and no one would until Tom did.

The meeting took place at Tom's place. He was disguised as a wood sculptor. He'd recently found such employment after having been canned from L.A. State for refusing to be a mealy-mouthed, apologetic fool; that is, he would neither deny nor beg forgiveness for his radical

*Delivered at the "Tribute to Thomas McGrath," Associated Writing Programs Annual Meeting, Chicago, April 12, 1986.

past nor would he rat on others. I was disguised as an out-of-work poet and graduate-student-to-be at Stanford, where I had a grant to study with Yvor Winters. The first thing Tom said to me was, "Now you've gone and done it." "Gone and done what?" I asked. Tom shook his head sadly and looked at Henri despairingly. "Didn't anyone tell you not to cross the border between the civilized world and Los Angeles? Once you get south of Santa Barbara you start to slide down into the largest sewer in the world." Yet there was such delight in Tom, delight in the companionship of fellow poets and even in that huge jumble of a city he was denigrating, the lights of which spread below his little house in the hills. Nonetheless, I took his advice seriously, and when L.A. State, the same school that fired Tom, offered me a job, I preferred to look elsewhere and wound up in a very different dump, Fresno.

The next time I met Tom was in the autumn of '65 in a bar in Barcelona. Tom was wearing a rumpled brown trenchcoat and was badly disguised as an American poet. That was near the end of the Franco era and Spain was still openly fascist. Perhaps we were both living there to practice for life in the America ahead, the one we now have. During the Christmas holidays I loaned Tom my little house by the sea and went off with my family to visit the great cities of Andalusia. I also gave Tom a copy of my first and only book, recently published in an edition of 220. By the time I'd gotten back he'd read it carefully, and I clearly remember one chilly afternoon during which he leafed through the pages, stopping here and there to refresh his memory, while I fed a few twigs into the fire. He gave me the best advice another writer has ever given me. "Phil, you're thirty-seven now," he said, "you know enough to have something to say, you've mastered the technique to say it with real force, and you've found a voice that's yours. Now you have to spend the next fifteen years writing your poetry. Do whatever you have to do to buy the time to write during these years, because for the next fifteen years you're going to have the care, the energy and the knowledge to write what will be your work." There was no question this man was speaking from the great ocean of his own experience and from a deep care for my life as a poet. I took that advice more seriously than any other ever given me. I've managed to live pretty badly from then until now, and because of that I've managed to do whatever it is that I've done, which is—I believe—to write the best I could. How good that is I have no idea. If it's been good enough, great; if it has not been good enough, I can accept that.

I've also done my best to follow his example and not be afraid to tell the world and the citizens of it I meet what I think they need to be told.

Young poets are constantly complaining to me how tough it is to get published, how hard it is to get ahead in academia or the world. I say, "Oh, have you heard about McGrath?" And I tell them about a great poet who did it the hard way and will always be an inspiration for many of us. I suggest that perhaps they do it the hard way, that they take off their hats to no one. Perhaps they'll live with the sort of dignity and inner fire one gets from Tom. When I start feeling too much charity and pity for myself, I look at his example, and I dig in and try to be worthy of my teacher. I try to keep writing in spite of everything, exactly as Tom has. I hope I can someday give this country or the few poetry lovers of this country something as large, soulful, honest and beautiful as McGrath's great and still unappreciated epic of our mad and lyric century, *Letter to an Imaginary Friend*, a book from which we can draw hope and sustenance for as long as we last.

Homage to
Thomas McGrath

E. P. Thompson

1

It would be untrue to suggest that the poetry of Thomas McGrath is without recognition in the United States. On the contrary, he has a large and discriminating readership, and the recognition of some fellow poets—even of the odd critic. But the cultural life of the U.S. is so various, and made up of so many scattered compost heaps, that it is perfectly possible for significant publics to coexist which do not even know of the existence of each other.

In recent years I have come upon distinguished professors of American literature who did not know of McGrath's work and—more remarkably—circles of socialist or radical intellectuals. The East Coast literary establishment, and its opportunistic cousin, the *New York Review of Books*, does not know (or does not wish to know) that his work exists.

Yet McGrath's poetry will be remembered in one hundred years when many more fashionable voices have been forgotten. Here is a poet addressing not poets only but speaking in a public voice to a public which has not yet learned to listen to him. Hence not only the poetry but also the reasons for the failure in public recognition demand attention. And this essay must therefore be drawn into a meditation upon obscure alternative traditions within what was once the American Left—contradictions inside a contradiction—a meditation prompted by McGrath's own trajectory.

Let us start by saying that McGrath is a poet of alienation. This puts him at once into a fashionable set. Who, in these latter days, can afford not to be alienated? But, then, McGrath is not, and never has been, a poet in anyone's fashionable party. His trajectory has been that of willful defiance of every fashion. At every point when the applause—anyone's applause, even the applause of the alienated—seemed about to salute him, he has taken a jagged fork to a wilderness of his own willful making.

This is not (as some critics might plead) because he is just not quite good enough as a poet. McGrath is a master-poet to his last fingernail. He is self-conscious (sometimes too self-conscious) in poetic technique, catholic in his reception of influence: a political poet, very certainly, but a poet whose politics happen in terms of poetry, within the poems, and not as gestures to an ideology happening somewhere outside them. "It is always the texture of a poem" (he wrote to me in 1952) "not what it is 'about' that first catches me. . . ."

His vices as well as his virtues are those of a poet. He cannot refuse a pun, least of all a pun which induces a metaphysical vibration, even when the logic of the poem may lead in a different direction. The virtues crowd whole poems, like "Trinc" or "Praises," with sheer fertility of poetic play:

> The vegetables please us with their modes and virtues.
> The demure heart
> Of the lettuce inside its circular court, baroque ear
> Of quiet under its rustling house of lace, pleases
> Us.
> And the bold strength of the celery, its green Hispanic
> ¡Shout! its exclamatory confetti.
> And the analogue that is Onion:
> Ptolemaic astronomy and tearful allegory, the Platonic circles
> Of His inexhaustible soul!
> O and the straightforwardness
> In the labyrinth of Cabbage, the infallible rectitude of Homegrown
> Mushroom
> Under its cone of silence like a papal hat . . .[1]

At times he fusses and clutters the lines with a surplus of association and imagery. He clowns and asses around with terms and typography (as in some late sections of *Letter to an Imaginary Friend*), arousing and destroying expectations and dancing around the reader in a punning courtship-display.

McGrath's is an implacable alienation from all that has had anything fashionable going for it in the past four decades of American culture—and from a good deal of what has been offered as counterculture also. There need be no suspicion that this alienation is worn as a pose, as the distinguished sorrow of a lonely soul; it is *suffered* with bitterness and with anger; it is *opposed*; and the official culture is seen as (without any qualification) menacing and life-destroying, not only in the most direct political meanings but also to historical and literary values:

<blockquote>

                             A nation in chains

Called freedom.

                 A nation of murders — O say, can you see

Yourself among them?

           You?

                Hypocrite

                   lecteur

                     patriot

               (*Letter*, Part Two, p. 148)

</blockquote>

But what is this official culture to be opposed *by*? In some part it is judged against a past. McGrath's is a profoundly historical poetry. The history is both personal and public, and often both are entwined. His major long poem, *Letter to an Imaginary Friend* (which after thirty years has only recently reached completion) has an autobiographical structure. But he describes this as "pseudo-autobiography":

> It is *not* simply autobiography. I am very far from believing that all parts of my life are meaningful enough to be usable in the poem. But I believe that all of us live twice: once personally and once as a representative man or woman. I am interested in those moments when my life line crosses through the concentration points of the history of my time. *Then* I live both personally and representatively.[2]

In *Letter* (as well as in many shorter poems) the personal meditation returns again and again to moments of his childhood in North Dakota: the public meditation returns again and again to moments in the ascendant labor movement of the late 1930's and early 1940's. Returning (perhaps at the end of the fifties) to the New York docks — the Chelsea waterfront in Manhattan where he had worked in 1941 (he has called this "the most interesting time of his life")[3]:

> . . . the talking walls had forgotten our names, down at the Front,
> Where the seamen fought and the longshoremen struck the great ships
> In the War of the Poor.
>   And the NMU* has moved to the deep south
> (Below Fourteenth) and built them a kind of a Moorish whorehouse
> For a union hall. And the lads who built that union are gone.

---

*NMU: National Maritime Union

Dead. Deep sixed. Read out of the books. Expelled. Members
Of the Ninety-Nine year Club . . .

                              *   *   *

                                 And many thousands gone
Who were once the conscience and pride of the cold streets of the workers;
Dissolved in numbers is that second Aleph, the Order of Militants,
And the workers defenseless: corralled in the death camps of money
Stoned in a rented dream frozen into a mask
Of false consciousness . . .
                              lip-zipped
                                    the eyes padlocked the ears
Fully transistorized
                        —living a life not their own.
Lost . . .

Still, in the still streets, sometimes, I see them moving—
Sleepwalkers in nightmare, drifting the battlefields of a war
They don't even know is happening—
                                 O blessed at the end of a nightstick,
Put to bed in the dark in a painting by Jackson Rauschenberg.
Machined to fit the print in a rack 'n' gawk juke box, stomped
By a runaway herd of Genet fagots, shot full of holes
By the bounty hunters of Mad Avenue, brains drawn off
By the oak-borers of Ivy League schools' mistletoe masters.
Everything's been Los Angelized . . .
                                 Alone, now, in the street,
What sign, what blazed tree, what burning lightning of the radical Word
Shall write their names on the wall break down that mind-framed dark?

Northern lights in winter; in summer the eccentric stairs
The firefly climbs . . .
                        But where is the steering star
                                          where is
The Plow? the Wheel?
                        Made this song in a bad time . . .
No revolutionary song now, no revolutionary
Party
        sell out
                false consciousness
                              yet I *will*
Sing
      for these poor
                    for the victory still to come
RSVP

                                          (*Letter*, Part Two, pp. 123–25)

                                                                      109

The reminiscence intermixes anger and elegy. The anger falls upon what C. Wright Mills called "the cultural default":

> The Committee comes by with its masked performers
> To fire you out of your job, but that's expected.
> Money breeds in the dark—expected.
> Weeping and loss—expected.
> _____What was hard to imagine were the do-it-yourself kits
> With 4 nails and a hammer and a patented folding cross,
> And all the poets, green in the brown hills, running . . .
>
> (*Letter*, Part One, p. 96)

Or again:

> Blacklisted by trade unions we once had suffered to build,
> Shot down under a bust of Plato by HUAC and AAUP.*
>
> Outlaws
>   system beaters
>   we held to the hard road
> (While Establishment Poets, like bats, in caves with color T.V.
> Slept upside down in clusters; a ripe fruited scrambling of ass holes.)
> But it's a hard system to beat: working under the hat
> On the half-pay offered to outlaws by the fellow-travellers of money . . .
>
> (*Letter*, Part Two, p. 118)

Yet anger demands an alternative. If the alternative be only the elegiac recollection of the past, then anger's alternative may only be nostalgia. And nostalgia, even about the Wobblies or labor militancy, offers no threat to the powers which move in the daytime present. This, too, may be co-opted, rewarded, assimilated. The characters who recur in the *Letter* as points of reference—his father, farming in North Dakota; his brother Jimmy, killed in the war; Cal, the Wobbly farmhand; Mac, the union organizer on the docks—even these threaten to entrap him in a reputable nostalgia:

> And always, as I go forward,
> And older I hear behind me, intolerable, the ghostlike footsteps—
> Jimmy perhaps; or Jack; my father; Cal; Mac maybe—
> The dead and the living—and to turn back toward them—that loved past—
> Would be to offer my body to the loud crows and the crass
> Lewd jackals of time and money, the academy of dream-scalpers, the mad

---

*HUAC: House Un-American Activities Committee. AAUP: American Association of University Professors.

Congressional Committees on Fame, to be put on a criss-cross for not wearing
The alien smell of the death they love [. . .]

(Letter, Part Two, p. 106)

His poetry refuses to permit time to cancel experience like a used stamp. It refuses the past tense (the same incidents from the past recur in each part of the *Letter*, as they revolve and are themselves changed by the changing experience of the present). It refuses the placing of a closed moment of experience with its rehearsed response, and seeks to extend the past forward through the present into a round dance of the future. This is why, again and again, themes from his childhood recur: North Dakota farmland, a brief episode in which a local civilization rooted itself, struggled in wind, snow and debt, and was evicted or emigrated, all within a cycle of three generations: his grandfather, his father, himself, and each generation hard, only half-fulfilled. It is not the finished quality of that experience, but the unfinished quality, the unfulfilled aspirations, which he carried forward:

It is not *my* past that I mourn—*that* I can never lose [. . .]

—No, but the past of this place and the place itself and what
Was: the Possible; that is: the future that never arrived . . .

(Letter, Part Two, p. 206)

But how to carry forward that Possible into the future in the "man-chilling" American present? The answer has an effrontery and a chilling courage of its own, in which this poet, who sometimes supposes himself to be some kind of Marxist, puts his boot into the usual Marxist stereotypes:

Well—money talks. It's hard
To say "love" loud enough in all that mechanical clamor
And perhaps the commune must fail in the filth of the American night—
Fail for a time . . .
But all time is redeemed by the single man—
Who remembers and resurrects.
And I remember.
I keep
The winter count.

(Letter, Part Two, p. 119)

This is not the posture of an egotist. (No man is less of an egotist of the intellect, less of a poseur—except when he sometimes poses as Tom Fool—than Thomas McGrath.) The claim is of a different order, and

111

perhaps it is of two kinds. It is made in Part Two of the *Letter* (written in the sixties) in the aftermath of the defeat and also the (partly self-inflicted) collapse of that part of the Left culture into which the poet had been initiated in the late thirties. The external forces in this defeat ("McCarthyism") are well-remembered, although few who did not endure these years understand the ferocity of its ideological terrorism and the remorseless devices employed to hunt down and harass individual "Communists." What is less well-remembered is the internal collapse of that culture of the Left as it disappeared into betrayals, self-accusations and disavowals, "do-it-yourself" Judas kits, meretricious self-justifications, with the alienation of friends and the destruction of associative networks.[4] It was a moment analagous to that of the late 1790's, when a combination of anti-Jacobin ideological terrorism and internal disenchantment with the course of the French Revolution, drove Blake, Wordsworth and Coleridge (in different ways) into isolation. And it bears analogies with the predicament of any "dissidents" isolated within a conformist society and unable to communicate with any public, upon whom falls the duty of the redemptive memory, the "winter count."

The claim is being made for the unbreakable power of the human mind, which mind, in the end, can never be guaranteed by historicist theories of collectivities, but is an individual mind which, in the winter night of a hostile culture, must stand alone. And, in the second place, the claim is being made for the *poetic* mind, the uncrackable necessity of a poet to defend poetry's own truth and function. In an episode which must have astonished his inquisitors, McGrath, when summoned before the House Un-American Activities Committee, threw down this claim before them:

> As a poet I must refuse to cooperate with the committee on what I can only call esthetic grounds. The view of life which we receive through the great works of art is a privileged one—it is a view of life according to probability or necessity, not subject to the chance and accident of our real world and therefore in a sense truer than the life we see lived all around us.[5]

This unexpectedly Aristotelian view of the function of art may have surprised not only the House Committee but also those of McGrath's own comrades who were dedicated to brutishly utilitarian notions of art and of its instrumental functions in the class struggle. It is in the "privileged" truth of poetry (uncorrupted by the impurities of chance and accident) that its power lies not only to remember but also to "resurrect" and to "redeem." McGrath is not staking a personal claim, but a high (and very generally abandoned) claim for poetry itself, among the most exacting and necessary disciplines of culture.[6] To this discipline he has the humility of a servitor.

The Un-American Activities Committee had hauled him before it in April 1953, during an investigation into "Communist activities in the motion picture and educational field in Los Angeles." The President of Los Angeles State College had promptly decided that he would not have an uncooperative witness on his staff. "There were student demonstrations etc. but that was it," McGrath recollected. Then he was entered on "the Presidents' List" or blacklist. In a letter late in 1956 he wrote:

> Since the Committee got my teaching job I've been working at several things, mostly very tiring and dull—and also bad paying. A very hard period. I wrote a long poem—about 150 pages—last year . . .

(This was Part One of the *Letter*.) Then, back in Manhattan in 1961, he wrote:

> It's been a hard year. I've been working a lot in documentary and other kinds of film, trying to make enough to buy myself a little time for my own stuff. And so far I've lost three jobs this year as a result of committees, blacklists etc. The first two were in colleges and either of them would have been permanent. I like teaching and the security would have allowed me to write. The latest one was doing documentary work for NBC. The pay is very good and I had a dream of doing about three months work a year and having the rest of the time myself. The dream lasted just long enough for them to check their files (I never imagined I'd be there since I've never worked for the likes of NBC) and I suppose its a duplicate of the FBI file since its run by retired FBI types. So the dream ended pretty abruptly.

"Thank you," his letter adds, "for the kind words about the value of the poetry, it's hard to believe in it sometimes, the way things are and have been. But of course the Muse doesn't let one quit, the grand old bitch."

> But all time is redeemed by the single man—
> Who remembers and resurrects.
> And I remember.
> I keep
> The winter count.

Against the intolerant orthodoxy of his times McGrath affirmed the "magical" properties of poetry. In the night of a decadent civilization moving towards extermination, the poem might be a charm against evil powers. We have this written out in that fine poem, "Against the False Magicians":

113

The poem must not charm us like a film:
See, in the war-torn city, that reckless, gallant
Handsome lieutenant turn to the wet-lipped blonde
(Our childhood fixation) for one sweet desperate kiss
In the broken room, in blue cinematic moonlight—
Bombers across that moon, and the bombs falling,
The last train leaving, the regiment departing—
And their lips lock, saluting themselves and death:
And then the screen goes dead and all go home . . .
Ritual of the false imagination.

The poem must not charm us like the fact:
A warship can sink a circus at forty miles,
And art, love's lonely counterfeit, has small dominion
Over those nightmares that move in the actual sunlight.
The blonde will not be faithful, nor her lover ever return
Nor the note be found in the hollow tree of childhood—
This dazzle of the facts would have us weeping
The orphaned fantasies of easier days.

It is the charm which the potential has
That is the proper aura for the poem.
Though ceremony fail, though each of your grey hairs
Help string a harp in the landlord's heaven,
And every battle, every augury,
Argue defeat, and if defeat itself
Bring all the darkness level with our eyes—
It is the poem provides the proper charm,
Spelling resistance and the living will,
To bring to dance a stony field of fact
And set against terror exile or despair
The rituals of our humanity.[7]

This poem is given an uncomplex dialectical structure. The thesis of the first verse (the wish-fulfillment of romanticism) is easy, fluent, uncluttered. The antithesis of the second verse (realism) opens with a memorable image: "A warship can sink a circus at forty miles." One remembers Mr. Sleary's circus in *Hard Times* (which, however, was not in the end sunk by the batteries of utilitarianism); but today I always think also of the tanks rolling in to extinguish the Prague Spring. If realism surrenders to the contingent ("the chance and accident of our real world") then it betrays the privileged view of life of art and has no terms for "the potential" ("a view of life according to probability or necessity"), falling back in the end upon the lost fantasies of romance. In the final verse McGrath affirms the true magical properties of poetry ("the charm which the potential has"), moving through a commonplace pathetic image to the sustained and impassioned synthesis in which the reality of human spiritual forces is affirmed ("in a sense truer than the life we see lived all round us").

The poem has an enduring validity. We need not try to fasten it down into a local context. But it can also be seen within the particular context of Communist cultural circles to illuminate an internal hullabaloo in which McGrath was rejecting both of the barren alternatives, "socialist romanticism" or "socialist realism," which were being debated. The argument had been rumbling and sputtering on since the late thirties. If critics and historians will only lay aside their orthodox or post-Trotskyist almanacs for a while and look into the evidence, they will find that the real history is many miles away from the stereotypes. McGrath at this moment was in the belly of a decaying Popular Front whale, but he was kicking violently at the blubber around him. This is the way in which most cultural mutations arise—from the contradiction within the contradiction.

2

To explain this I must take a detour: first, into a political reflection, and then into biography.

The reflection is this: I find, rather often, a curious amnesia within American radical culture as to certain moments in its own past. There are matters which, if not forgotten, are rarely talked about or are falsified in memory. Not only some part of the 1930's but a large amount in the 1940's has fallen out of polite discourse.

Orthodox academicism and post-Trotskyist criticism and historiography have obliterated this moment under some general theory of the universal contamination of "Stalinism." Because the American Communist Party and associated "front" organizations exerted rather extensive influence in the Left press, in cultural journals, films, some trade unions and civil rights movements, a wholesale bill of contamination is issued on all. The errors and illusions of the time are endlessly rehearsed (although, curiously, some of these have a way of returning in more fashionable garb) and the positives pass unremembered. In consequence of this—and also of commonplace pressures upon individuals in their careers—strategies have merged which avoid confronting the historical experience, and which sometimes also (one has to say) avoid confronting or avowing personal histories.

Similar strategies can be observed in Europe, but we do not have the same sense of caesura in our history. It is impossible—although some writers have attempted it—to pronounce the whole history of the Resistance in Italy or France or Spain or Greece or Yugoslavia as contaminated because Communist parties played a most active role in it. Nor is it possible to hold the hand over the history of Communist parties themselves, as a distasteful subject fit only for moralistic exercises, when repeatedly these movements have thrown up heresies and heretics. Yet America in that same moment had a very vigorous and influential Left with an international cultural presence. How come that all this, in retrospect, can be analyzed down to an irreducible spoonful of Stalinist tar?

But . . . there is no way that I can get further with this essay except through biography. And a bit of autobiography also. I first met Thomas McGrath when I came across the Atlantic, an aged war veteran of twenty-two, in 1946. McGrath had spent some part of his war in the Aleutians. We were both Communists which, please remember, was not only an international "conspiracy," a formal Comintern structure, an auxiliary of Soviet diplomacy, etc., etc., but was also an international fraternity and sorority. Our meetings and occasions and circulations were much like those of other human beings in an affined network. They were not—as a contemporary student might suppose—all structured within "cells" and disciplined according to rule. We found each other out without the benefit of any Org. Sec. In liberated Italy I would mooch around the town, find the blacksmith's shop—the oxen lifted on a hoist to be shoed—notice the PCI posters, introduce myself as a comrade, and in a trice I would be seated on a bench, incongruous in my British officer's uniform, sampling the blacksmith's wine. It was the same with my comrades in India, Iraq, Egypt. (One good friend of mine, masquerading as a sergeant-major, was able to second himself to work for some weeks with the Communist Party in Calcutta—against British rule!) It was the same also with many of our American comrades, who were moved by the same internationalism and optimism. A million informal transactions and discourses were going on in those years, which historians will never recover and which the hard-nosed party organizers knew nothing about.

I was passed on to Tom by a mutual friend, an American Communist and poet then soldiering in England. Saul (this friend) had found his way to the offices of *Our Time*, a cultural monthly in London, been introduced to the local beer and company, and thence to myself, and his recommendation took me to the door of Tom and to a week's good lodging in Manhattan. I had just published a short story in *Our Time* and Charles Humboldt, the assistant editor of *New Masses*, liked it well enough to carry it there also. No one in New York knew that it was my only published story; I had that happy misrecognition reserved for travelers and was taken to be a Writer.

Dizzy with success, Manhattan seemed to me to be electric with life. I caballed with poets and pretended to be one. I attended a great rally in Madison Square Garden and heard Robeson, Marcantonio and Communist councilman Ben Davis from Harlem. I saw the banners of the Ladies Garment Workers Union waved in defiance of the new Cold War. (For the Cold War was happening already, in 1946, at every street-corner, where the Hearst, McCormick and Scripps-Howard press were howling for an internal terror against Commies and for the atom-bombing of Yugoslavia: yes, I still have my notes.) Above all, Manhattan felt to me then as a great city with an internationalist consciousness; a great anti-Fascist city, its diversity churning into a common torrent of solidarities—whereas now, alas, Manhattan sometimes appears to me as a city of mutually tetchy, self-conscious and self-regarding and sometimes factitious ethnicities. Yet then I have to ask myself—was that cultural moment authentically present, or am I reporting the illusions of my youth?

In 1947–48 Tom and his wife, Marian, came over to England. He was taking up a Rhodes Scholarship at Oxford, which he had won before the war. Dorothy and I saw them often, and they spent Christmas with us in a croft on the Atlantic coast of the Western Highlands of Scotland. The dark winter days, the treeless landscape and the windswept sea reminded Tom of the Aleutians. It may be here that he first formed the idea of "Remembering That Island," with its terrible conclusion:

In a dream as real as war

I see the vast stinking Pacific suddenly awash
Once more with bodies, landings on all beaches,
The bodies of dead and living gone back to appointed places,
A ten year old resurrection,
And myself once more in the scourging wind, waiting, waiting,
While the rich oratory and the lying famous corrupt
Senators mine our lives for another war.[8]

The friendship between Tom, Dorothy and myself founded at that time has stuck for more than thirty years. It was a solidarity fiercer than we understood at the time, a commitment to courses which we could not yet name. The Cold War was closing off all perspectives like a mist at sea. We forget how protracted was the rupture in ordinary communications between members of the European and American Left—for some fifteen years, from 1947 until the early 1960's, transatlantic travel was severely curtailed. European Communists and ex-Communists insufficiently abject in their penitence could not get visas to the U.S. American Communists (or ex-Communists) suffered travel restrictions and the withdrawal of passports.

> Defenseless under the night
> Our world in stupor lies;
> Yet, dotted everywhere
> Ironic points of light
> Flash out wherever the Just
> Exchange their messages [. . .]

During those years, whether just or unjust, we exchanged "ironic points of light," as Auden so memorably put it in his "September 1, 1939," quoted above. At some time around 1960 McGrath at length touched England again, conversed in our New Left coffee bar and trod the Aldermaston Road in support of the Campaign for Nuclear Disarmament. Then the messages came to us not only from North Dakota but from Greece, Yugoslavia, Mexico. We have been poor correspondents. Yet we have felt—certainly Dorothy and I have felt—that all this time we have been walking shoulder to shoulder. And I am proud to find, in a letter from Tom of 1961, "I think of you both there as one of the few solid things in the world."

I do not mean—and it is important to say this—that we have adopted identical political or intellectual positions. But there has been a congruence of ulterior values and commitments, which arose from within the same double-contradiction. McGrath has reprinted in his Collected Poems, "Ars Poetica":

> Oh, it's down with art and down with life and give us another reefer—
> They all said—give us a South Sea isle, where light my love lies dreaming;
> And who is that poet come in off the streets with a look unleal and lour?
> Your feet are muddy, you son-of-a-bitch, get out of our ivory tower.[9]

But he has not republished "Thomas Paradox's Second Epistle to the Philistines," which probably belongs in the same period (between 1948 and 1953?) with its effective verse:

118

> The poet said to the bureaucrat: man creates
>   by the laws of beauty
> The artist creates the heart's face: an image
>   of all that's human.
> But he said: I've no time to argue—though it
>   sounds like a deviation—
>   On a hacienda
>   In San Fernando,
> I'm making the Revolution.

That is a version of the poem which appears in a raft of typescripts which McGrath sent us from the West Coast in the early fifties. My sole contribution to the full annotated text of McGrath's Complete Works in the Twenty-second Century (which century neither McGrath nor I expect to arrive) will be this. I cannot prove it, for I cannot find the earlier copy, but this is a West Coast, fifties, variant of a poem which in the late forties (and Manhattan) had ended the verse in this way:

>   Desk-deep in class war
>   On the eighteenth floor
> I'm making the Revolution.

The change was made, as the poet has recently acknowledged to me, for political and not for aesthetic reasons: "by the time the poem got to publication some of the people on the eighteenth floor were in jail or on their way or gone underground; but there were still a good many one-time radicals still alive and making money in the shadow of Hollywood."[10]

This illustrates the difficulties placed not only before an editor but also a critic. McGrath's texts often suggest a subtext which is tactfully diminished or even suppressed because the targets of his intellectual attack—the "bureaucrat," the instrumental Marxist ideologue—were themselves the objects of persecution by media and state. Meanwhile McGrath, himself persecuted by the same forces, was involved in sharp disputes within that cultural apparatus which both presented and contained, both expressed and repressed, an influential part of the American Left.

It is a curious situation, at odds with the stereotypes. On one side McGrath was being hounded by HUAC: "I expect to be fired from my job at the end of this term," he wrote to us from Los Angeles (1951?):

119

I'm certain someone will see "Crooked Mile,"* read it and decide I'm n.g. Which could mean (this is not for saying aloud) that I might go to jail. Possible.

But he was writing to us the next year:

All in all I think my career as the best or most promising or whatever it was left-wing poet in America** is due for some drastic revision. In fact, I feel pretty sure that it is no longer possible for me to publish in the left wing press any more. If that is too pessimistic, then I will emend it to say that it is only a matter of time. I suppose I was always suspect for being "difficult" and for being "bitter" . . . Unless you versify Daily Worker editorials in degenerate Whitmanesque, you're apt to seem like a formalist, and anything that is not a cliche is examined to see whether it might not be a political heresy. This is not just a lament for my own situation. For Christ sake, if you can get anyone to look into the stinking mess here, do so. All the writers I know regard Sillen and the literary commissars (like Fast) as idiots, but the only reaction to them is cynicism, since no one feels that anything can be done. It's absolutely strangling. Unless you are, like Neruda, a senator from Chile in exile, you're in a bad way. If you are Neruda, you get fawned on and editorialized over by bureaucrats who really hate all art but admire anything that succeeds. Help! Help!

But if the left-wing press was "strangling," there was no other: "My novel I think is done for—the pub. house where it was just had a red hunt and the editor was fired etc."[11]

It was at this time that McGrath, Philip Stevenson and a few friends founded the *California Quarterly*. It got "a mixed reception" (he wrote to us in 1953):

The agit-prop-and-idiot faction write us letters which say that the stories are negative and that we have no Negro writers—this group is a kind of self-appointed Committee of Public Safety, or better yet the Mrs. Grundys of the Revolution and apparently they never read poetry . . . Another group gives us hell for being so dedicated to uplift and betterment of the human race that we publish a story for its theme . . .

The only salvation of left writing in this country, I think, is to try to break the strangle-hold of the blue stockings who run left editing and criticism. But other editors are afraid to do anything. Unless we hold to orthodox views (views which no left-wing writer in the country accepts, but all are afraid to challenge for fear of a heresy trial) these editors think that Jerome and Sillen and the high panjan-drums (Fast et al) will attack and destroy us . . . It's a simply sickening situation. Everyone here assumes nothing can be done about it, refuse to stand together (that would be factionalism!) and adopt an attitude of pure cynicism toward

---

To Walk a Crooked Mile (New York: Alan Swallow, 1947).

**A jesting reference to the blurb of *Crooked Mile*.

Jerome & Co. regarding *Masses & Mainstream* as the idiot child: lame-witted and a little shameful to be sure, but nevertheless our own.

I am not competent to unravel the inner history of these disputes: I must leave this to others. My sympathies are with McGrath: yet I do not know that he was always "right," nor that he would always claim this himself. The protagonists whom he identified most often, among the party of "bureaucrats" or "philistines," were V. J. Jerome, Samuel Sillen and (on the West Coast) John Howard Lawson; and of his own party, Milton Blau and the generous-minded (and neglected) Charles Humboldt:

> Now that Charlie Humboldt and Milt Blau no longer have anything to do with *Masses and Mainstream* the present editors choose only the most thinned out kind of material. I pray for a new Duclos letter on American left criticism, but despair of getting it. When Mao wrote it for us (have you seen his pamphlet on Art and Literature?) there was what amounted to a suppression of it—no reviews, no discussion, nothing. Perhaps I am no longer quite sane on the whole subject. The Mao thing especially agitates me, since Mao says the same damn thing about the need for both a tactical and a strategic kind of writing which I have argued is the only solution to the dilemma of left writing under capitalism . . . I say in dead seriousness that we need help in the worst way.

No doubt the control exerted by the American Communist Party over its own cultural apparatus was unusually disciplinary and its instrumental attitudes towards art may have been unusually bleak. And the self-submission of some intellectuals to the mystique of the historical authority of the party, as the interpreter of revolutionary and class truth, may have been unusually abject. But McGrath was wrong to suppose that he was facing some local American difficulty, and that help might come from the advice of fraternal parties ("a new Duclos letter"). Duclos was quite as much part of the problem as were Sillen or Jerome. Little help could anyone in Europe bring as Zhdanovism extended its ideological and disciplinary reign throughout the international Communist apparatus. McGrath was contesting with symptoms which he had not yet diagnosed as those of Communism's mortal crisis; like his own workers he and his fellow protagonists were "drifting the battlefields of a war / They don't even know is happening." And one must add that not only party discipline (the "fear of a heresy trial") but also a stubborn loyalty to a party—and to comrades—who were the object of incessant public attack inhibited open intellectual confrontations.

Thomas McGrath had rendered his voluntary dues to the party's Caesar. He had offered to compromise with Caesar's demands, by developing a theory of "tactical" and "strategic" poetry. "Tactical" poetry might be about immediate political events: "the poet should give it as much clarity and strength as he can give it without falling into political slogans." "Strategic" poetry ("a poetry in which the writer trusts himself enough to write about whatever comes along") should be open and exploratory, "consciousness raising or enriching."[12] In 1949 he had unleashed a splendid charge of his own tactical cavalry in *Longshot O'Leary's Garland of Practical Poesie*. The title of this book has probably lost meaning to today's readers, although the fiercely political surrealism of the poems has enduring vitality. What has been forgotten is the precedent charge of the heavy brigade of T. S. Eliot, stationing their chargers on every campus and in every literary review. After the *Family Reunion* (1947) and the *Notes Towards a Definition of Culture* (1948) had come the reissue of *Old Possum's Book of Practical Cats*. McGrath's contestation with Eliot can be detected throughout his poetry of this decade, as allusion, irony, echo. And against Old Possum he sent out Longshot O'Leary onto the field.

These "tactical" poems McGrath wrote as immediate polemic. He did not expect them to last. His savage poem on the Marshall Plan, "First Book of Genesis According to the Diplomats,"[13] is—he wrote to us in 1948—"going to be completely useless in a few months possibly." But it has, in fact, long outlasted the Marshall Plan, perhaps because of its hilariously inventive surrealist polemic; and the poet has acknowledged this by including it in his (highly selective) *Collected Poems*.

But even poems such as these could not get into *Masses and Mainstream* by 1952–53. They were too "bitter." And where else could they find an outlet? I cannot, even today, turn away without a wry smile from the recollection of those know-all High Marxists and political Heavies who suppressed verses because they were *too bitter*! "Comrades, you must be more positive! You must have confidence in the international working-class movement!" And what if that movement was collapsing in ruins and bad faith all around us, did not poets then have the duty to warn?[14]

McGrath was right. But that did him no kind of good. Come 1956 and all that, and surely McGrath was at last liberated, freed from the Stalinist shackles, in touch once again with the new and ebullient radicalism of the 1960's, in accord with an audience once more? Well, no. That wasn't how it was. How exactly it was I do not exactly know. But a little I remember, something is in his letters, more is in his poems.

McGrath's break with the Communist Party was never as sharp or as polemical as was ours. This was partly plain pig-Irish stubbornness. When some of those very commissars of culture with whom he had been wrestling for years (in private) suddenly flaked out in public confessional mood, accusing "the party" of their own sins, he sat in the same place and was privately sick.[15] He had never, unless in one or two poems in *Longshot O'Leary*, romanticized the Soviet world.

His stance, in the matter of the Soviet Union, had, and maybe still has, a source in pure curmudgeonly opposition. If the official culture of the U.S. of A., which he found to be foul and mendacious, wanted to name Communism as its Satanic antagonist, then he was willing to vow himself a Satanist and place himself directly in front of Orthodoxy's polished self-satisfied nose.[16]

There was, in any case, a brief moment of honor in the American Communist Party in 1956, a revolt within the *Daily Worker*, a stirring of authentic self-reflection in the party. Tom was, with Charles Humboldt, one of the boarding-party who tried to set *Mainstream* onto a socialist humanist course. When the attempt failed he simply removed himself quietly and without public statement from the snarling comrades. In a letter which I cannot exactly date (probably 1961) he gave a rundown on the previous five years:

> I'm afraid that long letter will never arrive—somebody not paid by the post office dept here must have found it interesting reading. But anyway you must have gathered the main strands—and it's dreary to go over them (some jobs lost thru automation and some thru the high spirits of various quasi-governmental bodies: schools, films, etc. etc. . .) In the last three years I've moved around a lot—hardly six months in any one place—following jobs like a bindle stiff . . . To bring you up to date. For some years I was looked on by the *Mainstream* people as a very bad cat—largely because I had been fighting with John Howard Lawson, the grand panjandrum on the West Coast, a great culture faker. Then it was officially discovered that a lot of mistakes had been made etc. etc. Humboldt went as editor of *Mainstream* and asked me to join up with him, which I did. Then, over a period of time things went back to what they had been; it became more and more difficult for Humboldt to do anything with the magazine; there was a showdown and he lost. So I dropped off also—I was only a "contributor" whatever that means. I've had no organizational connection with the party for years, and the last years when I did have such a connection—god knows how long ago now—were ones where I spent most of the time fighting expulsion. Since then I've free-lanced in a few tactical things with other dissidents—there are a lot of us but there seems no way of getting everybody in any kind of concerted motion, although a few of us did dream for a while of organizing the Ramshackle Socialist Victory Party (RSVP). Somehow it seems that this might still be done, but I don't see how.
>
> Still, with all the trouble there was with the organization, the fact that it has

had such a terrible fight in the last years and has lost so much in members and power (more from bad politics than terror) has left a terrible terrible emptiness in the whole life of the country, an emptiness which I think everyone feels without knowing why. And an emptiness which has left a lot of writers and intellectuals in a bad way. I don't mean the ones who were in the organization (although they've been hard hit too); what I am thinking of is the kind of intellectual who never was with the organization and was always critical of it and even opposed to it. *But* who felt some kind of sense of comfort that on many of the big issues where he himself might do nothing, there was a group that was fighting for good causes . . .

> Northern lights in winter; in summer the eccentric stairs
> The firefly climbs . . .
>   But where is the steering star
>   where is
> The Plow? the Wheel?
>   Made this song in a bad time . . .
> No revolutionary song now, no revolutionary
> Party
>   sell out
>   false consciousness
>   yet I *will*
> Sing
>   for these poor
>   for the victory still to come
> RSVP
>   (*Letter*, Part Two, pp. 124–25)

So McGrath returns in the *Letter* back to Manhattan, the "stone city":

> An age of darkness has entered that stone
> In a few years between wars. The past holds,
> Like a sad dream trapped in granite: what foot can slip free what trail
> Blaze in that night-rock where the starry travellers search?
>   (*Letter*, Part Two, p. 125)

But before he returned to Manhattan (1960–61) something had happened in his last years on the West Coast: no less than a Renaissance! In 1958 he wrote to us about "a whirl of work"—a speaking-reading tour up the Coast, poetry with jazz in a nightclub, a record with Langston Hughes: "meanwhile I'm broke." Yet as this "Renaissance" bloomed, McGrath once again turned abruptly away on his own jagged fork. If anything he had found the civilization of the West Coast more threatening than the East. Los Angeles gets a singularly savage handling in the *Letter*:

Windless city built on decaying granite, loose ends
Without end or beginning and nothing to tie to, city down hill
From the high mania of our nineteenth century destiny—what's loose
Rolls there, what's square slides, anything not tied down
Flies in . . .
              kind of petrified shitstorm.

(Letter, Part Two, p. 112)

He recalled his time on the West Coast as:

Ten years—doing time in detention camps of the spirit,
Grounded in Twin Plague Harbor with comrades Flotsom & Jetsam:
Wreckage of sunken boats becalmed in the Horse Latitudes
Windless soul's doldrums Los Angeles AsiaMinor of the intellect
Exile.

(Letter, Part Two, p. 111)

The "exile" was made the more anguished by the loss of his two most valued and sustaining relationships: with Marian, and then with his second wife, Alice. It was made endurable by the small "commune" of resistance, the "Marsh Street Irregulars," the circle of friends, fellow-outlaws and poets, which he was later to recall in elegiac mood.[17] But the pervading memory is one of nightmare, the nightmare of *The Gates of Ivory, The Gates of Horn* (1957). This terrible futuristic extrapolation of a capitalist, consumerized subtopia, governed by the invigilations of a surrealist HUAC, ought never to have passed out of print. Much superior to *Animal Farm* (that exemplary case of ideology masquerading as art), its fertile symbolic code disallows any simplistic ideological printout—when published in Czech it was no doubt read as a savage satire upon Stalinism. It carries no local political "message" but a warning that human creativity was under threat from external repression and internal self-betrayal, and that civilization might pass "into some kind of surrogate existence."

McGrath's hostility to West Coast civilization extended not only to its dominant consumer culture but also to a good part of the self-styled oppositional culture also—an "opposition" which he often gestures at as one of "culture-fakers," exhibitionists, egotists, and "the dreamers, crazed, in their thousands, nailed to a tree of wine" (*Letter*, Part Two, p. 116)—an "opposition" only too easily to be bought or co-opted by money and power. What happened to destroy McGrath's accord with the West Coast "Renaissance" I do not know. But he explained some part of it to us after his return to New York in 1960. For a while he had "had some hope" for "the Beat mob":

There was in fact a lot of social critical thinking in the group (never a group, just a bunch of people who were on the scene). Then *Life-Time* discovered the thing and invented their own version of it. The censors helped by making *Howl* and Ginsberg into an icon. Barney Ross of Grove Press and Lawrence Lipton (he wrote a book called *The Holy Barbarians*) cut the balls off the "movement," substituting "disaffiliation" and (as if there weren't enough to go around) "alienation," dada, obscenity etc. etc. The Beat Movement became a little club of crazies, very exclusive; and the younger ones accepted "disaffiliation" etc. etc. as the official program, grew beards, went back to the big war against their parents and all social content was lost. All positive social content any way. What a son-of-a-bitch Rimbaud was! He gave a program to a century of petit bourgeois psycho-anarchists.

*   *   *

> What! All those years after the Annunciation at Venice
> And no revolution in sight?
>   And how long since the lads
> From West Stud Horse Texas and Poontang-on-the-Hudson
> Slogged through the city of Lost Angels in the beardless years
> Led by a cloud no bigger than an orgone box, whence issued—
> Promising, promising, promising (and no revolution and no
> Revolution in sight) issued the cash-tongued summons
> Toward the guru of Big Sur and San Fran's stammering Apocalypse?
>
> I do not know how long this thing can go on!
> —Waiting for Lefty, waiting for Godot, waiting for the heavenly fix.
> In my way of counting, time comes in through my skin—
> Blind Cosmos Alley, charismatic light
> Of electric mustaches in the Deep Night of the Gashouse gunfire
> From enormous imaginary loud cap pistols of infinitely small caliber
> Anarcholunacy—how long, in that light, to read what signposts?
> When all that glows with a gem-like flame is the end of Lipton's cigar?[18]

For a year or two (1960–61) he was back in New York (now with Genya), an unaffiliated and agnostic revolutionary:

> I remain unconvinced of everything except that (under what auspices now I cannot imagine) the revolution has got to come. And it had better come pretty soon here or we will have passed into some kind of surrogate existence—unless we have already—in which regeneration is impossible . . . We live in Manhattan—lower East side—lower than it's ever been, very poor, luminous poverty and a phosphorescence of non-literary alienation in the streets. We have a terrible sort of place. Would be unbearable to think of living here for a long time—but I feel that way about the whole city.

And, in the same letter:

No movements about. The pacifists keep fairly busy and I've given them a hand on a few things now and again. The biggest thing I think that has happened in quite a while is the action which the women took a couple of weeks ago. Demonstrations took place all across the country, some of them pretty sizeable (a couple of thousand Americans involved in a *good* cause is pretty sizeable to us nowadays).

Several letters exchanged at this time related to his attempt to visit—perhaps to stay a while and work—in Cuba. We furnished credentials from *New Left Review* for Tom and Genya to serve in Cuba as, respectively, journalist and photographer, but to no avail: the State Department evidently consulted up-to-date files and permits were refused.

It is at around this time that McGrath's pessimism about urban American civilization appears to deepen: "I don't belong in this century—who does?"

> Now, down below, in the fire and stench, the city
> Is building its shell: elaborate levels of emptiness
> Like some sea-animal building towards its extinction.
> And the citizens, unserious and full of virtue,
> Are hunting for bread, or money, or a prayer,
> And I behold them, and this season of man, without love.
>
> If it were not a joke, it would be proper to laugh.
> —Curious how that rat's nest holds together—
> Distracting . . .
>   Without it there might be, still,
> The gold wheel and the silver, the sun and the moon,
> The season's ancient assurance under the unstable stars
> Our fiery companions . . .
>   And trees, perhaps, and the sound
> Of the wild and living water hurrying out of the hills.[19]

Later, back in North Dakota, in one of his rare essays on his poetic intentions, he discussed the matter:

What is there, out here on the edge, that makes our experience different from that of the city poet? First there is the land itself. It has been disciplined by machines, but it is still not dominated. The plow that broke the plains is long gone and the giant tractor and the combine are here, but the process of making a living is still a struggle and a gamble—it is not a matter of putting raw materials in one end of a factory and taking finished products out of the other. Weather, which is only a nuisance in the city, takes on the power of the gods here, and vast cycles of climate, which will one day make all the area a dust bowl again and finally return it to grass, make all man's successes momentary and ambiguous. Here man can never think of himself, as he can in the city, as the master of nature. Like it or not he is subject to the ancient power of seasonal change: he cannot avoid being *in* nature; he has an heroic adversary that is no abstraction. At a level below immediate consciousness we respond to this, are less alien to our bodies, to human and natural time.

The East is much older than these farther states, has more history. But I believe that that history no longer functions, has been forgotten, has been "paved over." In the East man begins every day for himself. Here, the past is still alive and close at hand—the arrowheads we turn up may have been shot at our grandfathers. I am not thinking of any romantic frontier. The past out here was bloody, and full of injustice, though hopeful and heroic. It is very close here—my father took shelter with his family at Fort Ransom during an Indian scare when he was a boy. Later he heard of the massacre at Wounded Knee. Most of us are haunted by the closeness of that past, and by the fact that we are only a step from the Indian, whose sense of life so many of the younger people are trying to learn.[20]

*   *   *

Why my grandmother saw them—
And saw the last one perhaps: ascending the little river
On the spring high water in a battered canoe.
Stole one of her chickens
(Herself in the ark of the soddy with the rifle cocked but not arguing)
Took the stolen bird and disappeared into history.

(*Letter*, Part Two, p. 190)

But it was not only that in the cities the sense of history was "paved over." McGrath also argued—and perhaps still argues?—that urban civilization in the U.S. had entered into a "surrogate existence":

Supposing he already knows the facts of life and the class struggle, the poet has nothing to learn from the city. Where once it was a liberating place it is now a stultifying one. Only in the ghettos is something "happening," as the great proliferation of Black, Chicano and Indian poetry shows. For such poets the ghettos are a source of strength. But the white poet can enter the ghetto only with great difficulty and in any case the ghettos are only beginning to work through to revolutionary politics. At the moment they are still involved (with important exceptions) in cultural and political nationalism, dead ends which it seems must be explored before a serious politics becomes possible. When that time comes the cities will again be the place of the central experience of the time and the poets will have to go back . . .

The point is to find, during these years of "wandering in the desert," the link with the revolutionary past in order to create, invent, rescue, restructure, resurrect the past. This may be our gift to the city.[21]

Yet McGrath did not retire from New York to North Dakota gracefully and in elegiac mood. He stormed out with the first number of an irregular journal, *Crazy Horse*, "edited by a dead Sioux chief"—the chief who helped to defeat General Custer. *Crazy Horse* announced that it wasn't interested "in either the shrunken trophies of the academic head-hunters nor in those mammoth cod-pieces stuffed with falsies, the primitive inventions of the Nouveau Beat. We believe that poverty is real, that work is real, that joy and anguish and revolution are real."

> We, the Irregulars of Crazy Horse, Ghost Dancers of the essential existential Solidarity, now summon into being the hosts of the new resistance. Give up those bird-cages built for lions! Alienation is not enough![22]

McGrath's own poems and those of Alvaro Cardona-Hine came closest to meeting the extravagant prescriptions of the manifesto. There is a violence of desperation, a mood of willful self-isolation, invective and blasphemy about this moment: a total rejection.

Crazy Horse was published sporadically over the next years, from North Dakota, and then passed from Tom and Genya's editorship into other hands. McGrath half turned back to his own state and he was half-driven there. First the University of North Dakota and then Moorhead State University (Minnesota) to their honor (and their own good fortune) found places for this most distinguished poet. In the past twenty-odd years there have been dark patches and patches of sun, and in all times McGrath has continued to be prolific, innovative, poetically "Live-O." These years are still too close to both of us to discuss with objectivity.

3

As I have followed the tracks of this remarkable poet through a dozen tiny and short-lived journals on the margins of official (or "official" oppositional) culture it has been impossible not to reach for a comparison. The experience of isolation, of the loss of relations with a public, of blacklisting and of survival through a succession of casual jobs,[23] is one which calls into mind the experience of many Czech intellectuals who were evicted from their professions in the "normalization" which succeeded upon 1968. McGrath has been the outlaw of American normalization.

Of course, the proper and important qualifications must be made. McGrath was hounded around the place but he was not imprisoned, his work was not actually suppressed (except by the self-regulating censorship of editors and publishing houses), and if he was hounded at length back into North Dakota, Dakota—he would be the first to insist—is no

Siberian *gulag*. He has even, of late years, received a little recognition: an Amy Lowell and a Guggenheim fellowship came his way.

Yet, for all that, the trajectory of his life and work offers the sharpest kind of critique of the dominant culture. His work has been barely permitted to continue, sometimes circulating to a readership of a few hundreds on an outlaw margin. Students in the next century may savor the "metaphysical" wit of the poet who, hounded from one job to another in California in the 1950's, wrote "Figures in an Allegorical Landscape" from his temporary refuge as a board marker on the Stock Exchange:

> Where number farmers plant their hope
> In the dark of the moon of ignorance,
> He guards their fractionated sleep:
> A sad vaquero, riding fence
>
> Like a good shepherd. Sacred cows
> Graze on the ranges of his lack.
> In his high patrol he binds the strays
> From Anaconda to Zellerback,
>
> While all Dow's children clap their hands
> For the Eucharist of their golden feast.
> But he is bound in stocks and bonds,
> Who writes the Number of the Beast.[24]

And I will predict with greater confidence that students will read with pride McGrath's multifaceted refusal to cooperate with the House Un-American Activities Committee in 1953, as a teacher, poet and citizen — a statement which commences:

As a teacher, my first responsibility is to my students. To cooperate with this committee would be to set for them an example of accommodation to forces which can only have, as their end effect, the destruction of education itself . . . I am proud to say that a great majority of my students . . . do not want me to accommodate myself to this committee. In a certain sense, I have no choice in the matter—the students would not want me back in the classroom if I were to take any course of action other than the one I am pursuing.[25]

And they will note with pleasure that McGrath's students fulfilled his confidence in them, publishing a tribute to him in the form of a collection of his own poems, *Witness to the Times!* In a "Comment" prefaced to the collection, McGrath wrote:

130

I hope that the poems will be a witness to a continuing liaison with the world, an affair that is not without its up and downs but which is as secure as a sacred marriage. I believe that this figure of the world's lover is the best image for the poet—that he may succeed where the Neutral Man (whom it shall not profit to gain his soul if he lose the world) is certain to fail. The poet always has this task, it seems to me: to bear witness to the times; but now especially when the State is trying by corruption, coercion, and its own paltry terror to silence writers, or dope them or convert them into the bird sanctuaries of public monuments—now especially the artist should be responsible to the world.[26]

McGrath's good friend and mentor, Charles Humboldt, had a more savage comment on "the witnesses" who made their terms with "the confessors of the sacred state":

> Now they are kind to children and at the least
> Rebuff burst into tears, reproach and follow
> The hunted as though *they* were being holloed
> Through halls and borders like a tired beast.[27]

"Why does the persecution in mass of Communist and progressive intellectuals arouse no protest among the partisans of 'the liberty and integrity of the individual'?" he asked. And he indicated the "latent conservatism" of even the "pseudo-revolutionary" movements of modern art, "self-absorbed and devoid of all realistic material perspective":

> Their goal was freedom *from* society, not freedom *within* society to be won in alliance with its progressive forces. After all, one could still crawl in the cracks of the police state. So the fire eaters now drink at their masters' tables while the prophets compose cautious prayers for their own salvation.[28]

McGrath perhaps will have said "amen" to that, yet it will not have satisfied him. He was not euphoric about "the progressive forces" of society, and his "realistic material perspectives" lay more in the past than in the present or future:

> I sit at the beach, in the light of a gone day,
> And I wait for the hunters [. . . .]
>
> . . . Dark, now, all the States,
> And night on the west coast.
> Darkness and exile [. . . .]
>
> For they will hunt you, O revolutionaries!
> Hunt you in darkness—the slogan chalked on the wall
> Is your magical sign, icon of terrible love,

The dark of the calendar. They hunt you, listening
For a sound of gunfire.

But, now, the silence, and the neutral stars on the sea.
Sirens. Waiting. The waves' long lamentation.
Endured by millions—this darkness and the hunting:
Capture   Death   Victory. Like the struggle, the changeless sea,
Like the constant stars: Endure   Resist   Endure[29]

Here, waiting for the hunters, he turned inward upon himself and
commenced the *Letter to an Imaginary Friend*. In such a moment of
isolation and defeat, Wordsworth at Goslar in 1799 commenced *The
Prelude*, a poem to which *Letter* can be justly compared. There is the
same autobiographic structure (and the same indefiniteness as to bio-
graphic detail); the same recovery of childhood experience, seen both
through the child's eye and the adult poet; the same central concern
with political experience; the same strenuous attempt to settle mytholog-
ical accounts with the poet's own time.

Yet to mention *The Prelude* in the same breath as *Letter* is not only to
provoke academic hilarity. It is also to snag one's foot on the widespread
misunderstanding that *Letter* (in its "valid" parts) is some kind of "pasto-
ral" offering from "the West." It is this (I suspect) which has closed the
urban and academic readership against a due recognition of the poem: it
is difficult to perceive that a poem with "agrarian" themes, by a poet who
has chosen to "withdraw" to North Dakota, might possibly be addressed
to their immediate history and their own malaise. When McGrath pub-
lished *The Movie at the End of the World*, a selection from a lifetime's
verse, the *New Republic* noted that this revealed the poet as "an old-time
dustbowl radical out of the Dakotas of the '30's" who had passed
through "characteristic romantic progression from illusion to disillusion"
(April 21, 1973). Seven years later the *New York Times Book Review* got
around to awarding the same book the high fame of a seven-line notice
(April 13, 1980) which said that "the spirit that animates [the poems] is
of the West, whether it is in the form of tough modern verse or that of
the simple, oldtime ballad."

The misrecognition here is spectacular. McGrath's first published
poems belong to the last years of the thirties. His first volume, *First
Manifesto*, was published by Alan Swallow at Baton Rouge in 1940, and
a brief scrutiny will show that dominant influences upon the poems
were those of Hart Crane and of the English left-wing poets of the
thirties: Auden, Day Lewis, Spender, MacNeice. It is not so much the
"oldtime ballad" as Auden's reinvention of it in *Look, Stranger* and

Another Time which gave to McGrath an inspiration for his own rein-
ventions in *Longshot O'Leary*. In McGrath's subsequent poetry he draws
upon Western agrarian themes and a Wobbly vocabulary, but the poetic
and intellectual influences are in no way "regional." A very long way
back there may be Whitman, or the voracious appetite and universal
self-license of Whitman, but

> Whitman, he thinks, deserves to be sung.
> His imitators should all be hung.[30]

Influences which I have myself noted include Lorca, Eluard, Neruda,
Brecht, Pasternak. The strongest intellectual influence of "Marxism"
came to him, not through Marx, but through Christopher Caudwell:

> *Longshot O'Leary Says a Square Is a Person*
> *Who Cannot Read Caudwell*[31]

Among his contemporaries he was clearly in touch with the group of
British poets of the Left around *Our Time* and *Arena* (some of whom he
had met in 1947–48): Edgell Rickword, Randall Swingler, Jack Lindsay,
Hamish Henderson, Arnold Rattenbury, Jack Beeching, Roy Fuller.
And close poetic colleagues and friends in America are often summoned
into the round dance of his verse: among them Charles Humboldt,
Edwin Rolfe, Naomi Replansky, Don Gordon, Alvaro Cardona-Hine,
Robert Bly.

But I have written myself into a ridiculous corner: in noting influences
which might be overlooked, I have suggested far too narrow a grid of
reference for this deeply-cultured mind. He has received, no doubt, two
hundred influences per week, and some he has received and rejected (as
Eliot, Pound and Beckett) while others, like the *haiku*, he has submitted
himself to as a discipline.[32] His poetry is enriched by sufficient mythic
and literary (as well as political) allusion to keep, alas, whole Eng. Lit.
Faculties at work through the twenty-first century. I wish only to
emphasize that Part Two of the *Letter*, which some people suppose to be
"about" North Dakota, is signed off "North Dakota-Skyros-Ibiza-Agaete-
Guadalajara, 1968." It is true that McGrath's *politics* are given a very
distinct American location; they are not the extrapolation of some
theorized cosmopolitan prescription. But these are interpreted through a
poetic grid of reference which, if not universal, is as universal as his
selection of poetic values allows it to be.

As he insists, "North Dakota is everywhere." And what is "every-
where" is not that complacent and self-important entity, "the human

condition," but the condition of men and women in their labor, in their love and their loss, in their "somatic" relation to nature, in their exploitation and oppression, in their thwarted aspirations for "communitas" (their faculty for dreaming and myth-making), and at times very specifically in their common imbrication in the capitalist nexus.[33]

Nevertheless, it is *Dakota* which is "everywhere," and if we are to understand the *Letter* that is where we must start. The history of the Dakotas and the biography of the McGrath family is an extraordinarily compressed episode, almost a parable of capitalism. His grandparents on both sides were Irish and on his mother's side (the Sheas) they were Gaelic-speaking. His maternal grandfather came, by way of Ellis Island, up to North Dakota, working on the railway, carting and freighting. His paternal grandfather came through Canada, carrying with him savage anti-English recollections of the Great Potato Famine; he also came following the railway, doing freighting work with a contractor of oxen. Both pairs of grandparents became homesteaders, the Sheas in the neighborhood of Sheldon, where McGrath grew up. The family passed on to the growing poet a vigorous inheritance from the Irish oral tradition. His paternal grandfather was a notable "curser"[34] and his father a great teller of "tall stories"—such stories as recur in the *Letter*, as when the winds from the dust bowls of the West darken the Dakota skies:

> And the dust blowing down your throat like a fistful of glass—
> And *that* not so bad, but pushing down on your hat
> Were the vagrant farms of the north: Montana, Saskatchewan,
> With the farmers still on them, merrily plowing away,
> Six inches over your head . . .
>
> (*Letter*, Part One, p. 47)

In the evenings at the farm, when the battery set ran out, his father would entertain the children with songs and stories, some traditional, some (about local personalities and events) of his own making. To this McGrath could add the scanty resource of the local school—Pope's *Iliad*, Halkett and Laing versions of the classics, *The Burnt Njal*—and the ambiguous inheritance of the Catholic church, which is resurrected and roasted in Part Three of the *Letter* (p. 62):

> And now comes the Holy Father a-flap in his crowdark drag!

The Dakota farms are laid out like geometric patterns on a drawing board, allocation upon identical allocation. They seem to have been planted on top of the natural environment, not to have grown up in relation with it. Here and there are densely packed clumps of woodland ("woodlots"), for homesteaders who agreed to raise timber received a small additional grant of land. The trees do not follow the lanes and hedges, they are simply dumped into isolated corrals: utility plants for fuel. Here a civilization was planted, with immense hardship, in one generation; struggled to maintain itself in the face of dust bowls and mortgages in the next; and gave way to collapse and emigration in McGrath's own generation. Moreover, the first generation entered into that hard world of labor only after expelling their forerunners:

> It was here the Sioux had a camp on the long trail
> Cutting the loops of the rivers from beyond the Missouri and Mandan
> East: toward Big Stone Lake and beyond to the Pipestone Quarry,
> The place of peace.
> A backwoods road of a trail, no tribal
> Superhighway; for small bands only. Coming and going
> They pitched camp here a blink of an eye ago.

*　　*　　*

> From Indians we learned a toughness and a strength; and we gained
> A freedom: by taking theirs: but a real freedom: born
> From the wild and open land our grandfathers heroically stole.
> But we took a wound at Indian hands: a part of our soul scabbed over:
> We learned the pious and patriotic art of extermination
> And no uneasy conscience where the man's skin was the wrong
> Color; or his vowels shaped wrong; or his haircut; or his country possessed of
> Oil; or holding the wrong place on the map—whatever
> The master race wants it will find good reasons for having.
> (Letter, Part Two, pp. 189–90)

And, even more savagely, in Part Three:

> [. . .] the deep, heroic and dishonest past
> Of the national myth of the frontier spirit and the free West—
> Oh, nightmare, nightmare, dream and despair and dream!
>
> A confusion of waters, surely, and pollution at the head of the river!
> Our history begins with the first wound: with Indian blood
> Coloring the water of the original springs—earlier, even:
> Europe: the indentured . . .
> (p. 36)

It was in his father's generation that this episode came to its climax. yet the climax was not one of promised prosperity after hardship and toil, not that of prairie middle peasantry or New England individualists.

What took place instead was a climax of exploitation, by banks, millers, dealers and railways, leading these Irish, Scandinavians, Germans and assorted Americans into a huge social movement of wrath and solidarity. The Dakotas and Minnesota, so easily to be seen from the East or West Coasts as being way out there beyond the uttermost sticks, were in fact the heartland of a great and effective popular movement, inadequately described in the misty all-inclusive term as "populist." It was an active and democratic movement; the North Dakota Non-Partisan League was socialist in its origins, and demanded the state ownership of banks, grain elevators, etc. In 1919 the NPL caucus dominated the state legislature, created a state bank and grain elevators, imposed income and inheritance taxes, introduced assistance to home buyers, legalized strikes and brought in mines safety regulations. In the judgment of a contemporary historian, "no more dramatic demonstration of democracy has occurred in American history."[35]

This movement was one of the few great impulses on the North American continent in the twentieth century which afforded premonitions of an American socialism or "communitas." And it contained within it even sharper forms of political consciousness. McGrath's father read the *Industrial Worker* and the migrant farmhand, Cal, so important in the structure of the *Letter*, is a Wobbly and McGrath's childhood mentor. It is from Cal also that young Tom first encounters the savage scepticism of the freethinker in the face of the Catholic formation of his boyhood: "All peace on earth for about five seconds" (*Letter*, Part Three, p. 58).

These are some of the materials for the "pastoral" (or sometimes "anti-pastoral") themes of McGrath's poetry. And there are in fact many themes, which the urban reader—encountering coulees and horses and Indians and the stars—allows his eye to pass across too inattentively. Not one of them should be treated with that kind of disrespect, and least of all McGrath's horses, which are sometimes horses, sometimes nightmares or outlaws, and very often Pegasus, the Crazy Horse. (In one of his first published poems he noted: "I have known personally horses / Who were more alive than many college professors.")[36]

Within this "pastoral" mode we find, certainly, the keenest eye for natural beauty and for the rightness, but also mercilessness, of natural things; a "somatic" sense of human transience, a cutting-down of humankind to size against the cyclonic weather and the stars; a sense of contest, the small farmsteads pitted against the vast Dakota winters. And we find other things also. We find the central theme of labor, a male world of agrarian labor with its glimpsed solidarities; and the

136

theme of exploitation, for the winds which blow incessantly over Dakota are two, the wind of nature and the wind of *money*, of mortgages and interest-rates and bankruptcies, "continual wind of money, that blows the birds through the clocks" (*Letter*, Part One, p. 92). There are other themes also, among them the glimpsed "communitas" of the farmer-labor alliance and the Wobblies—a communitas which found, in the thirties, a further and sadder extension in the moments of solidarity of the unemployed.

So this is not altogether what one has come to expect from the term "pastoral." "*Letter* is not a poem that comes out of the sensibility of the city middle-class intellectual."[37] Yet this is not pastoral's negation, anti-pastoral or urban face-making either. The moments of agrarian experience—of joy, terror, hardship in labor—are unqualified values. In *Letter*, Part One, there is a moment of sudden transition when McGrath moves (1939) from Dakota to his first contact with High Culture in Louisiana:

> And they got hold of Agrarianism—
> Salvation—40 acres and a mule—the Protestant Heaven,
> Free Enterprise! Kind of intellectual ribbon-development [. . .]

> *   *   *

> And all of them
> On Donne. Etc.
> And all of them sailing on the Good Ship Tradition . . .
> For the thither ports of the moon.
> High flying days
> I'll tell you right now!
> And me with my three ideas
> With my anarchist, peasant poverty, being told at last how bright
> The bitter land was.
> How the simple poor might lift a laud to the Lord. [. . .]

> *   *   *

> O architectonic colloquy! O gothick Pile
> Of talk! How, out of religion and poetry
> And reverence for the land the good life comes.
> Some with myth, some with Visions out of
> That book by Yeats would dance the seasons round
> In a sweet concord.
> But never the actual seasons—
> Not the threshing floor of Fall nor the tall night of the Winter—
> Woodcutting time—nor Spring with the chime and jingle
> Of mended harness on real and farting horses,

Nor the snort of the tractor in the Summer fallow.
Not the true run of the seasons.

(Letter, Part One, pp. 60–62)

Labor, then, the "real and farting horse" (which might still be Pegasus), exploitation (the "wind of money"), glimpsed communitas:

> But I was a peasant from Sauvequipeuville—
> I wanted the City of Man.
>
> (Letter, Part One, p. 60)

All these are at odds with customary urban expectations. For McGrath's pastoral verse lacks one almost-obligatory element, that of ultimate reconciliation (of man with nature, or of men and women in a shared consensus). I can point to this by means of a contrast with Robert Frost's *The Code*, a poem which I highly regard. Frost often acknowledged in his poetry dimensions of labor and of hardship. In this poem we have a moment of sudden conflict between a small working farmer and his hired hand. Storm clouds threaten the taking-in of harvest: the farmer urges on and chides his skilled laborer who, sharing equal commitment to the task and equally aware of the weather's threat, knows better than to change his steady measured pace, since there is no way in which that long-learned pace can be mended. At length the laborer is goaded to throw down the whole load upon the farmer's head. But, then, notice how the poem ends:

> "Weren't you relieved to find he wasn't dead?"
>
> "No! and yet I don't know—it's hard to say.
> I went about to kill him fair enough."
>
> "You took an awkward way. Did he discharge you?"
>
> "Discharge me? No! He knew I did just right."[38]

The poem has established conflict to the edge of murder, but has then reconciled that moment within a shared consensus of values, of shared agrarian skills, which are acknowledged by both master and man.

Contrast this with the episode of Cal at the opening of Part One of *Letter*:

> Then, one day—windy—
> We were threshing flax I remember, toward the end of the run—
> After quarter-time I think—the slant light falling
> Into the blackened stubble that shut like a fan toward the headland—

138

The strike started then. Why *then* I don't know.
Cal spoke for the men and my uncle cursed him.
I remember that ugly sound, like some animal cry touching me
Deep and cold, and I ran toward them
And the fighting started.
My uncle punched him. I heard the breaking crunch
Of his teeth going and the blood leaped out of his mouth [. . .]

(*Letter*, Part One, p. 18)

The episode violates any notional consensus of agrarian values, not only as between employers and hands, but also carrying the conflict right into the poet's own family, for McGrath's father quarrels with his brother:

Outside the barn my father knelt in the dust
In the lantern light, fixing a harness. Wanting
Just to be around, I suppose, to try to show to Cal
He couldn't desert him.
                              He held the tubular punch
With its spur-like rowel, punching a worn hame strap
And shook the bright copper rivets out of a box.
"Hard lines, Tom," he said. "Hard lines, Old Timer."
I sat in the lantern's circle, the world of men,
And heard Cal breathe in his stall.
                              An army of crickets
Rasped in my ear.
                              "Don't hate anybody."
My father said.
I went toward the house through the dark.

That night the men all left.

(*Letter*, Part One, p. 23)

There is a reconciliation here between son and father, for both carry the conflict unresolved inside them. But for that conflict itself there is no resolution:

There were strikes on other rigs that day, most of them lost,
And, on the second night, a few barns burned.
After that a scattering of flat alky bottles,
Gasoline filled, were found, buried in bundles.

(*Letter*, Part One, p. 24)

And never, in any poem, is it resolved. That past is never "paved over" and finished. It remains, tormented by conflict, but also pregnant with "the possible that never was." It is this which confronts the expectations

139

of pastoral verse and which prevents McGrath's *Letter* from being nostalgic, a retrospective meditation upon or a celebration of a finished way of life. Both conflict and potential coexist in the poem's present tense.

The theme of the potential indicates the point at which McGrath departs from prevalent notations—and also anxieties—as to what is called "populism." He has always been more watchful, more accusatory of the "cultural default" of the intellectuals than the default of "the people." The Western intelligentsia has increasingly found refuge in theories (some of these even in the form of Marxisms) which predicate the inexorable determinist force used by structures to expropriate the people of self-activity. The people are thus regarded as stamped with an ideologically confected false consciousness, leading to the view that "populism" is always threatening and only the islands of intellect, the reviews and academies, are able to liberate themselves from determinist process. McGrath has, in contrast, held the intelligentsia as themselves co-partners of the expropriators and co-authors of false consciousness. Even the revolt of the *New York Review of Books* intelligentsia during the Vietnam War did not convince him:

> Out of so much of this temporary "war politics" rises a terrible spiritual smell which signals to the enemy: "I'm not really like this. Just stop bombing Hanoi and I will go back to my primary interests: flowers, early cockcrow, the Holy Ghost, wheelbarrows, the letter G, inhabitable animals, the sacred mysteries of the typewriter keyboard, and High Thought including the Greater, the Lesser, and High, Low, Jack-in-the-goddam-game mysticism." Worthy enough subjects in themselves . . .[39]

I am not wholly clear what is being argued here. Perhaps it is that the "revolt" engaged with certain symptoms—symptoms too embarrassing to ignore—but did not identify nor engage with the cause? Perhaps that the cause, if identified, would have indicted the artificers of false consciousness themselves? Maybe the criticism is even more bluntly political?

> I suppose I ought at once to name the villain who has stolen our past—or tried to steal it: we don't admit anything but temporary defeat—in order as soon as possible to activate the rage of those critics and those readers who feel that politics is vulgar and revolutionary marxism anathema. The villain is capitalism in all its material and magical forms. How sad for me that I cannot name something nicely and safely metaphysical![40]

Yet McGrath's political stance derives less from revolutionary Marxist theory than he may himself suppose, simply because it does not ultimately derive from theory at all: "in the beginning was the *world!*[41] And the "world," the experience in which his politics are rooted (and which his poetry strives to recover) is "a very *American* kind of radicalism":[42] not that of "populism" but of the most radical—sometimes socialist, sometimes anarcho-syndicalist—and the most militant anti-capitalist affirmations within Labor-Farmer, Wobbly and early American Communist traditions. In retrospect he has become critical of the Popular Front of the thirties and early forties: "the more sectarian politics before the Popular Front were more 'American' than the politics which followed":

> In the '20s the Left had many of its origins further west than New York, and out there some of us had been living with the dark side of American experience for a long time. In the late '30s and even more the '40s the Left got coralled in the Eastern cities. And I think some of the writers were unprepared for the late '40s and '50s because they had taken in too much of the Popular Front and watered down their radicalism . . . It led people into an optimistic notion of what *was* going to happen, although after 1946, it should have been perfectly plain what was going to happen. Perhaps it was some sense of this that made me, if not prepared for the long night, at least unsurprised.[43]

The radical intelligentsia inhabited an exciting metropolitan culture, taking some of their bearings from a cosmopolitan Communist mythology, and found themselves quite unprepared for the "man-chilling dark" of subsequent decades. They were unprepared for the mercilessness of American capitalism "in all its material and magical forms." Nor were they sustained by the experience of the solidarity of anti-capitalist struggle (although the poet himself had found this in dockside Manhattan in 1940) and its glimpsed "communitas." For radicalism had begun to drift, from the Popular Front onwards, into complicity with the same divisive ego-psychology that is the legitimating operative drive of capitalist ideology itself: the multiple "I wants" of the claims to equality of ego-fulfillment. And working-class militancy itself was engulfed as the full employment and easy money of the war years dissolved the bonds of solidarity:

> Out of the iron thirties and into the Garden of War profiteers.
> Once it was: *All of us or no one!* Now it's *I'll get mine!*
> (*Letter*, Part Two, p. 146)

"Here's the first / Sellout from which the country is a quarter century sick," and one made the more possible because Popular Front radicals turned away from the class war to "that other war / Where fascism seemed deadlier and easier to fight—but wasn't" (*Letter*, Part Two, p. 148).

Against this loss of militancy and solidarity, McGrath's poems perform their incantatory charms, searching backwards for the "we" of shared labor and hardship, the "we" of active democratic process, the "we" of historical potential, the "we" of casual labor sawing wood in the bitter cold of a Dakota winter, when "the unemployed fished, the fish badly out-numbered"—among the coffee-guzzling Swedes, the moon-faced Irish, the lonesome deadbeats:

> Those were the last years of the Agrarian City
> City of swapped labor
> Communitas
> Circle of warmth and work
> Frontier's end and last wood-chopping bee
> The last collectivity stamping its feet in the cold. [. . .]
>
> The solidarity of forlorn men [. . .]
>
> The chime of comradeship that comes once maybe
> In the Winter of the Blue Snow.
> (*Letter*, Part One, pp. 45–46)

This sense of solidarity . . . in the community is one of the richest experiences that people can have. It's the only true shield against alienation and deracination and it was much more developed in the past than it is now.[44]

Communality or solidarity—feelings which perhaps are more important to us than romantic love . . .[45]

So he recalls—writing in Los Angeles in 1955—the rising mood of militancy, solidarity and hope of the late thirties, in a poetic mood half-angry, half-elegiac:

> Wild talk, and easy enough now to laugh.
> *That's* not the point and never was the point.
> What was real was the generosity, expectant hope,
> The open and true desire to create the good.
>
> Now, in another autumn, in our new dispensation
> Of an ancient, man-chilling dark, the frost drops over
> My garden's starry wreckage.
> Over my hope.
> Over
> The generous dead of my years.
>
> Now, in the chill streets
> I hear the hunting and the long thunder of money. [. . .]

142

                    To talk of the People
Is to be a fool. But they were the *sign* of the People,
Those talkers.
                              Went underground about 1941

Nor hide nor hair of 'em since [. . .]

                              (*Letter*, Part One, 52–53)

As I have gone over this lifetime of work and have touched upon some moments when the poet's life intersected with the crises of his own society, I have been more and more possessed by a sense of the stature of McGrath's achievement. I will say without qualification that we are dealing, with McGrath, with a major talent. To sustain over forty years a principled alienation from the dominant culture; to turn away from every seduction which could have co-opted him to the modes of an official opposition, a "two-party system"[46] of Academy and anti-Academy which the dominant culture could accommodate; to face directly the terror and defeat of those years in which that culture seemed to move inexorably towards an exterminist consummation; to refuse romanticism or easy answers, and yet at the same time to refuse the options of pessimism or empty face-making—all this is an achievement to which I do not know an equal.

A major talent, who has marked his trail through the forest of forty dark years with the blazes of his poems. But can we say that the achievement of his art has matched the achievement of his integrity? It is my own view that we can; that McGrath must be measured as a major poet. But I am perhaps too close both to the poet and to the times to be the necessary "Good Critic who, even now, may be slouching towards" his poems.[47] His shorter poems employ the whole keyboard of technique and tone: lyrical, polemical, satirical, meditative, elegiac, metaphysical. They convey, cumulatively, a unique and consistent view of life and, with this, an inversion of official descriptions of reality, a demystification of American normalization:

                The street rolls up til his office reaches him
                And the door puts out its knob and drags him in.
                His desk-trap is baited with the kill of the day.
                He sets it off by touching it and can't get away.[48]

From this "Poor John Luck" of the forties to his most recent poetry, there is a characteristic McGrathian imagery of determinism, in which persons are acted on by impersonal forces:

143

The streets bulge with ambition and duty—
Inhaling the populace out of exhausted houses.
The drowsy lion of money devours their calendars [. . .][49]

—until the metropolitan civilization itself carries its inert human freight to disaster:

Below me the city turns on its left
Side and the neon blinks in a code I can all too clearly
Read. It will go down with all hands.[50]

And yet, with swift inversions, these massive determinist structures themselves are seen as resting upon the frail spiritual and emotional powers of those who inhabit them:

The city lifts toward heaven from the continent of sleep
This skin of bricks,
      these wounds,
            this soul of smoke and anguish,
These walls held up by hope and want [. . .]

          insubstantial
Structures, framework of dream and nightmare, a honeyed static
Incorporeal which the light condenses.[51]

I do not know any contemporary poet with comparable range of tone and theme, and sureness of touch with all. Nothing is predictable. On one page we have a hilarious celebration of beer ("*Guinness Stout* with its arms of turf and gunfire"),[52] on another a meditation upon the Heisenberg Principle.[53] The characteristic imagery invites by turn the description "metaphysical" (by bringing into conjunction opposing mythologies or belief systems) and "surrealist" (by implanting will and intention in inanimate objects): one is tempted to coin, for McGrath, the term "metasurrealist."

From start to finish of his *oeuvre* there is one recurrent theme: war, the losses of war, the threat of nuclear war, the celebration of war and the means of war in the official culture, the "heavy dancers." And here also "Dakota is everywhere," for, if Dakota were to secede from the United States, it would be, with its battery of Minutemen, the third most powerful nuclear state in the world:

As in the silos waiting near Grand Forks North Dakota—
O paradise of law and number where all *money* is armed!
                    (*Letter*, Part Three, p. 5)

But even this terrible theme—and a distinct essay would be needed to follow its development—is handled with extraordinary versatility, like a crystal tossed into the air so that the sun glints now from one facet, now from another. He can move from lament to jest to invective to the quiet and beautiful "Ode for the American Dead in Korea" to the low-keyed meditation of "The Fence Around the H-Bomb Plant": "the fence proclaims / A divorce between yourself and a differing idea of order":

> [. . .] it creates out of your awareness a tension
> Wire-drawn, arousing a doubt as to whether
> It is the bomb that is fenced in, you free,
> Or whether you mope here in a monster prison
>
> As big as the world may be; or a world, maybe,
> Which has everything but a future [. . .][54]

A world "which has everything but a future." Is it possible for a poet who is ever-sensitive to that threat to write great poetry? It is a question which McGrath has asked himself; he has spoken with respect of poets (his contemporaries) who, overcome with the sense of political emergency, set aside their talents for more direct forms of engagement.[55] And the injury of living in such times can be sensed within his own poetry. The times offered to him few affirmative evidences capable of carrying authentic symbolic power. There are such evidences to be found, for example moments in *Letter*, Part Two, when the movement of the sixties can be felt:

<pre>
                                        I tell you millions
        Are moving.
                    Pentagon marchers!
                                Prague May Day locomotives
        With flowers in their teeth!
                                (Letter, Part Two, p. 107)
</pre>

But the weight of evidence falls always the other way, and he has been too honest to romanticize the record.

He has turned in his verse to three kinds of affirmatives. First, to the elementary alphabet of love, of work, of the rightness of natural things, and, more recently, of his growing son, Tomasito. This is always effective. Second, to a more metaphysical assertion of the exploited as the absolute negation of capitalist process: "Labor His Sublime Negation," "the accursed poor who can never be bought,"[56] who must ultimately confront their exploiters. This (it seems to me) comes through with

145

increasing strain, as a proposition whose confirmation by history is continually postponed, and hence can only be affirmed by recourse to the past, and sometimes to an antique Wobbly vocabulary of "bindle-stiffs" and "jungling tramps." McGrath has perhaps less emotional insight into newer and more complex forms of social contradiction: his world of labor and of exploitation is predominantly male, and (as we have seen) he has considered "cultural and political nationalism" to be "dead ends" which must be worked through before "serious politics" is reached:

> At the congress of the color blind
> I put up the communist banner my father signed and sang:
> LABOR IN A BLACK SKIN CAN'T BE FREE WHILE WHITE
> SKIN LABOR IS IN CHAINS!
> (*Letter*, Part Two, p. 130)

Yes: but something of the positives of "black skin" civil rights has been left unsung. And there is at times a dated stereotyping of gender roles — perhaps authentically recollected from his Dakota youth — which suggest a pose of tough masculinity which undoubtedly presents a resistance to younger readers. (They should overcome their resistance, since a refusal of McGrath's verse on these grounds — even if the grounds have some validity — is bigoted and to their own loss.)

The third affirmative is central to the organization of the *Letter to an Imaginary Friend*. It consists in the magical or "charm" properties of poetry itself:

> It is the charm which the potential has
> That is the proper aura for the poem . . . [57]

The poet, in revealing the human potential, is the vector of (we remember) "a view of life . . . in a sense truer than the life we see lived all round us." He prefaced to *Letter*, Part Two, a passage from Claude Lévi-Strauss as a figure of the poet:

The man who wishes to wrest something from Destiny must venture into that perilous margin-country where the norms of Society count for nothing and the demands and guarantees of the group are no longer valid. He must travel to where the police have no sway, to the limits of physical resistance and the far point of physical and moral suffering. Once in this unpredictable borderland a man may vanish, never to return; or he may acquire for himself, from among the immense repertory of unexploited forces which surrounds any well-regulated society, some personal provision of power; and when this happens an otherwise inflexible social order may be cancelled in favour of the man who has risked everything.

146

This rather grand prescription is perhaps cited, not as an exemplar for the poet so much as an indication of poetry's function. But it is important that McGrath sees the "immense repertory of unexploited forces" as lying in the unrealized *past*. It is the past which is the reservoir for potential for the present and the future.

> I am only a device of memory
> To call forth into this Present the flowering dead and the living
> To enter the labyrinth and blaze the trail for the enduring journey
> Toward the rounddance and commune of light . . .
> (*Letter*, Part Two, p. 103)

From the past also the poet draws the resources for the mythic or magical properties of poetry. In the *Letter* these come in three forms: autobiographical; in terms of Hopi myth and the *kachina* ritual; and in terms of the Christmas ritual. The balance of these three varies in the long period of the poem's composition—about thirty years. And the tone of the poem varies markedly. In a sense, *Letter*, Parts One and Two, is a different poem from *Letter*, Parts Three and Four, although there are autobiographical and thematic bridges which carry us from one to the other. In my own view some of the very finest work belongs to Part Two, and One and Two are intellectually the most taut, as well as the most engaged. They are poems of resistance. *Letter*, Parts Three and Four, have surrendered nothing to no one, yet there is a sense in which they have passed beyond polemic and resistance to a "philosophical" acceptance of the tragicomedy of things. In the first volume the injustice and repression of the rulers of this world made McGrath angry and embattled; in the second volume it can as often make him laugh.

In conception the poem was to be structured by reference to Hopi myth: "It is concerned with the offering of evidences for a revolutionary miracle and with elaborating a ceremony out of these materials to bring such a miracle to pass."[58] Yet while this myth is remembered in Part Four, it has come to share its place with the Christmas myth (which was scarcely evident in One and Two).

In origin McGrath's use of myth may have been influenced by Christopher Caudwell's *Illusion and Reality*, and perhaps by the discussions around the book in England and New York in the late forties. Caudwell's was a heavy book to throw at the heads of the philistines and bureaucrats of the Communist Party. It provided a full charter against utilitarian views of art, and the most complex claims for the function of the artist then available in the Marxist tradition.[59] To simplify, *Illusion and Reality* offered a materialist vindication of the primacy of spiritual

147

forces in human development. The function of poetry and art was seen as partly "adaptive," socializing and adapting the "instincts" to changes in material being; and partly that of summoning up the spiritual energies of the group prior to any collective action. Part Four of *Letter* is preceded by a passage from Caudwell describing how, through verse or dance, the "simplest tribe" creates emotionally a collective "phantastic object"— such as the anticipated harvest—in order to summon up the energies to grow the real harvest. In this sense the phantastic world is more real than the material world of social being, which depends upon "magic" to give it form and energy.

Caudwell's speculations on the origin and functions of art were enforced at the end of World War II by advances in scholarship, by the discovery of the treasury of cave paintings at Lascaux, and by the publication (1948) of G. R. Levy's *The Gate of Horn*, with its examination of totemism and cave art. The totem is "a focus of the life-energy of a group embodied in the immortal ancestor":

> That is why art is necessary to such a religion, and why approach to the forms or symbols is so strictly guarded, since they are nearer to reality than the separated lives.[60]

Perhaps it was in the postwar excitement of the debates around Caudwell, Levy and Lascaux that McGrath grounded his materialist vindication of poetry's spiritual power and function. In his encounters with utilitarian "politicos" he was able to argue "that I was the *real* political type and that they were vulgar marxists." He refused to accept the loftier authority of the political theorist: "It would be a good thing if both sides recognized that while they're both political animals, one is dog and one is cat."[61] And this Caudwellian respect for the powers of magic will have predisposed him to borrow from Hopi myth those symbols of resurrection and renewal which recur in *Letter*, Parts Two, Three and Four. Yet these symbols are embodied in the spirits of the past, "that power of the dead out of which all life proceeds" (*Letter*, Part Two, p. 104), a power which can be liberated by the ceremonies of poet or artist. This task is

> . . . not so much [one] of rescuing the past (and not just my own) but of *creating* it, since it was stolen from us, malformed, a changeling substituted. I do this, of course, as do all my comrade Kachinas and resurrectionists, to rescue the future.[62]

And the "ghost dances" or *kachinas* of the Hopi provide a vocabulary of symbolism for this, since "*kachinas* are properly not deities . . . They are respected spirits: spirits of the dead . . . spirits of all the invisible forces of life."[63] Tom's father and Mac and Cal and all the *dramatis personae* of *Letter* may therefore be called up into the dance. A blue star will signify the transition from the Hopi's Fourth World (McGrath's capitalism) to *Saquasohuh*, the Fifth World:

> The Blue Star Kachina will help these spirits to bring in the new world. . . . All of us should help to make this Kachina. I think of the making of my poem as such a social-revolutionary action. In a small way, the poem *is* the Kachina.[64]

It is a happy conceit to warm the poet at his work, although I am less certain that so contrived a conceit can operate as warmly on the feelings of the reader. It is perhaps for this reason that the poem seems to change direction midway. Between Parts Two and Three, Hopi mythology is supplemented by important-sounding personages from medieval occultism, and the *kachina* plays (in *Letter*, Three and Four) a less significant part in the structure of the poem than may at first have been intended. It is replaced by the more familiar vocabulary of Christmas ritual, which affords the narrative structure for both Parts Three and Four.

At the most lucid (and beautifully recovered) level this Christmas narrative spans both books in the sled ride of the poet as a young boy from the family farm to his grandparents' home in Sheldon, the nearby town; confession and midnight mass; the boy's recollections and visions (and the grown poet's reflections on the boy); episodes, anecdotes and a Homeric Christmas dinner at Sheldon; and the return to the home farm. At another, polemical, level the poem explores the child's notions of Christian mythology and satirizes Catholic faith and ritual. Christmas brings two opposed worlds into tension: the "World of Down," a world of natural things, of the child's excitement, of commensality, of the (somewhat pagan) Christmas tree; and the "World of Up," a world of false consciousness, draining the spirit:

> Upward.
>   Outward.
>   Away.
>   Toward the black hole of Holy Zero,

> To that Abstract absolute of Inhuman and Supernatural Power:
> Not Father nor Mother nor Son nor Daughter but old Nobodaddy . . .
>   (*Letter*, Part Three, p. 63)

149

And in a complex dance, occult personages, revolutionary heroes and Hopi incantations join with Christian symbolism to reconcile the opposing worlds. This is to be done by acknowledging or "angelizing" the demons of the natural world, and demystifying or "demonizing" the abstractions of the "Heaven-Standard-Time":

> And so, act unto act, we pass through the ancient play
> And the little godlet tries to be born to our fallen world,
> To the poor in this ramshackle church, to insert himself, crisscross,
> Between this world of the poor and that Heaven & Earthly World
> Of Power and Privilege owned by the eternal Abstract One
> Who is not even the Father.
>
> (*Letter*, Part Three, p. 63).

Is *Letter* a major poem, a "great" poem? Does the spirit-dance of incompatible mythic personages convince? How can anyone tell yet? Such matters take time to settle. Parts Three and Four, in particular, have a complexity of reference which must be tested by a discourse among readers.[65] There are places where I must confess to my own difficulties, places where the poet appears to lose direction, passages of "mock-hearty hoorahing" (his own self-criticism). There is a tendency to fall back on revolutionary incantations ("to free the Bound Man / Of the Revolution," *Letter*, Part Two, p. 209) which arouses suspicions. It suggests a philosophical or political irresolution—an inhibition against working through in public his accounts with the illusions and self-betrayals of his own tradition of the Left. The "Bound Man of the Revolution" is proposed as self-evident proletarian Natural Man who is everywhere in chains; but the evidence of the past half-century must call in question any such Natural Man.[66] One wonders at times whether those occult personages or the blue haze of the Hopi's Saquasohuh might not be put in there to obscure the fact that the poet has found certain matters too painful to examine.

But if there are evasions these are not of such an order as to diminish the poem's stature. *Letter to an Imaginary Friend* is a remarkable achievement. It tears down all the curtains which lie between "poetry" and "life"; it opens directly upon the pandemonium of reality, the stubborn issues of history, work, morality, politics. It discovers a long, broken, accented rhythm of extraordinary versatility, which can pass from invective or humor into lyrical or contemplative mode. The childhood recollections (especially in *Letter*, Parts One and Three) bear comparison with the early books of *The Prelude*. (But Wordsworth would never have been capable of the hilarious passage of the boy's boastful attempt at a truly horrific adult confession). The poem has markers throughout which will be followed by historians in the future. *Letter*, Part Two, is superbly constructed and is a definitive statement of the deathward-tending malaise of a civilization. *Letter*, Part Four, is a sustained incantation—a summoning of spiritual energies—which concludes with a lyric of the chastest beauty. And in the unfolding of *Letter*, the only poem I know of which is built to the size of our times, the miracle of the resurrection of the past actually begins to take place:

> It is *not* daybreak
> Provokes cockcrow but cockcrow drags forth the reluctant sun   not
> Resurrection that allows us to rise and walk but the rising
> Of the rebel dead founds resurrection and overthrows hell.
> (Letter, Part Two, p. 210)

In this resurrection an alternative present begins to appear; if we cannot see an alternative future through the blue *kachina* haze, we can see the elements from which that alternative might be made. In despite of the "man-chilling dark," Thomas McGrath has fashioned an alternative self-image for America. He has deployed his poem as "a consciousness-expanding device":

> The most terrible thing is the degree to which we carry around a false consciousness, and I think of poetry as being primarily an apparatus, a machine, a plant, a flower, for the creation of real consciousness . . .[67]

In a letter to us of 1949, when he first reached the West Coast, McGrath describes sharing a house and garden in Los Angeles with friends; since they had no access to an automobile "we are pretty well cut off from everyone, and it is a little bit like being all alone on an island, although we are only about five miles from Hollywood." And I have thought of the extraordinary juxtaposition at that time, and through the ensuing "Great Fear" in Hollywood, with Ronald Reagan and Thomas McGrath almost as neighbors and as visitants within the same hysteric culture; and of the genesis of opposed self-images of America.[68]

The future President was at that time steadily working his way up the "levels" of Los Angeles:

> . . . at the ten
> Thousand a year line (though still in the smog's sweet stench)
> The Johnny Come Earlies of the middling class:
> morality
> fink-size

Automatic rosaries with live Christs on them and cross-shaped purloined
Two-car swimming pools full of holy water . . .
                                                From here God goes
Uphill.
            Level to level.
                            Instant escalation of money—up!
To Cadillac country.

                            Here, in the hush of the long green,
The leather priests of the hieratic dollar enclave to bless
The lush-working washing machines of the Protestant Ethic ecumenical
Laundries: to steam the blood from the bills—O see O see how
Labor His Sublime Negation streams in the firmament!
                                        (*Letter*, Part Two, p. 113)

Here was manufactured the approved self-image of America, as television opened its "poisoned eye" within the heads of millions, carrying that poison image from Hollywood to far Dakota:

                    The houses blacked out as if for war, lit only
With random magnesium flashes like exploding bombs (TV
Courtesy REA)
                    Cold hellfire
                                screams
Tormented, demented, load the air with anguish
                                                invisible
Over the sealed houses, dark, a troop of phantoms,
Demonic, rides: the great Indians come in he night like
Santa Claus
                    down the electronic chimneys whooping and dead . . .
                                        (*Letter*, Part Two, p. 192)

And so those lush-working washing machines laundered the "American dream" and washed the blood out of the American past. It was McGrath's neighbor who won, and who, in his triumph, threatens the whole world. At the lowest level, the poet sat by the beach and waited for the hunters. But, with the help of the "Marsh Street Irregulars" and the network of little resistance magazines, McGrath commenced his long labors of fashioning an alternative self-image. And America is moving today, surely, towards a moment of contradiction, of confronting images. "Everyone everywhere in the States" (McGrath wrote in 1972) "senses that the whole system is finished, though it may endure for a time. Meanwhile there is this great emptiness that can never be paved . . ."[69]

If this moment should come, then it will be in such material as *Letter* that an alternative America will discover her features. It is still possible that a miracle will take place, and that the hunted poet will triumph over the powerful impostor—as Blake wrote, when discussing miracles, did not Paine "overthrow all the armies of Europe with a small pamphlet?"

The world may now be too old and lost for such miracles. But, confronted with McGrath's lifetime of loyalty to his Muse, "the grand old bitch," I can only celebrate his stamina. His loyalty has been not only to his own talent, at a time when in the scanty *samizdat* of hunted outlaws, poetry itself seemed to be an obsolescent trade. It has been also a loyalty to a notion of poetry as still, despite every evidence of defeat, a major art, a major vector of consciousness, and a major guarantor of an unextinguished human potential:

> [. . .] all time is redeemed by the single man—
> Who remembers and resurrects.
> And I remember.
> I keep
> The winter count.
>
> (*Letter*, Part Two, p. 119)

He has kept the count well. Homage to Thomas McGrath.

There is a valuable Selected Bibliography by Fred Whitehead in *North Dakota Quarterly*, Vol. 50, No. 4 (Fall 1982), a *festschrift* issue for McGrath. This also includes many useful memoirs and essays. *The Movie at the End of the World* (Chicago: Swallow Press, 1972) is subtitled *Collected Poems*, although it is in fact an economical selection from earlier collections. Parts One and Two of *Letter to an Imaginary Friend* (Chicago: Swallow Press, 1970) have been followed by sections of Part Three in *Passages Toward the Dark* (Port Townsend: Copper Canyon Press, 1982) and *Echoes Inside the Labyrinth* (New York and Chicago: Thunder's Mouth Press, 1983). These abbreviations have been used in text or notes: *Movie; Letter; Passages;* and *Echoes. Letter*, Parts Three and Four, was published by Copper Canyon Press, Port Townsend, 1985.

It will be unusually difficult to establish any canon of McGrath's work. From typescripts sent to us in the fifties I have found poems which appear in *Movie* as "new poems"; and one or two of them turn up in *Passages* or *Echoes*. This might sometimes be important to the historian, perhaps also to the critic: Warning, handle each "new poem" with agnosticism as to its genesis and context. The poet himself appears to have lost some of his own copies which, however, survive in the hands of friends or in the pages of scores of little journals in which he has published.

1. "Trinc" is in *Echoes*, pp. 13–18, "Praises" in *Movie*, pp. 157–58.
2. *Passages*, p. 93.

3. See Joe Doyle's interesting essay on "Tom McGrath's Years on the New York Waterfront," *North Dakota Quarterly*, Vol. 50, No. 4 (Fall 1982), pp. 32–40.

4. The evidence is fully presented in Victor S. Navasky, *Naming Names* (New York: Viking, 1980).

5. Reprinted in *North Dakota Quarterly*, Vol. 50, No. 4 (Fall 1982), pp. 8–9.

6. "Probability or necessity"—McGrath here and elsewhere is grounding his view on Aristotle, *On the Art of Poetry*, Chapter 9, "Poetic Truth and Historical Truth": "It is not the poet's function to describe what has actually happened, but the kinds of thing that might happen, that is, that could happen because they are, in the circumstances, either probable or necessary . . . For this reason poetry is something more philosophical and more worthy of serious attention than history; for while poetry is concerned with universal truths, history treats of particular facts": T. S. Dorsch, ed., *Classical Literary Criticism* (New York: Penguin, 1965), pp. 43–44.

7. *Movie*, pp. 121-22.

8. Ibid., p. 100.

9. Ibid., p. 59.

10. McGrath to author, November 27, 1980. Of his cultural "bureaucrats," V. J. Jerome was imprisoned under the Smith Act and John Howard Lawson was one of the "Hollywood Ten." Navasky (op. cit.) has a valuable discussion in Chapter 9, "The Reasons Considered," of the internal cultural disputes of the CPUSA, especially the "heresy trial" and recantation of Albert Maltz (with Maltz's own recollections). When I first met McGrath in the summer of 1946, the Maltz case had already taken place, and I remember his anger about it.

11. A subsequent letter (1952?) notes that "novel [*This Coffin Has No Handles*] now being considered by Liberty Book Club, but editor there wants Sam Sillen to read it to get his opinion—and I figure Sillen will kill it off." It was published as a special issue of *North Dakota Quarterly*, Vol. 52, No. 4 (Fall 1984).

12. When McGrath first tried out this not-very-threatening revision in *New Masses* he "got a terrific shower of shit as a result": see interviews in *Another Chicago Magazine*, 5, (1980), and in *Cultural Correspondence*, 9 (Spring 1979) and *North Dakota Quarterly*, Vol. 50, No. 4 (Fall 1982), p. 28. I have not tracked down the original exchanges in *New Masses*.

13. *Movie*, pp. 55-56.

14. McGrath recalls the years after 1946: "There was nothing to do to prepare, except as an isolated individual. All one could do was to warn, and those were warnings that no one wanted to hear, often seen as a kind of pessimism or defeatism": *Cultural Correspondence*, 9, p. 43.

15. Tom does not recall exactly when he left the CPUSA. Around 1955–57 he was quarreling with West Coast organizers about cultural matters and trying to transfer from an "intellectual" to an industrial branch. When this failed, his membership lapsed but he continued to write for *Masses and Mainstream* and *People's World*. He became a sort of "charmed quark" on the unaffiliated far left, and was interested for a while in the Progressive Labor Party until it turned out that his main contact was an FBI spy (conversation with author, 1980).

16. See *Letter*, Part Two, p. 150:

> . . . having come by blacklist degrees
> To the bottom: dropped out of the labor market as unsafe

> To a government at wars ie the cold, the Korean, the Pretend
> (Against Russia) the Holy (against Satanic citizens the likes of
> Myself).

This suggests that the Pretend War against Russia was only a cover for the Holy War of internal social and intellectual control. Cf. *The Gates of Ivory, The Gates of Horn* (New York: Mainstream Publishers, 1957), p. 100, where the generals come and ask the Sybil, "How long will the Pretend War last?" and the Sybil replies: "How long do you want it to last?"

17. See "Return to Marsh Street," *Movie*, pp. 142–44; *Letter*, Part Two, pp. 120–22; Gene Frumkin, "A Note on Tom McGrath—The Early 50s," *North Dakota Quarterly*, Vol. 50, No. 4 (Fall 1982), pp. 46–55.

18. "After the Beat Generation," in *Crazy Horse*, 1, no date (but published from Tom and Genya's address at 220 East 14th Street, New York, which they left in 1961 or early 1962); also *Movie*, p. 162.

19. "Poem," *Movie*, pp. 130–31. But I think this poem also dates back to the fifties.

20. "McGrath on McGrath," *Epoch*, 22 (1973), p. 217; also in *North Dakota Quarterly*, Vol. 50, No. 4 (Fall 1982), pp. 23–24.

21. *Epoch*, op. cit., pp. 218–19. See also "Poetry and Place," interview McGrath and Mark Vinz, in *Voyages to the Inland Sea*, Vol. 3, ed. John Judson (LaCrosse: Center for Contemporary Poetry, Murphy Library, University of Wisconsin—LaCrosse, 1973), pp. 33–48.

22. Most of the *Crazy Horse* manifesto is in *North Dakota Quarterly*, Vol. 50, No. 4 (Fall 1982), p. 10. I am indebted to the archivists at the poetry collection in Brown University Library, where I consulted some numbers of *Crazy Horse*, the *California Quarterly* and *Witness to the Times!*

23. McGrath's work ranged from some pulp-writing and movie moonlighting (see Mike Hazard, *North Dakota Quarterly*, Vol. 50, No. 4 (Fall 1982), pp. 101–06) to casual labor and semi-skilled work in furniture and ceramics workshops. He found the physical work ("if it is not too bloody physical") pleasant and compatible with writing poetry. He commenced *Letter*, Part One, while working "in a little factory for making decorative sculpture"—"the things we were working on were beautiful things . . . it was a very good situation"—and completed it in a few weeks: interview in *Dacotah Territory*, cited in *North Dakota Quarterly*, Vol. 50, No. 4 (Fall 1982), p. 122, and McGrath to author, 1980.

24. "Figures in an Allegorical Landscape: Stock Brokerage Board Marker," typescript in our own collection. Ironically his job as board marker was one of the only ones he was not blacklisted out of: he was simply "automated out."

25. *North Dakota Quarterly*, Vol. 50, No. 4 (Fall 1982), pp. 8–9. McGrath refused to cooperate with HUAC as a teacher and as a poet. "When I was notified to appear here, my first instinct was simply to refuse to answer committee questions out of personal principle and on the grounds of the rights of man and let it go at that." However, on "further consideration," and to support the stance of other witnesses, he also cited the first, fourth and fifth amendments.

26. *Witness to the Times!*, a mimeographed typescript "conceived and edited by students of Thomas McGrath," Los Angeles, 1953 or 1954.

27. *California Quarterly*, Vol. II, No. 1 (Autumn 1952), p. 50.

28. *California Quarterly*, Vol. II, No. 2 (Winter 1953), pp. 8–9.

29. From Sections 1 and 4 of "The Hunted Revolutionaries," first published in *California*

Quarterly, Vol. IV, No. 1 (Autumn 1955). Sections 2 and 3 are republished in *Movie*, pp. 172–73, dedicated to Henry Winston, the black national chairman of the CPUSA who lost his eyesight while in prison under the Smith Act; see Frederick C. Stern in *North Dakota Quarterly*, Vol. 50, No. 4 (Fall 1982), p. 108. I do not think that Sections 1 and 4 have been republished.

30. Alice McGrath, "Longshot O'Leary Says It's Your Duty to Be Full of Fury" (November 1952) in *North Dakota Quarterly*, Vol. 50, No. 4 (Fall 1982), p. 45.

31. Ibid., p. 44.

32. See *A Sound of One Hand* (St. Peter: Minnesota Writers Publishing House, 1975) and *Open Songs: Sixty Short Poems* (Mount Carroll, Ill.: Uzzano Press, 1977).

33. See interview in *Voyages*, note 21 above.

34. Extravagant play upon his grandfather's alliterative cursing is in *Letter*, Part Three, pp. 50–52.

35. David Montgomery, in *In These Times* (October 8–14, 1980).

36. "Letter to Wendell" in *First Manifesto* (Baton Rouge: Swallow Pamphlets No. 1, 1940).

37. Note in *Passages*, p. 93.

38. Robert Frost, *Selected Poems* (London: Jonathan Cape, 1936), p. 190.

39. *Epoch*, op. cit., p. 214.

40. *Measure*, 2 (Bowling Green: Bowling Green State University, 1972), unpaginated.

41. *Epoch*, op. cit., p. 213.

42. *Voyages to the Inland Sea*, op. cit., p. 38.

43. *Cultural Correspondence* (see note 11 above), p. 43.

44. *Voyages*, op. cit., p. 41.

45. *Passages*, p. 93.

46. McGrath, "Some Notes on Walter Lowenfels," *Praxis* 4 (1978), p. 90.

47. *Epoch*, op. cit., p. 208.

48. "Poor John Luck and the Middle Class Struggle Or: The Corpse in the Bookkeeper's Body," *Movie*, p. 89.

49. "The Histories of Morning," *Echoes*, p. 45.

50. "The News around Midnight," *Movie*, p. 138.

51. "Dawn Song," *Passages*, p. 9.

52. "Trinc: Praises II," *Echoes*, p. 17.

53. "Living on Faith," *Passages*, p. 148.

54. For lament, see among other examples his poems for his brother Jimmy, "Blues for Jimmy," *Movie*, pp. 73–78, and "The Last War Poem of the War," Ibid., p. 180; for jest, see "Mottoes for a Sampler," Ibid., p. 159; for invective, see "Song for an Armistice Day," Ibid., p. 161 and *Letter*, Part Two, pp. 147–48. "Ode for the American Dead in Korea" (subsequently changed to "Asia") is in *Movie*, pp. 102–03, and "Reading the Names of the Vietnam War Dead" ("thousands of dense black stones fall forever through the darkness under the earth"), Ibid., pp. 180-81. "The Fence Around the H-Bomb Plant" is in *Passages*, p. 56.

55. *Cultural Correspondence*, op. cit., p. 42, and *Praxis*, 4, 1978, where he writes "there are some particularly interesting examples in England," perhaps thinking (among others) of Edgell Rickword's long poetic silence?

56. *Movie*, p. 57.

57. "Against the False Magicians," *Movie*, p. 21.

58. Note preceding *Letter*, Parts One and Two (1970).

156

59. I have discussed this moment in "Caudwell," *Socialist Register* (London, 1977). ↓ Grath has not revised his high opinion of Caudwell.

60. G. R. Levy, *The Gate of Horn* (London: Faber & Faber, 1948), p. 39.

61. *Another Chicago Magazine*, 5 (1980), p. 73.

62. *Measure*, 2, op. cit.

63. Frank Waters, *Book of the Hopi* (New York: Viking, 1963; rpt. New York Penquin, 1977), p. 167.

64. Note preceding *Letter*, Parts Three and Four.

65. The most helpful guides as yet known to me are Dale Jacobson, review of *Letter*, Parts Three and Four, and Joseph Butwin, "The Last Laugh: Thomas McGrath's Comedy," both in *North Dakota Quarterly* Vol. 55, No. 1 (Winter 1987).

66. But please note the poet's comment, when I first published this criticism in *The Heavy Dancers: Writing on Wars Past and Future* (London: Merlin Press and New York: Pantheon, 1985): "You are hopeful where I always felt the Revolution had to be firmly grounded in despair (however hopeful) and in the end I expect more of humankind than you do. In a few words: you are a protestant revolutionary and I'm a catholic-revisionist-buddhist one": McGrath to author, March 13, 1985. (He also remains Irish!)

67. *Voyages to the Inland Sea*, op. cit., p. 48.

68. This should have been clear from the title of his remarkable collection, *Figures from a Double World* (Denver: Alan Swallow, 1955) which, as he explains in a Note prefaced to *Movie*, was a publisher's error for his chosen title, *Figures of the Double World*, "the emphasis on the dialectic, on process, on states of the world rather than states of mind."

69. *Measure*, 2, op. cit. Among those who read early drafts of this essay I benefited especially from the comments of my friend, the late Warren Susman. He suggested that, while McGrath's poetry is unique, I have overstated the uniqueness of his experience. Between the "twin poles of the academy" ("The 1940's and 1950's saw the triumph of the New Criticism and its favorite poets on virtually every American campus") and its "official" opposition, McGrath was not exceptional in being ignored and isolated. The forest of little journals in most parts of the States—in many of which McGrath found refuge and hospitality for his own poems—is witness to a different story, and (Susman suggests) "for the cultural historian his *typicality* as well as his uniqueness are important cultural facts."

Thomas McGrath

Terrence Des Pres

"America is too terrible a subject for an American . . ."

"Then we can forget the West."

"No, no. We cannot forget the West. There is no America outside the West, and there never will be. It is the dream, and that dream is the only hope. No, we cannot forget the West. Where all the races meet in a place of beauty, not in a place of blood. The land cannot grant amnesty."
—from "McGrath on McGrath"[1]

Sweetened with a harvest song, the work goes well.
—Christopher Caudwell[2]

Thomas McGrath has been writing remarkable poems of every size and form for nearly fifty years. In American poetry he is as close to Whitman as anyone since Whitman himself, a claim I make with care. McGrath is master of the long wide line (wide in diction, long in meter), the inclusive six-beat measure of America at large. The scene of his work is the whole of the continent east to west with its midpoint in the high-plains rim of the heartland. His diction, with its vast word-stock and multitude of language layers, is demotic to the core yet spiced with learned terms in Whitman's manner, a voice as richly American as any in our literature. But for all that, McGrath is little known. He has been championed by one no less worldly than E. P. Thompson, and those who have praised him, Kenneth Rexroth and Donald Hall among them, have been devoted to his work. In the main, though, McGrath hasn't had the attention that a whole flotilla of our lesser poets enjoy, a situation out of joint with the facts of the matter and a scandal to those who know McGrath's four-part epic, *Letter to an Imaginary Friend*, a poem of witness to the radical spirit—"the generous wish," as McGrath calls it—of American populist tradition.[3]

158

If McGrath remains an outsider, his humor might be part of the reason. Apart from Stevens's wispy playfulness and some of Auden's wit, we don't expect an important poet to be broadly comic, especially when the same voice rails in earnest against the time's worst abuses. McGrath holds high expectations for poetry—he wants to see it change the world by calling us to recovery of our finest dreams—yet he delights in excess and in punning and is, seemingly, hyperbolic by conviction. Humor of this kind supports irreverent freedom and a desire to pull things back "down to earth." In his will to dislodge prevailing pieties, McGrath aligns himself as Twain did in *Huckleberry Finn*, with oddity and outcasts:

> —I'm here to bring you
> Into the light of speech, the insurrectionary powwow
> Of the dynamite men and the doomsday spielers, to sing you
> Home from the night. (p. 105)

That is a diction more expansive than the sort now in fashion. Mc-Grath's vigorous vocabulary might therefore be a jolt to genteel readers, who will probably be shaken still further by a bawdy argot of physical frankness informing the whole. McGrath's language is an amalgam of field-hand grit and Oxbridge nicety seasoned by working-class dialect from the 1930's and 1940's. These choices give him an almost fabulous voice, at least on occasion, and a range of lyrical textures uniquely his own. Finally, there is the singular way he manages materialism (Marxist) and sacramentalism (Roman Catholic) side by side as if they composed a doctrinal continuum that surely they don't—except in McGrath's special usage.

We are allowed our hesitations, but the moment of truth comes with McGrath's geography and then his political convictions, both of which enter his art decisively. He identifies himself mainly with the western side of the country and sets much of his best work in the place and rural spirit of the Dakotas, a region by definition graceless and provincial to dominant eastern-urban sensibility, a place and spirit that to many among us is no place and thus a sort of utopian badlands politely forgot. On top of that comes McGrath's politics—an insurrectionary stance that in its Marxist emphasis might have been international but which, nourished by the grainland countryside west of Fargo, is decidedly home-grown, a radicalism that McGrath calls "unaffiliated far Left."

From the beginning, McGrath's geography and politics have set him apart from the orthodoxies of literary culture, starting with the program he and Alan Swallow encountered in 1939 when they were students together at Louisiana State. Straight off the blasted farmland of the Depression years, McGrath ran into a critical agenda on its way to becoming the New Criticism:

> And they got hold of Agrarianism—
> Salvation—40 acres and a mule—the Protestant Heaven,
> Free Enterprise! Kind of intellectual ribbon-development—
> But I was a peasant from Sauvequipeuville—
> I wanted the City of Man. [. . .]
>
> And all of them
> On Donne. Etc.
> And all of them sailing on the Good Ship Tradition . . .
> For the thither ports of the moon.
> High flying days
> I'll tell you right now!
> And me with my three ideas
> With my anarchist, peasant poverty, being told at last how bright
> The bitter land was.
> How the simple poor might lift a laud to the Lord. [. . .] (pp. 60,62)

Coming to manhood in a time when the land was no way bright nor the poor in a mood to be thankful, McGrath could see that between life and art a no-man's-land of romance was being confected. The lines above continue for a good page more, contrasting "reverence for the land [and] the good life" with the spirit-maiming work of seasons in their "true run," juxtaposing criticism's "gothick Pile / Of talk" with "machine guns down at the docks" where labor organizers, McGrath's friends among them, were getting beat up and murdered.

When McGrath says in *Letter* that "North Dakota is everywhere," one can fairly hear the strain upon an urbane sensibility that isn't easily able, and may in fact be unwilling, to imagine that the West (outside of California) exists. McGrath says that his own family had to deal with "Indian scare[s]"; that "the past out here was bloody, and full of injustice, though hopeful and heroic."[4] What, after all, is *American* about America if not the frontier experience and how the fate of the Indians questions ours:

From Indians we learned a toughness and a strength; and we gained
A freedom: by taking theirs: but a real freedom; born
From the wild and open land our grandfathers heroically stole.
But we took a wound at Indian hands: a part of our soul scabbed over[....] (p.190)

160

As a boy McGrath saw "the Indian graves / Alive and flickering with the gopher light." In his art the landscape is weighted with the human world. Even when abandoned, the land is not empty. Nature is peopled, strife-ridden and—"where the Dakotas bell and nuzzle at the north coast"—of surpassing beauty. For most of us, however, these early defeats and distant splendors are of little consequence; and in this way geography and politics put McGrath at a disadvantage with prevailing sensibility. Yet he is exactly on target. His untoward and seemingly marginal themes are part of his labor to keep a core of national memory active. The marvel of his poetry is how it persists, how in spite of changing times and timely despair McGrath keeps the vision he inherited, a "minority of one" in Emerson's durable sense.

As a poet who conceives the future as a redemptive dream worth pursuing through a lifetime's work, McGrath is pledged to "the Fifth Season," to a new order beyond the cyclical entrapment of society in its twilight servitude to capital. But while most Americans pretend freedom from history and would go weightless into tomorrow like leaves in a wind, McGrath's practice is to summon the past of his own time and place, the essential history of personal, and then of national, experience insofar as each—the private and the public testaments—bear witness to each other. Like any bard, he keeps the record of his tribe, especially the memory of events in danger of being repressed or forgotten. This is not an easy job, given the trials of recovery. The starting point is acceptance of estrangement, then recognition that much worth recalling is gone for good. Keeping in his mind that McGrath's grandparents homesteaded the farmland that his family worked and his own generation was forced to leave, here (from *Echoes Inside the Labyrinth*) is "The Old McGrath Place":

> The tractor crossed the lawn and disappeared
> Into the last century—
> An old well filled up with forgotten faces.
> So many gone down (bucketsful) to the living, dark
> Water . . .
>   I would like to plant a willow
> There—waterborne tree to discountenance earth . . .
> But then I remember my grandmother:
> Reeling her morning face out of that rainy night.[5]

McGrath plants the poem instead, and his attention turns from cursing to blessing. The outcome is a praise-poem in the manner of elegy, its nostalgia nipped in the bud by "bucketsful." The scene is the dead site of

161

a family farm—of which, in America, there are still sights countless. The aim of the poem is to regenerate the past through memory's witness; or rather, to claim that task as the poet's mission. The "faces" won't be forgotten. The farmyard well is still there, still alive, and becomes an entrance to ancestral sources, a complex emblem of death and rebirth. In its dark water abide the mothering powers of farm and family that McGrath grew up with and from which, as a poet, he draws his strength.

Thomas McGrath was born in 1916 on a farm near Sheldon, North Dakota, of Irish Catholic parents. Every aspect of this heritage—the place, the hard times, the religious and political culture—informs his art in a multitude of ways. His religious upbringing figures centrally in Part Three—"the Christmas section"—of *Letter*, and in his poetry at large there is a steady preference for the ritualistic forms and sacramental language of the Church. Being Irish also worked in his favor when, in 1941, he entered the maritime world of seamen and longshoremen—the Irish community that worked Manhattan's West Side docks—where the fight for reform went forward on the piers and in the bars and walkups of Chelsea. There McGrath worked as a labor organizer and, briefly, as a shipyard welder. His politics led him into a world of experience that, in turn, backed up his political beliefs in concrete ways. To be a Red on the waterfront was to be the natural prey of goon squads patrolling the docks for the bosses and the racketeers. It was also to see the world of industrial work at firsthand. In Part Two of *Letter* McGrath recalls his job as a welder at Federal Drydock & Shipyard:

> "After the war we'll get them," Packy says.
>   He dives
> Into the iron bosque to bring me another knickknack.
> The other helpers swarm into it. Pipes are swinging
> As the chain-falls move on their rails in.
>   Moment of peace.
> The welders stand and stretch, their masks lifted, palefaced.
> Then the iron comes onto the stands; the helpers turn to the wheels;
> The welders, like horses in fly-time, jerk their heads and the masks
> Drop. Now demon-dark they sit at the wheeled turntables,
> Strike their arcs and light spurts out of their hands.
>
>   "After
> The war we'll shake the bosses' tree till the money rains
> Like crab-apples. Faith, we'll put them under the ground."
> After the war.
>   Faith.

                    Left wing of the IRA
       That one.
              Still dreaming of dynamite.
                                        I nod my head,
       The mask falls.
              Our little smokes rise into roaring heaven. (p. 142)

These lines are full of commotion and wordplay, for example the
double meanings in "faith" and "war" and the "nod" at the end. The
scene itself suggests McGrath's larger figure of the "round-dance," his
emblem of communal action wherein his double vision — materialist and
sacramentalist at once — is reconciled with itself. In the passage above,
the rites of work become an act of prayer, a moment of *working together*
beneath the hegemony of a faith now defeated. After the war the bosses
had won and it was Packy O'Sullivan gone, him with his curse on
capital. McGrath returned to Chelsea to find everything changed, his
friends dead or departed, the vigorous radicalism of the National Mari-
time Union bought off and a new breed of "labor-fakers" running the
show:

> And the talking walls had forgotten our names, down at the Front,
> Where the seamen fought and the longshoremen struck the great ships
> In the War of the Poor.
>   And the NMU had moved to the deep south
> (Below Fourteenth) and built them a kind of Moorish whorehouse
> For a union hall. And the lads who built that union are gone.
> Dead. Deep sixed. Read out of the books. Expelled. (pp. 123-24)

McGrath's family immigrated from Ireland and the Shea's (his moth-
er's side) were Gaelic-speaking. Some arrived by way of Ellis Island,
others through Canada. Both grandfathers worked their way west as
immigrant laborers on the railroad. They got as far as the Dakota
frontier and settled as homesteaders, living at first in the ubiquitous dirt-
built "soddies." For young McGrath, the specific gifts of family and place
included the liturgical richness of Catholicism to fill up frontier empti-
ness, but also the political richness of farming in a part of the country
and at a time when the broad-based Farmers' Alliance was strong
enough (during the 1880's and early 1890's) to pursue the first and only
nationwide attempt at a national third party, the People's Party, thereby
awakening radical consciousness and endorsing a spirit of grassroots
insurgency. From Texas up through Kansas and into the great north-
west, the Farmers' Alliance gave rural populations their first taste of
dignity. For the first time power was more than a courthouse coterie.

Decent life for a while looked possible. And from early on, this unique addition to American political culture, now called Populism, was strong in the Dakotas.[6]

Neighborhood, for McGrath growing up, was part of an adversary culture with collective traditions including self-help and sharing. This state-within-a-state gave countless small farmers a defense against the unchecked plundering of grain companies, banks and the baronial railroads. When McGrath curses wealth and the money system, we should keep in mind that his family was working to get a foothold in America during the depths of the Gilded Age, our most ruthless era of capital accumulation. Boom and bust were the signs of the time, when economic depression and political helplessness ruined "plain folks" by hundreds of thousands and, an important point, made every year's harvest—each autumn's race with nature and the money supply—a time of national crisis.

The glory days of the Farmers' Alliance were over by McGrath's time, but the political imagination of the populist tradition was ingrained and open to new forms of expression each time economic disaster shredded the nation. Until World War I, members of the Industrial Workers of the World—the Wobblies—were a strong and often strong-armed force in key sectors of labor (lumber and mining most firmly), carrying forward the tradition of "agrarian revolt." After the war the Non-Partisan League (started in 1916, the year of McGrath's birth) organized the vote and worked toward the public ownership of vital facilities. In North Dakota the League came to control the state legislature and established a public granary system. The populist spirit thrived on these successes; it also counted on a tradition of communal work that rural peoples have known since the dawn, maybe, of independent yeomanry. This broader background, as McGrath suggests in an interview, underwrites his own kind of visionary populism:

The primary experience out in these states, originally, anyway, was an experience of loneliness, because the people were so far away from everything. They had come out here and left behind whatever was familiar, and you find this again and again in letters that women wrote out here. The other side of that loneliness was a sense of community, which was much more developed—even as late as thirty or forty years ago—than it is now. The community of swapped labor. This was a standard thing on the frontier; everybody got together and helped put up a house or put up a soddy when a new family came along. You helped with this, that or the other, and you swapped labor back and forth all the time and that community was never defined. It wasn't a geographical thing; it was a sort of commune of people who got along well together, and right in the same actual neighborhood there might be two or three of these. . . . This sense of solidarity . . . is one of the

richest experiences that people can have. It's the only true shield against aliena-
tion and deracination and it was much more developed in the past than it is now.[7]

In McGrath's poetry this "community of swapped labor," and the
populist sentiment rising from it, cannot be overestimated. This was the
political milieu, or simply the spirit of place, that he inherited. Parts One
and Two of Letter to an Imaginary Friend, in which McGrath evokes his
roots, are devoted to moments of compact drama recalling the populist
legacy as it spun itself out and into his soul. The Great Depression was
the definitive learning experience for McGrath's own generation, the
testing ground for political belief of any kind and, as it seemed to him
from his own encounters, the historical proof of populism's capacity to
endure as a force. Drifters of every sort filled the land, men from differ-
ent backgrounds, some of them schooled, others not, all of them angry
and talking politics nonstop. Companionship with laborers like these
provided the forum for McGrath's education—working, for example,
with a logging team:

> All that winter in the black cold, the buzz-saw screamed and whistled,
> And the rhyming hills complained. In the noontime stillness,
> Thawing our frozen beans at the raw face of a fire,
> We heard the frost-bound tree-boles booming like cannon,
> A wooden thunder, snapping the chains of the frost.
>
> Those were the last years of the Agrarian City
> City of swapped labor
> Communitas
> Circle of warmth and work
> Frontier's end and last wood-chopping bee
> The last collectivity stamping its feet in the cold. [. . .]
>
> The weedy sons of midnight enterprise:
> Stump-jumpers and hog-callers from the downwind counties
> The noonday mopus and the coffee guzzling Swedes
> Prairie mules
> Moonfaced Irish from up-country farms
> Sand-hill cranes
> And lonesome deadbeats from a buck brush parish.
>
> So, worked together. (p.45)

Diction shoves and bristles within a theme of solidarity, affording
McGrath's figuration of harmony-in-conflict another lively example.
The object of praise is again a community united through work—a
further glimpse of "the round-dance"—and again, the world it comes

from is gone. Some hundred lines later McGrath's mood turns elegiac as he remembers the collective rapport of a time when people of all sorts came together in common need to help out; and then how they lost and disappeared. I quote the following passage at length to discover the tonal shifts, the conjunction of blessing and cursing, the reach of language and then the historical complexity of events being rendered:

> The talk flickered like fires.
> The gist of it was, it was a bad world and we were the boys to change it.
> And it *was* a bad world; and we might have.
>
> In that round song, Marx lifted his ruddy
> Flag; and Bakunin danced (And the Technocrats
> Were hatching their ergs . . .)
>   A mile east, in the dark,
> The hunger marchers slept in the court house lobby
> After its capture: where Webster and Boudreaux
> Bricklayer, watchmaker, Communists, hoped they were building
> The new society, inside the shell of the old—
> Where the cops came in in the dark and we fought down the stairs.
>
> That was the talk of the states those years, that winter.
> Conversations of east and west, palaver
> Borne coast-to-coast on the midnight freights where Cal was riding
> The icy red-balls.
>   Music under the dogged-down
> Dead lights of the beached caboose.
> Wild talk, and easy enough now to laugh.
> *That's* not the point and never was the point.
> What was real was the generosity, expectant hope,
> The open and true desire to create the good.   (pp. 51–52)

Passages of this kind epitomize McGrath's poetic enterprise. No mere catalog, this is a kind of lyrical documentation at which McGrath excels, and through which he preserves his firsthand sense of the nation at odds with itself. He bears witness to "the generous wish," and curses the McCarthy plague ("the hunting" conducted by HUAC) that put an end to "talk of the states those years":

> Now, in another autumn, in our new dispensation
> Of an ancient, man-chilling dark, the frost drops over
> My garden's starry wreckage.
>   Over my hope.
>   Over
> The generous dead of my years.
>   Now, in the chill streets

I hear the hunting, the long thunder of money.
A queer parade goes past: Informers, shit-eaters, fetishists,
Punkin-faced cretins, and the little deformed traders
In lunar nutmegs and submarine bibles.
And the parlor anarchist comes by, to hang in my ear
His tiny diseased pearls like the guano of meat-eating birds.
But *then* was a different country, though the children of light,
                                                    gone out
To the dark people in the villages, did not come back . . .
But what was real, in all that unreal talk
Of ergs and of middle peasants (perhaps someone born
Between the Mississippi and the Rocky Mountains, the unmapped country)
Was the generous wish.
                        To talk of the People
Is to be a fool. But they were the *sign* of the People,
Those talkers.

                                                    (pp. 52–53)

The parts of *Letter* I've been quoting give the poem its authority. They mark episodes of personal importance to McGrath's political development. They are also—the impassioned talk of the Depression years, the welders on nightshift during the war—representative moments in the life of the nation. McGrath has deliberately stationed himself to document the populist spirit *in action* from the thirties on through the forties and fifties, and then beyond into our own time. He is on the lookout for evidence of political promise, and a witness to communal possibilities. His care is for people working and living together—the productive spirit of *Communitas*. Without question, this is McGrath's grand theme, based on his poetry's recollection of his own experience as a boy, as a young man and then active poet. His art is motivated by a visionary care for the future, but also by "grief for a lost world: that round song and commune / When work was a handclasp."[8]

When McGrath began publishing in the early forties, his work was shaped by the strain and agitation of the thirties. For political visionaries it had been a painful but exciting time to come of age. On the disheartening evidence of events, the future was bound to be a glory. After the lament, the exaltation. This doubling—first the bad news, then the good—is the form of the American jeremiad, a type of political-visionary stance that thrives on unfulfillment.[9] It owes much to our founding fathers and little to Marx, but yields an enlarged notion of consensus when recast in Marxist terms. For McGrath, in any case, the jeremiad is a natural vehicle; it allows him to rail and reconfirm, to deplore the failures and backsliding of his tribe without abandoning hope.

In the poems of the forties, McGrath announces and proclaims. His language is abstract and mythic, a style distinct from the kind of line and language in *Letter*. Repeatedly, in these early poems, the poet calls to his tribe and predicts redemptive apocalypse. In "Blues for Warren," a poem of 197 lines with the inscription "killed spring 1942, north sea," the dead man is praised as one "who descended into hell for our sakes; awakener / Of the hanging man, the Man of the Third Millenium."[10] A political prophecy is informed by traditional archetypes, while Marx and the Church are made to join in common cause. Here the hero, a "Scapegoat and Savior," is united—in spirit and in body—with the dispossessed multitudes his death will help redeem:

> Those summers he rode the freights between Boston and Frisco
> With the cargoes of derelicts, garlands of misery,
> The human surplus, the interest on dishonor,
> And the raw recruits of a new century.

Much of McGrath's work in his early style—collected in *The Movie at the End of the World*—declares belief, addresses action and actors in the political arena, blesses and blames. Many of these poems are informed by a sense of humor that is tough and playful at once, a manner that reaches a comic highpoint and takes on a new, easy-going confidence with a little volume of poems printed by International Publishers in 1949. Entitled *Longshot O'Leary's Garland of Practical Poesie*, the book is dedicated to the friends of McGrath's waterfront days in New York. Most of these poems express the spirit enacted by the title. The center-piece is a ballad of nineteen stanzas, "He's a Real Gone Guy: A Short Requiem for Percival Angleman,"[11] celebrating the death of a local gangster. Like Brecht, from whom he learned a great deal, McGrath often praises renegades and losers, figures that rebuke the prevailing order as part of capital's bad conscience. "Short Requiem" is an exercise, so to say, in jocular realism, a satire that goes to the tune of "The Streets of Laredo." The violence of the west comes east and this is stanza one:

> As I walked out in the streets of Chicago,
> As I stopped in a bar in Manhattan one day,
> I saw a poor weedhead dressed up like a sharpie,
> Dressed up like a sharpie all muggled and fey.

The poem portrays a man who was a worker getting nowhere and who turned, therefore, to the profits of crime. Here is the core of dialogue between the poet and the crook:

"Oh I once was a worker and had to keep scuffling;
I fought for my scoff with the wolf at the door.
But I made the connection and got in the racket,
Stopped being a business man's charity whore.

"You'll never get yours if you work for a living,
But you may make a million for somebody else.
You buy him his women, his trips to Miami,
And all he expects is the loan of yourself."

"I'm with you," I said, "but here's what you've forgotten:
A working stiff's helpless to fight on his own,
But united with others he's stronger than numbers.
We can win when we learn that we can't win alone."

In the uproar and aftermath of the Depression, a poem like this would find its grateful audience. But by the time it appeared in 1949, labor was damping down and in the schools the New Criticism was setting narrower, more cautious standards of literary judgment. McGrath, with his Brechtian huff, was out in the cold, although any reader nursed on Eliot might still appreciate the poem's hollow-man ending:

He turned and went out to the darkness inside him
To the Hollywood world where believers die rich,
Where free enterprise and the lies of his childhood
Were preparing his kingdom in some midnight ditch.

I have cited this poem because I like it, but also because in ways not expected it surpasses its Marxist scene (the world as classes in conflict) with a vision of community (the workers of the world united) that in the last stanza translates a political predicament into spiritual terms. I take it that McGrath, in *Longshot O'Leary*, was after a style at once streetwise and jubilant. He begins to count on slang and local patois more directly to invigorate his diction. A distinctly "Irish" note (nearly always at play in the later poetry) is struck in namings, allusions and parody. Humor becomes a leavening element, and the comedy of wordplay keeps the spirit agile in hard situations. And now McGrath can imagine his audience, lost though it might be. His model derives from the men and women he worked with in New York before the war, tough-minded socialists devoted day by day to the cause, a working commune worth tribal regard. To call this tribe back into action, to witness its past and praise its future, becomes McGrath's poetic task.

In 1954 McGrath took a job at Los Angeles State College, a teaching position that did not last long. The spirit of McCarthy was closing down "the generous wish," and McGrath, after declaring to a HUAC committee that he would "prefer to take [his] stand with Marvell, Blake, Shelley and García Lorca,"[12] found himself jobless and without recourse. Being blacklisted was an honor of sorts, but money and prospects were in short supply. So was hope for a better world. It was then that McGrath began his thirty-years' work on *Letter*. It was then, too, that the earlier, more formal style gave way to the lyrical expansiveness, rooted in his Dakota heritage, that marks McGrath's best poetry. As a friendly critic puts it, "we can at least make an honest guess that McGrath's direct experience of repression in the early fifties threw him back into touch with his earlier experiences."[13] Counting his losses, it must have seemed that praise and blame were not enough, that the defense of his art would require enlargement of resources as a witness—some way, that is, of speaking for the nation as well as for himself, a song of self valid for all.

What he discovered is that each of us lives twice: not only that we are first in the world and then make of it what we can through the word, but also that each of us bears a representative (political) as well as an individual (private) life. The representative parts occur when self and history intersect, and to make these distinctions is to suggest one way that politics and poetry converge. By the time he came to write *Letter*, McGrath saw that "In the beginning was the *world!*"[14] and that he would have to locate himself exactly at the crossroads where self and world meet:

> All of us live twice at the same time—once uniquely and once representatively. I am interested in those moments when my unique personal life intersects with something bigger, when my small brief moment has a part in "fabricating the legend."[15]

By way of "fabricating the legend," *Letter* begins: "—From here it is necessary to ship all bodies east." McGrath has said the line was given to him by poet and friend Don Gordon during the blacklisting fifties when, out of work and uncertain in spirit, McGrath was living "in Los Angeles at 2714 Marsh Street, / Writing, rolling east with the earth." The opening sequence of *Letter* continues with a shift in voice: "They came through the passes, / they crossed the dark mountains in a month of

170

snow, [. . .] Hunters of the hornless deer in the high plateaus of that country." Then the two voices join as McGrath goes on to declare his relation to the grandest of our native themes—America's heroical westering:

> Aye, long ago. A long journey ago,
> Most of it lost in the dark, in a ruck of tourists,
> In the night of the compass, companioned by tame wolves, plagued
> By theories, flies, visions, by the anthropophagi . . .
>
> I do not know what end that journey was toward.
> —But I am its end. I am where I have been and where
> I am going. The journeying destination—at least that . . . [.] (p.1)

At the onset of *Letter*, the poet stations himself at land's end, but he does not yearn in the way of Whitman or Jeffers for further passage, some intenser rapport of solitary Self with the Universe at large. Rather he turns, faces back to consider where he's been and what he's learned and how, in some added stretch of time, this northern continent might become the great thing it has always symbolized. America, having fulfilled its claim to manifest destiny, having defined itself through westward migration, finds itself in some way finished. This terminus is either a dead end or a new beginning, and simply put it comes to this: the vision of ourselves that Whitman strained to realize, McGrath aims to recover. *Letter* is a poem of remembrance and what it celebrates is the American Dream in its first freshness, countless times exploited, countless times betrayed, but still alive in memory and actual terrain; the covenant and promise, not of a city on a hill like a fortress, but of a loose-knit neighborhood upon a spacious plain. And McGrath will approach this mighty task by summoning—out of a farmyard well, maybe—the voices of family, companions, co-workers; the chorus, in short, of what he calls his "generous dead."

McGrath's distinction between "personal" and "representative" kinds of experience suggests that the voices in *Letter* address events larger than the person or persons speaking, events in which private and political destinies intersect or collide to reveal political as well as private spheres of meaning. These points of intersection are generally shared by more than one voice, and from them comes an enlarged view—an "expanded consciousness," in McGrath's formulation—of the nation's definitive gains, losses and wrong turns, together with the seeds of possible redress and renewal. In Part Two, for example, McGrath confronts the historical irony of "the Dakota experience": how, that is, a land of pioneer farms was bled and broken to make way for the ranges of missile sites (the ICBM's) that now infest the landscape. The poet looks out upon "the abandoned farmhouses, like burnt-out suns, and around them / The planetary out-buildings dead for the lack of warmth," and asks: "where / Have *they* gone? Those ghosts that warmed these buildings once?" The missiles hum in their silos, but "the people?" In answer comes this voice:

> "First they broke land that should not ha' been broke
> > and they *died*
> Broke. Most of 'em. And after the tractor ate the horse—
> It ate *them*. Most of 'em. And now, a few lean years,
> And the banks will have it again. Most of it. Why, hellfar,
> Once a family could live on a quarter and now a hull section won't do! (p.197)

Disastrous economic policy has cleared the land for a weaponry of global destruction. The point of McGrath's topography begins to be clear, and reveals the sweep of his poetic enterprise. As E. P. Thompson says: "If Dakota were to secede from the United States it would be, with its battery of Minutemen, the third most powerful nuclear state in the world."[16] He isn't joking. As recently as 1985, the nuclear count in McGrath's part of the country stood this way:

North Dakota ranks 3d with 1510 nuclear warheads deployed and 10th with 19 facilities in the nuclear infrastructure. It houses two main SAC bases, Grand Forks AFB and Minot AFB, both housing a B-52 bomber wing as well as a Minuteman missile wing, two of only three such bases in the world.[17]

That North Dakota, one of the first and firmest of our populist states, one of the few places in America where democracy was more than a sham of consensus—that North Dakota should now bear the brunt of our nuclear arsenal is an irony replete with American consequence. McGrath's sense of Indian genocide as the nation's first "wound" suggests that our prevailing culture might really re-enact the country's primal scene, that the Original Sin of the Republic permits more recent evils like Hiroshima, Vietnam, or death-squad governance in our Latin vassal states. The Battle of Wounded Knee, which eliminated the Sioux nation and ended our "Indian Wars," would be replayed in whiteface with the defeat of rural populism, and then replayed again, this time in the noface of nuclear weaponry taking control of the land. These are events of national magnitude, but *in the same place?* Three stages of destiny inflicted one on top of another in McGrath's own neighborhood? Searching throughout *Letter* for examples of "the wrong turn," moments when the American dream went bad, McGrath has concrete reasons for saying "Dakota is everywhere."

But he is even more concerned with moments when the nation's dream was decently realized. At the heart of *Letter to an Imaginary Friend* beats the rhythm of work in the rural countryside of McGrath's youth, reminding us how narrow our habitual poetics has been. The theme of work has been indispensable to the nation's sense of itself, but in our poetry it has seldom appeared. One can go back to Whitman, in a vague sort of way, and Gary Snyder's celebration of work has been exemplary—almost a poetics in itself. Some of Frost's New England pieces, and Philip Levine's vision of Detroit, have taken work seriously. More recently, feminist poets, Adrienne Rich among them, have insisted on the theme of work, in particular the thankless labors necessary to life of the body. Apart from these, however, McGrath is alone in his insistence on the primacy of work to American experience.

He is most concerned with the community-creating aspect of work— the "erotics of labor," if I might put it so, having in mind the notion of Eros as the binding energy shaping social units into larger and larger productive wholes. There were, for example, the work teams that assembled haphazard every fall for harvest, matter on the face of it unpromising, but from which McGrath takes moments of real and mythical beauty. In Part Two, Section IV, there are a number of episodes from the earth-bound world of that time, some of which I quote below, starting with a barnyard version of *in principio*. Note the active character of McGrath's wordplay, and then the multiple destinies within a common fate:

> Morning stirring in the haymow must: sour blankets,
> Worn bindles and half-patched soogans of working bundle-stiffs
> Stir:
>   Morning in the swamp!
>   I kick myself awake
> And dress while around me the men curse for the end of the world.
>
> And it *is* ending (half-past-'29) but we don't know it
> And wake without light.
>   Twenty-odd of us—and very odd,
> Some.
>   One of the last of the migrant worker crews
> On one of the last steam threshing rigs.
>   Antedeluvian
> Monsters, all.
>   Rouse to the new day in the fragrant

Barnloft soft hay-beds: wise heads, grey;
And gay cheechakos from Chicago town; and cranky Wobblies;
Scissorbills and homeguards and grassgreen wizards from the playing fields
Of the Big Ten: and decompressed bankclerks and bounty jumpers
Jew and Gentile; and the odd Communist now and then
To season the host.
                    Stick your head through the haymow door—
Ah!
    A soft and backing wind: the Orient red
East. And a dull sky for the first faint light and no sun yet.

4:30. Time to be moving.   (p.160)

The scene as a whole is the last of America's unfallen moments, before the flood but with the Crash of '29 on its way. The men don't see what's arriving and yet they do not seem lost; "without light" they may be, but with the wind for "backing" and the "new day" coming at them out of the "red / East." And it's no accident that the Crash comes now, at *this* time of the year. When McGrath says Dakota is everywhere, let us not forget that the Depression—which in the long run allowed Hitler to come to power and World War II to transpire and the nuclear order to rise from those ashes—let us keep in mind how much the economy owed its instability to the inequities of the market and then in particular to the financial crisis, every autumn, as western banks put too much strain on eastern banks for loans to process the buying, shipping, selling and profit-taking for the year's harvest.

But here the Fall has not yet occurred, and McGrath goes on to depict his boyhood's descent into a "green" world of purely animal existence, a prelapsarian realm recalling Whitman's praise for dumb and placid beasts. Here is the still unfallen earth-world of animals as McGrath recalls it from his youth:

                  Into the barnfloor dark
I drop down the dusty Jacob's ladder, feeling by foot,
The fathomless fusty deep and the sleepy animal night
Where the horses fart, doze, stomp: teams of the early
Crewmen: strawmonkey, watermonkey (myself) and the grain haulers.
They snort and shift, asleep on their feet.
                                I go, carefully,
Down the dung-steamy ammonia-sharp eye-smarting aisle
Deadcenter: wary of kickers, light sleepers and vengeful wakers.

A sleep of animals!
              Almost I can enter:
                        where all is green [. . . .] (p.161)

The barn with its "aisle" becomes a holy place. But to enter the green world's hush, and then to sense its otherness, is directly to recoil at humankind's intrusion, as the imperatives of work tie man to beast and beast to man. And thus the moment of the green world's fall:

                    But, in the world
Of work and need that sacred image fails.
                    Here,
Fallen, they feed and fast and harrow the man-marred small acres
Dull; and dulled.
                    Alas, wild hearts, we have you now:
—Old plugs
        hayburners
                crowbait
                    bonesack
                        —Hail!   (pp.161–62)

The longer passage I've been quoting is pure McGrath in its substance of praise and sympathy, in its wide range of line-play and then the way language levels mingle and weld into a spacious diction that is slangy, sacral, traditional and nonce, with the universality of ancient pastoral images alongside grassroots patois that only a namer could know— having grown up, as McGrath did, on the strength in names such as *crowbait, bonesack, hayburner*, ambivalent terms that curse and bless at once, thick with echoes of pathos and fate.

There are many passages in *Letter* devoted to scenes of physical labor and to the theme of communal order that work inspires. The finest of these occurs early in the poem—the whole of Section III in Part One. I would like to suggest, moreover, that this long episode constitutes the poem's primal scene or center. Section III opens out of childhood's sleep, with the call of the steam-driven thresher usurping the mother's call—no soothing voices of nurse and stream, as in Wordsworth, but the blast and clamor of a vast machine. On this day, during the harvest season of McGrath's ninth year, the bitter knowledge of work and politics begins:

Out of the whirring lamp-hung dusk my mother calls.
From the lank pastures of my sleep I turn and climb,
From the leathery dark where the bats work, from the coasting
High all-winter all-weather christmas hills of my sleep.
And there is my grandfather chewing his goatee,
Prancing about like a horse. And the drone and whir from
        the fields
Where the thresher mourns and showers on the morning stillness
A bright fistful of whistles.   (p.11)

175

The field teams are short a man and the boy must take his place. There is, moreover, greater urgency in this moment than might at first appear. Harvest is each year's season of crisis, the time of time running out with all life governed by the twin gods of machinery and the sky:

The machine is whistling its brass-tongued rage and the jack-booted weathers of autumn
Hiss and sing in the North.
The rains are coming, the end of the world
Is coming.   (p.11)

If the rains come, if the harvest fails, the end of *this* world is certain; the banks will foreclose and the farm will be lost. Thus a child steps into a man's job "too soon, too young," with no allowance for playful rites of passage:

                                            Aloft on the shaking deck,
                Half blind and deafened in the roaring dust,
                On the heaving back of the thresher,
                My neck blistered by sun and the flying chaff, my clothes
                Shot full of thistles and beards, a gospel itch,
                Like a small St. Stephen, I turned the wheel of the blower
                Loading the straw-rack.
                The whistle snapped at my heels: in a keening blizzard
                Of sand-burrs, barley-beards and beggars-lice, in a red thunder
                Where the wheat rust bellowed up in a stormy cloud
                From the knife-flashing feeder,
                I turned the wheel.   (p.13)

This is the harvest of savage work and ruthless circumstance described by Christopher Caudwell, a thoughtful Marxist critic during the thirties, whose book, *Illusion and Reality*, McGrath has praised and often cites. Harvest is Caudwell's primary example of our collective struggle with nature, the historical contest that defines reality and social relations. Poetry was born of this struggle, or so Caudwell believes. Around actions essential to survival—chiefly war and harvest—the tribe builds festivals of dance and song to generate the energy, enthusiasm and communal focus necessary to the hard days ahead. Caudwell puts it this way:

In the collective festival, where poetry is born, the phantastic world of poetry anticipates the harvest and, by doing so, makes possible the real harvest. But the illusion of this collective phantasy is not a mere drab copy of the harvest yet to be: it is a reflection of the emotional complex involved in the fact that man must stand in a certain relation to others and to the harvest, that his instincts must be adapted in a certain way to Nature and other men, to make the harvest possible.[18]

176

Caudwell argues that ancient harvest was poetry's first occasion, that art mediates, collectively, the ceaseless struggle between need and reality. His stress is on *need*, not on *desire* merely. And no need is stronger or more often in jeopardy than feeding the tribe—true even now, as famine sweeps the sub-Sahara or, during the Reagan era, as the American family farm goes down the drain, some 3,000 lost per month as I write. Caudwell claims that poetry in a festival setting gives—or did once give—humankind the heart and communal will to work in common and accomplish urgent tasks.

One sees that Caudwell's ideas would be useful to McGrath, for whom the harvest, in boyhood experience, had been both traumatic and exalting. One sees also the fine result as McGrath goes on, in Section III, to write a twenty-two-line stanza that mixes festive mood and gritty detail into a superlative image of harvest with the threshing rig at its center:

> Feathered in steam like a great tormented beast
> The engine roared and laughed, dreamed and complained,
> And the pet-cocks dripped and sizzled; and under its fiery gut
> Stalactites formed from the hand-hold's rheumy slobbers.
> —Mane of sparks, metallic spike of its voice,
> The mile-long bacony crackle of burning grease!
> There the engineer sat, on the high drivers,
> Aloof as a God. Filthy. A hunk of waste
> Clutched in one gauntleted hand, in the other the oil can
> Beaked and long-necked as some exotic bird;
> Wreathed in smoke, in the clatter of loose eccentrics.
> And the water-monkey, back from the green quiet of the river
> With a full tank, was rolling a brown quirrly
> (A high school boy) hunkered in the dripping shade
> Of the water-tender, in the tall talk and acrid sweat
> Of the circle of spitting stiffs whose cloud-topped bundle-racks
> Waited their turns at the feeder.
> And the fireman: goggled, shirtless, a flashing three-tined fork,
> Its handle charred, stuck through the shiny metallic
> Lip of the engine, into the flaming, smoky
> Fire-box of its heart.
> Myself: straw-monkey. Jester at court.   (p.14)

The threshing machine with its steam engine is at the heart of the scene, or rather *is* the scene. And what a vast thing it is. In the fifties, when McGrath began *Letter*, there were still threshing machines to be seen, belt-driven by combustion engines. Even these were mammoth, but the earlier steam-driven threshers were by all accounts awesome—and dangerous too, as Willa Cather reminds us in *My Antonia*. In Mc-

Grath's rendering, however, the dread machine possesses festive features; it laughs and dreams and complains. It slobbers like a monstrous animal with sparks for a mane. Its voice is a steam whistle, always described in metallic images, signalings a boy might take to heart. Clearly McGrath *likes* machines, the threshing rig first of all. Machines are the primary site for the world of work, and this one stands in union with the land like a blessed and blessing monster—"its whistling brass commandments" amid "the barb-tongued golden barley and the tents of the biblical wheat."

Those who work the rig take from it even identity—names like water-monkey, straw-monkey, spike-pitcher—carnival figures ranged from mock-God to mock-devil, in this case a dirty engineer and a fireman armed with a pitchfork. To dwell on these images, so grotesque and accurate ("Aloof as a God. Filthy. A hunk of waste"), is to see what's meant by suggesting, as I shall in a moment, that McGrath's later style is *carnivalesque*. He creates a monstrosity of a world, brimming with abundance and unruly beauty, full of ambivalent names and exaggerated figures, set forth in language that brings "down to earth" all that would otherwise be fearful or official, a communal world seething with energy. And over all of it, the straw-monkey poet as "Jester at court."

Once the boy begins his job in the fields, even dreaming is occupied by the threshing rig: "the whistle biting my ears, / The night vibrating, / In the fog of the red rust, steam, the rattle of concaves"—becoming a permanent part of McGrath's imaginative world:

> So, dawn to dusk, dark to dark, hurried
> From the booming furious brume of the thresher's back
> To the antipodean panting engine. Caught in the first
> Circle.   (p.14)

Hell's first circle, of course, one of *Letter*'s many echoes of Dante. But also the circle to be transformed into commune and round dance. The boy's overriding desire is to work his way into manhood, to go as an equal in the circle of men who run the rig and move the grain. Impossible, of course, for a child of nine years; he can be a "man to the engine's hunger, to the lash of the whistle," but not to the young toughs, the old-timers, or to his uncle who is "boss of the rig." His luck is to have a mentor: "Cal, one of the bundle teamsters, / My sun-blackened Virgil," who would teach him to take his time, not grow too fast, a field hand whom McGrath calls a "good teacher, a brother." The figure of Cal becomes one of the tutelary spirits of *Letter*, a quiet man aged about thirty, with a "brick-topped mulish face," who reads The *Industrial Worker* and is one of "the last of the real Wobs." Initiation into the world of work will thus be compounded by a bitter first taste of politics. When Cal leads the men against McGrath's uncle, any notion of rural romanticism—the spacious skies and amber grain of our collective pastoral fantasy—is dispelled from McGrath's view of the heartland:

> We were threshing flax I remember, toward the end of the run—
> After quarter-time I think—the slant light falling
> Into the blackened stubble that shut like a fan toward the headland—
> The strike started then.   (p.18)

Cal speaks for the men, is cursed by McGrath's uncle; a fight starts between them and the boy is appalled:

> I heard their gruntings and strainings
> Like love at night or men working hard together,
> And heard the meaty thumpings, like beating a grain sack
> As my uncle punched his body—I remember the dust
> Jumped from his shirt.   (p.18)

This is Eden invaded by real-world conflict, a primary instance of political intrusion. What happens next is remarkable and signals the coming together of two voices, McGrath's and the metallic blast of the rig. Shaken by the violence, the boy runs in anger to the idling machine and tries to throw it into gear:

> And the fireman came on a run and grabbed me and held me
> Sobbing and screaming and fighting, my hand clenched
> On the whistle rope while it screamed down all of our noises—
> Stampeding a couple of empties into the field—
> A long, long blast, hoarse, with the falling, brazen
> Melancholy of engines when the pressure's falling.   (p.19)

Here, it seems to me, McGrath allies himself *with* the voice of the machine. Then directly after the drama of the fight comes a long lyrical expanse of the poem (nearly three pages) in which the boy goes off toward the river, alone in the gathering dusk:

> Green permission . . .
>   Dusk of the brass whistle . . .
> Gooseberry dark.
> Green moonlight of willow.
> Ironwood, basswood and the horny elm.
> June berry; box-elder; thick in the thorny brake

The black choke cherry, the high broken ash and the slick
White bark of poplar.
                              I called the king of the woods,
The wind-sprung oak.
                              I called the queen of ivy,
Maharani to his rut-barked duchies;
Summoned the foxgrape, the lank woodbine,
And the small flowers; the wood violets, the cold
Spears of the iris, the spikes of the ghostflower—
It was before the alphabet of trees
Or later.
                              Runeless I stood in the green rain
Of the leaves.
        Waiting.   (p.20)

He enters the "green world," hoping for contact with peace at life's
heart. Instead, "under the hush and whisper of the wood, / I heard the
echoes of the little war" as hawk and mink go about their separate hunts.
Later he goes for a swim and "under the river the silence was humming,
singing." Finally his grief breaks into weeping and he encounters for the
first time the burden of the mystery, the gore amid grandeur of life's
rapacious innocence. He hears "the night hawk circling," but also the
"comfort of crickets and a thrum of frogs." For the first time, the horror
and the glory exist together:

        The crickets sang. The frogs
        Were weaving their tweeds in the river shallows.

        Hawk swoop.
                    Silence.
                                        Singing.
        The formal calls of a round-dance.
        This riddling of the river-mystery I could not read.   (p.22)

This is, I think, the primal figuration in McGrath's poetry, this coming
together of violence and harmony in ways that serve to keep his knowl-
edge of class conflict and his vision of communal oneness united. Ameri-
can pastoral is ersatz without its historical disruptions; at the same time,
political violence cannot be redeemed—or perhaps even borne—without
the festive dream of pastoral solidarity. When, finally, the boy returns to
the farmyard his father is kneeling in the dust, fixing a harness by
lantern light outside the barn—his gesture of atonement to Cal lying
hurt inside:

180

"Hard lines, Tom," he said. "Hard lines, Old Timer."
I sat in the lantern's circle, the world of men,
And heard Cal breathe in his stall.

                                An army of crickets

Rasped in my ear.

                            "Don't hate anybody."

My father said.   (p.23)

All unexpected, this has been the passage into manhood; that same night the men leave in "a rattle of Fords." The harvest is ended, far from the spirit of festival that for a moment emerged. Referring to the strike in the fields, McGrath concludes by letting the momentum of his narrative carry him forward in time, in jumps of quick transition that anchor other of the poem's episodes and voices in this one strong incident—as if what had just happened were opening remembrance into the future:

                      They had left Cal there
In the bloody dust that day but they wouldn't work after that.
"The folded arms of the workers" I heard Warren saying,
Sometime in the future where Mister Peets lies dreaming
Of a universal voting-machine.

                         And Showboat
Quinn goes by (New York, later) "The fuckin' proletariat
Is in love with its fuckin' chains. How do you put this fuckin'
Strike on a cost-plus basis?"   (pp. 23–24)

The condition of the workers—their will to join ranks, their fear and hesitation—is seen both in the episode of the strike and again in the voices at the end of Section III, a raucous outburst cut short by a tone growing somber and quieting out. What happens, in these last fading lines, links the pioneer dream (populist) to the newer vision of justice (socialist). Both are tangled in violence, both rooted in the meaning of the West and with the lofty, meat-eating hawk for an emblem:

"The folded arms of the workers."
I see Sodaberg
Organizing the tow boats.

                         I see him on Brooklyn Bridge,
The fizzing dynamite fuse as its drops on the barges.
Then Mac with his mournful face comes round the corner
(New York) up from the blazing waterfront, preaching
His strikes.

              And my neighbors are striking on Marsh Street.
(L.A., and later)

                     And the hawk falls.

A dream-borne singing troubles my still boy's sleep
In the high night where Cal had gone:
                              They came through
The high passes, they crossed the dark mountains
In a month of snow.
Finding the plain, the bitter water, the iron
Rivers of the black north . . .

Hunters

                              in the high plateaus of that country . . .

Climbing toward sleep . . .

But far

                    from the laughter.   (p.24)

   And there, no doubt, McGrath stood: far from the laughter but in
sight of the mystery—a burden to be shouldered and, somehow, made
light of. And finally that's what happens: McGrath goes on to make
light of the sorrowing world by a laughter that brings it down to earth.
This notion of making-light-of, moreover, is not an easy pun but the key
to McGrath's remarkable combination of contrary states, Marxist mate-
rialism and Catholic sacramentalism on the one hand, historical neces-
sity and frontier freedom on the other, and then his serious recovery of
the American dream to be carried out, more and more as works pro-
gress, by comic means.

McGrath's importance as a poet resides partly in the political themes to
which he bears witness, and partly in the way he deploys language to
purge and reconfirm the nation's historical program. He introduces,
gradually, a jocular spirit composed of praises and curses together. He
envisions the human predicament as an extended Feast of Fools and
himself as the "Jester at Court." Drawing on old-world traditions, he
turns to the rites of festival and feast day, and takes up a carnival style.
And always his choices have political as well as poetic implications. Here
is a humor no hierarchy can digest or tolerate. Nor can any imposition
stamp it out. When this sort of laughter takes effect, "the great night and
its canting monsters turn[s] holy around [us]. / Laughably holy." Mc-
Grath possesses a comic charity that precludes *hysterica passio*, but also a
grotesque, expansive laughter tuned to the Stevensian notion of imagi-
nation as a "violence within" that pushes back against the world intrud-
ing. The name for this—the carnivalesque—derives from Mikhail

Bakhtin, the Russian theorist for whom laughter, precisely in its most rampant, freely ruthless mood, is "the world's second truth," and whose book on Rabelais is central to my sense of the comic spirit as I find it in McGrath.[19]

In *Letter*, the first sign of carnival comes early, in Section I of Part One, where McGrath turns to the matter of his family. At age five he ran away from home, as children will. He says he has never been back; but says also he "never left." Running from family, he took them along and "had the pleasure of their company":

> Took them? They came—
> Past the Horn, Cape Wrath, Oxford and Fifth and Main
> Laughing and mourning, snug in the two seater buggy,
> Jouncing and bouncing on the gumbo roads
> Or slogging loblolly in the bottom lands—
> My seven tongued family. [. . .]
>
> Conched in cowcatchers, they rambled at my side.
> The seat of the buggy was wider than Texas
> And slung to the axles were my rowdy cousins;
> Riding the whippletrees: aunts, uncles, brothers,
> Second cousins, great aunts, friends and neighbors
> All holus-bolus, piss-proud, all sugar-and-shit
> A goddamned gallimaufry of ancestors.
> The high passes?
> Hunter of the hornless deer?   (pp. 3–4)

Excess and exaggeration are primary signs of carnival style. As a diction, the lines above might be called the magnified colloquial, a colorful popular idiom found almost anywhere (at one time) in rural America, certainly in the middle south and heartland plains, where people slog over gumbo roads even now. Some of McGrath's diction appears literary, like "gallimaufry," and some, like "loblolly," might be archaic, but who's to say these very words didn't come off the boat with McGrath's grandparents. The point about obscurity is that most *spoken* language, the local speech of a place and its spirit, goes unrecorded. When found in literature it tends to be discounted as regionalism and remains "unofficial." For McGrath, however, the unofficial forces in language are best suited for utopian attack against the press of the established world. Terms for bodily functions, the primary four-letter words, remain off the record despite the fact that they have been the argot of all times and places, the core of nonconsensus (but universal) speech. These are the anchor-words of carnival style, and one or more of them will be operative, setting the earthward pitch of the whole, in any unit (passage, scene, grouping of images) from McGrath's later poetry. Often, as in the example above, an entire batch comes at us holus-bolus, at once in a lump. Language like this is in league with the tall tale (the buggy "wider than Texas") and is decidedly *of the people*, even of the *folk* in the American sense of "just plain folks."

The primary "curse words," as they are often called, can be relied on to upset prevailing taste and established decorum, while at the same time they can *also* convey covert alliance and express goodwill or solidarity. This is an idiom that can be used both to curse and to bless, to reduce and magnify, to pull down and elevate. It is, furthermore, a language independent of scene, wording in no way tied to a specific place or time or class or subject matter, language as available and packed with loamy energies as earth itself. When McGrath calls his family "sugar-and-shit" and "piss-proud," he casts blame while expansively showering praise. This part of McGrath's idiom is, so to say, the spit 'n' image of Mark Twain, the first master of American vernacular. Whitman had that goal as well, but only as a goal; and Twain, of course, had to contend with censorship. With McGrath an American Vulgate comes into its own, a *basso continuo* of the populace at large.

The remarkable thing about this kind of language, slang and curse words especially, is that its status as an agency of symbolic action, in Burke's sense, exceeds any referential or descriptive function it might also have. And being "unofficial," it is invested with powers of the border, wickedly alive. One sees, then, that in the questions at the close of the passage above, McGrath has in mind his piss-proud family, but also the oddity of his linguistic inheritance generally. Of both he asks a crucial question: Is this the stuff of heroes? Was it people like these, with this kind of raucous talk, that set out to take the West and make good the American dream? His answer is "Yes" and *Letter* is his evidence.

To judge from the likes of Whitman, Twain and McGrath, to be an American poet is to speak the language of the hard-pressed but irrepressibly optimistic masses. It's at this linguistic gut level that the "violence within" pushes back at the "violence without." To *speak American* is to combine one's regional idiom with the vernacular at large. It's also to appropriate any other language that seems apt, be it learned, technical, foreign, or just the day's jargon. And to speak American is to exaggerate routinely, to talk in a larger-than-life voice megaphoned by the continent itself. In an interview McGrath has said that "one of the modes of this poem is exaggeration." He is referring to *Letter*, and goes on to say:

"exaggeration in terms of language, the exaggeration of certain kinds of actions to the point where they become surreal, fantastic—yes."[20] The element in his style that earlier critics identified as "surreal" is, in the later poetry, the distortive aspect of carnival excess. The result is what Bakhtin calls "grotesque realism"—as in McGrath's bardic image of himself from Book Four of *Letter*:

> And now, out of the fog, comes our genealogizer
> And keeper of begats. A little wizened-up wisp of a man:
> Hair like an out-of-style bird's nest and eyes as wild as a wolf's!
> Gorbellied, bent out of shape, short and scant of breath—
> A walking chronicle: the very image of the modern poet!   (p.81)

McGrath's combination of excess and vulgarity might puzzle or offend some readers, and we see the excuse it affords to deny him his seriousness. But then we see as well that McGrath's language has earnest, even valiant, purposes. *In the beginning is the word, the curse word; the new world starts by getting down to earth.* That is the logic of carnival. Certainly it's the order that governs McGrath's epic poem, a logic writ large in the following example. Out of the depth of the Second World War (McGrath was in the air force, stationed on a snowblind island in the Aleutians) he extracts "a hero" who is destroyer and builder, who gets rid of and creates, a figure most lowly and therefore most high. I quote at length because the following lines (from Book X of Part One) make a typical unit in the rhythm and expanse of *Letter*:

> —From those days it's Cassidy I remember:
> Who worked on the high steel in blue Manhattan
> And built the top-most towers.
>
>   Now on our island [Amchitka],
> He was the shit-burner. He closed the slit-trench latrines
> With a fiery oath.
>   When they had built permanent structures
> And underlaid them with the halves of gasoline drums,
> He took the drums out on the tundra in the full sight of God
> And burned them clean.
>   Stinking, blackened, smelling
> Like Ajax Ajakes, he brought home every night
> (Into the swamped pryamidal, where, over two feet of water,
> Drifting like Noah on the shifting Apocalypse
> Of the speech of Preacher Noone, I read by the ginko light)
> Brought home mortality, its small quotidian smell.

There was a hero come home! (The bombers swinging
Around his neck, the gunners blessing his craft
From dropping their load in comfort!) Him, who on the high and windy
Sky of Manhattan had written his name in steel, sing now,
Oh poets!

But that's a hard man to get a line on.
Simple as a knife, with no more pretension than bread,
He worked his war like a bad job in hard times
When you couldn't afford to quit. He'd had bad jobs before
And had outwon them.
                            Now in a howl of sleet,
Or under the constant rain and the stinking flag of his guild,
He stood in his fire and burned the iron pots clean.   (p.79)

Meanwhile: "Into the gun-colored urine-smelling day, heroic, / The bombers go," and when the crews returned in their shot-up planes "we ran like rabbits down the dead flat road of their light / To snatch them home to the cold from the fiery cities of air." The war, for McGrath, was just such a city of air, a sky in need of clearing and renovation. Between the dead and unborn worlds comes Cassidy, construction worker, shit burner, time's hero—except that he too is gone. Hit by an off-track aircraft, he never came back:

                            Nowhere, now, on the high
        Steel will he mark on the sky that umber scratch
        Where the arcing rivet ends.   (p.85)

An "umber scratch," the color of rust, feces and fertilization, scrapes the sky and maps the next reach of creation. It is the hero's signature blazing the heavens—an image not without its grotesque majesty. Or so it would seem to Bakhtin, who reminds us that "in the images of urine and excrement is preserved the essential link with birth, fertility, renewal, welfare."[21] This is a primary case of earth reasserting its claims against the worldly cities of air; life and the sources of life must be free and uncowed, particularly in bad times like war, when the official world demands complete submission. Then especially the earth pushes back. There can, furthermore, be no overestimating the degree to which the human body is the foremost location of this earth-world antagonism. The body is earth's domain in creatural terms but equally the world's insofar as social-political order inscribes itself in bodily functions through sexual mores, eating habits and excretory rites of the kind over which McGrath's Cassidy presides. To readers who suppose that emphasis on bodily functions is "degrading," Bakhtin suggests that laughter

186

always "degrades and materializes," that "degradation here means coming down to earth," and that in a carnival context it "relates to acts of defecation and copulation, conception, pregnancy, and birth".[22]

The point of carnival — its symbolic action — is to turn the world "inside out"; to pull down ranks, privileges, pretentions; to suspend official hierarchy in favor of a radical equality, wherein everything is laughed at and anything can be said. No power setting itself above the community escapes ridicule, and the lower forms of humor prevail — jokes, puns, parody, slapstick and clowning. In this festive manner contact with earth is renewed at the gross level all men and women share. Consciousness is anchored in the physical foundation of life, the belly and the genitals especially. If this is "obscene" it is also the key to festive affirmation. Crucial to our understanding, however, is the communal character of such references. As Bakhtin puts it: "The material bodily principle is contained not in the biological individual, not in the bourgeois ego, but in the people, a people who are continually growing and renewed. This is why all that is bodily becomes grandiose, exaggerated, immeasurable."[23]

Bakhtin's constant reference to "the people" did not sit well with the Soviet authorities of his time; the inheritors of revolution were no longer interested in their utopian pledge. In America, too, "the people" meets with objection; we are, most of us, torn between our genuine populist impulse and an economically rewarding self-interest that cannot serve itself and protect its privileges while at the same time taking seriously the dream of a country held in common. To point to "the people," moreover, is to summon something that hardly exists apart from the rhetoric of its summoning, especially if what's meant is some sort of inclusive, like-minded group organized to act on its own behalf toward emancipation and enlarged consensus. All the same, "the people" is a valuable and very American idea. The early successes of populism in the West suggest that those who are exploited and powerless will eventually reach a collective sense of themselves. When they do, they discover a courage not available in isolation, a resilience reflected, as Bakhtin observes, in festive forms: "Speech and gesture are gradually freed from the pitifully serious tones of supplication, lament, humility, and piousness, as well as from the menacingly serious tones of intimidation, threats, prohibition."[24] The interesting point is that victory over fear, and the purging of self-pity, are registered in speech officially proscribed. Not only *what*, but also *how* we praise and blame positions us in the world. What this comes down to, finally, is enlistment of the powers of earth against whatever world is pressing to extradite its earthly foundation.

The case with carnival language is not praise *or* blame but *both together*. McGrath's poetics makes no sense apart from this double-edged freedom of unsanctioned speech. Cassidy, in *Letter*, flies "the stinking flag of his guild" and works "in the full sight of God." Blessing-cursing sets the earth-based frame of McGrath's language-field. His fusion of praise and blame then magnifies the contrary thrust of his other key words—"stiff," for example, which is McGrath's routine name for field-hands and laborers. The workingman is a "stiff," a "bundle-stiff," part of "the circle of spitting stiffs." At first it sounds demeaning, slang for "corpse"; "to stiff" or "be stiffed," moreover, suggests victimization, in particular the plight of workers under capital. But the plain "working stiff" can be reborn, can rise again, in the manner of the male sexual member; in which case "stiff" also signifies erection and the generative powers of life. The word is multivalent and perfectly suited to a Marxist perspective. Through work the matter of earth is transformed into shapes of world. At the heart of this miracle is the worker, the lowly "stiff," and one day the last shall rise up and be first.

The extraordinary energy of "curse words" in familiar talk, their explosive power in formal situations, their vigor (and valor) in poetic usage—all this is obvious from daily observation. In McGrath's case this multivalent energy is the key to his diction: in *Letter* there are *no neutral words*. That must be true for poetry in general, but in McGrath's work especially. He is always praising or blaming, often both together. Benediction is his final goal, but first comes the need for descent, the poet blazing a path into song with a curse:

Listen:

Under the skin of dark, do I hear the singing of water?
The trees tick and talk in the almost windless calm
And the stream is spinning a skein of an old and lonesome song
In the cold heart of the winter

constant still.
One crow

Slowly goes over me

—a hoarse coarse curse
—a shrill

Jeer: last of the past year or first of the new,
He stones me in appalling tongues and tones, in his tried
And two black lingoes.

A dirty word in the shine,

A flying tombstone and fleering smudge on the winter-white page
Of the sky, my heart lightens and leaps high: to hear
Him.
    And the silence.
               That sings now: out of the hills
And cold trees.
        Song I remember.   (pp.188–89)

The entirety of *Letter to an Imaginary Friend*, in two volumes, adds up to a total of 329 pages, a very large work. The first two parts, published in 1970, are under the sign of Easter, inside the carnival time of Shrovetide festival. The third and fourth parts of *Letter*, published together in 1985, are under the sign of Christmas, within the time of feasting and glad tidings. In medieval practice, Eastertide and Christmas differed from other modes of carnival; during these two seasons sacred dogma and liturgical forms could be openly mocked, and there was a definite name for this license: *risus paschalis* or "paschal laughter." When one is looking for the formal unity of *Letter* as a whole, therefore, points of departure should include the popular-festive form of carnival, the occasion of paschal laughter in particular; then the underlying rites of death and resurrection; and last the spectacle of earth in endless becoming with, always, a new world verging into view.

Moving from the first to the second half of *Letter*, the change in tone and style is decisive. In all ways extravagant, this latter part is the collective belly laugh of high feasting on ancestral holy days, a comic mode from which nothing is spared. In a commentary on the poem, McGrath has said that the two halves of the poem share a common content, but that in the second half "the method will be wilder."[25] Certainly it is. Whereas language in *Letter's* first half is mimetic in principle, in Three and Four it is joyously antithetical or anti-mimetic, a language hostile to the status quo and pushing for new birth. I have, however, concentrated mainly on the poetry of One and Two. *Letter's* first half, I think, reveals McGrath at his finest in terms of witnessing and his art of lyrical documentation. However, the language of One and Two cannot be wholly appreciated without a sense of its final purpose (its symbolic action in broadest terms), which only comes into view in Parts Three and Four, where McGrath aims to subsume and *go beyond* the historical world, arrived at the edge of apocalypse.

For an epigraph to *Letter's* last part, McGrath cites Caudwell and includes this remark:

> . . . the instincts must be harnessed to the needs of the harvest by a social mechanism. An important part of this mechanism is the group festival, the matrix of poetry, which frees the stores of emotion and canalises them in a collective channel. The real object, the tangible aim—a harvest—becomes in the festival a phantastic object. The real object is not here now. The fantastic object is here now—in phantasy. . . . That world [of phantasy] becomes more real, and even when the music dies away the ungrown harvest has a greater reality for him, spurring him on to the labours necessary for its accomplishment.[26]

Poetry creates images of renovation so real and compelling that we are spurred onward "to the labours necessary." That, I take it, is the political justification for carnival poetry in a visionary mode. It also reminds us of the main point in *Letter*: that at the back of McGrath's epic we find the harvest festival. And at the ritual's center stands a godlike machine that together with the weather determined the pace and shape of life in rural Dakota when McGrath was coming of age. The powerful earth-image of the threshing rig holds the whole of the poem in place and gives us, his readers, an anchor for a text that is otherwise wildly expansive. But who shall receive such a "letter"? McGrath's "generous dead" to begin with, the ancestral part of his tribe; and then any reader called by the poem as McGrath was called by the blast of a monstrous machine in the remembered fields of his youth. The "imaginary friend" is you, me, the whole of the disbelieving world. McGrath calls us "friend" and I take him at his word. For all his cursing and "hard lines," his public stance is genial, outgoing, utopian by nature as well as conviction. In a "Note" on *Letter* McGrath says: "Work, for example, is not something which most poets write about. Also communality and solidarity—feelings which perhaps are more important to us than romantic love—never appear in our poetry."[27] He means to sort his kind of poetry from the *other* kind, the kind enamored of self and self's inconsequence.

When McGrath addresses "communality and solidarity," he is talking about Eros in its political, all-embracing form. This kind of love—call it charity, *caritas*, communal husbandry—is at the heart of his poetic enterprise. Generosity and hopefulness go together in his work, modes of blessing made way for by laughter. With these things in mind, I conclude by citing "The End of the World," published in 1982 in *Passages Toward the Dark*:

> The end of the world: it was given to me to see it.
> Came in the black dark, a bulge in the starless sky,
> A trembling at the heart of the night, a twitching of the webby flesh of the earth.
> And out of the bowels of the street one beastly, ungovernable cry.

190

Came and I recognized it: the end of the world.
And waited for the lightless plunge, the fury splitting the rock.
And waited: a kissing of leaves; a whisper of man-killing ancestral night—
Then: a tinkle of music, laughter from the next block.

Yet waited still: for the awful traditional fire,
Hearing mute thunder, the long collapse of sky.
It falls forever. But no one noticed. The end of the world provoked
Out of the dark a single and melancholy sigh

From my neighbor who sat on his porch drinking beer in the dark.
No: I was not God's prophet. Armageddon was never
And always: this night in a poor street where a careless irreverent laughter
Postpones the end of the world: in which we live forever.[28]

The poem might be read in a number of ways, but in one way principally if McGrath's charity is as steady as I think. The onset of "traditional fire" would be the final Biblical Wrath that even today (or especially today) the Fundamentalists among us forecast. But while Men of God call for brimstone, McGrath does not. The only end of the world is the one we all feel daily, life's senseless silent wasting, its sad predictable blundering that seems, often, too beastly to go on. But it goes on, and while much is dying, much else is coming to birth. The world feels open and closed, final and full of possibility. That, as I take it, is the point of the poem: that once we admit the perpetual burden upon us, we might then begin to reach out, make an effort, work on ways of making light of it and sharing it about. Meanwhile, what keeps this life-in-death from death itself is "a tinkle of music, laughter from the next block." Against the old ultimatum, not thunder and the fall of sky, but the street's careless laughter and the sigh of a neighbor next-door.

1. "McGrath on McGrath," *North Dakota Quarterly*, Vol. 50, No. 4 (Fall 1982), pp. 22–23. McGrath attributes these remarks to William Eastlake, "from Arizona."

2. Christopher Caudwell, *Illusion and Reality: A Study of the Sources of Poetry* (London: Lawrence & Wishart, 1977), p. 38. First published, 1937.

3. McGrath, *Letter to an Imaginary Friend*, Parts I & II (Chicago: Swallow Press, 1970); Parts Three & Four (Port Townsend: Copper Canyon Press, 1985). Unless otherwise noted, all citations are from Parts One and Two.

4. McGrath, *North Dakota Quarterly*, p. 23.

5. McGrath, *Echoes Inside the Labyrinth* (New York and Chicago: Thunder's Mouth Press, 1983), p. 33.

6. For a history of the populist movement in relation to our political culture more

generally, see Lawrence Goodwyn, *Democratic Promise: The Populist Moment in America* (New York: Oxford University Press, 1976).

7. Mark Vinz, "Poetry and Place: An Interview with Thomas McGrath" (July 25, 1972), *Voyages to the Inland Sea, Vol. 3*, ed. John Judson (LaCrosse: Center for Contemporary Poetry, Murphy Library, University of Wisconsin—LaCrosse, 1973), pp. 39,41.

8. McGrath, "Trinc: Praises II," in *Echoes*, p. 14.

9. See especially Sacvan Bercovitch, *The American Jeremiad* (Madison: University of Wisconsin Press, 1978).

10. McGrath, *The Movie at the End of the World: Collected Poems* (Chicago: Swallow Press, 1972), pp. 47-53.

11. McGrath, *Longshot O'Leary's Garland of Practical Poesie* (New York: International Publishers, 1949), p. 14.

12. McGrath, "Statement to the House Committee on Un-American Activities," *North Dakota Quarterly*, op. cit., p. 9.

13. Rory Holscher, "Receiving Thomas McGrath's *Letter*," *North Dakota Quarterly*, op. cit., p. 118.

14. "McGrath on McGrath," *North Dakota Quarterly*, op. cit., p. 19.

15. Ibid., p. 25.

16. E. P. Thompson, "Homage to Thomas McGrath," *The Heavy Dancers* (London: Merlin Press, 1985), p. 324. Reprinted in *TriQuarterly* No. 70 (Fall 1987), p. 106.

17. William M. Arkin and Richard W. Fieldhouse, *Nuclear Battlefields: Global Links in the Arms Race*, (Cambridge, Mass.: Ballinger Publishing Co., 1985), p. 203. The scale of comparison is global.

18. Caudwell, op. cit., p. 81.

19. Mikhail Bakhtin, *Rabelais and His World*, tr. Helene Iswolsky (Bloomington: Indiana University Press, 1984). This book was written in the late 1930's, but not published in the Soviet Union until 1965. First published in English, 1968.

20. *Voyages to the Inland Sea*, p. 47.

21. Bakhtin, op. cit., p. 148.

22. Ibid., pp. 20-21.

23. Ibid., p. 19.

24. Ibid., p. 380.

25. McGrath, *Passages Toward the Dark* (Port Townsend: Copper Canyon Press, 1982), p. 94.

26. Caudwell, *Illusion and Reality*, p. 34.

27. McGrath, *Passages*, p. 93.

28. Ibid., p. 22.

More Questions:
An Interview with
Thomas McGrath,
June 4, 1987

Joshua Weiner

Language and Audience

JW: You've said that the history of all hitherto existing societies is the history of class struggles, and the history of history is language and in language. And, in your discussions of Pound, Eliot and Yeats, you have said that their language generates what you've suggested is a fog of false consciousness. I was wondering if you could elaborate on that. How would you differentiate your own sense of language, and its attempt to empower and raise consciousness?

McGRATH: The first thing is that both Pound and Eliot were defending defunct systems. Pound, in the sense that he was a fascist, was at least talking about a system that was still in existence. Eliot was a much more polite kind of fascist, and I think he was in many ways an anti-Semite like Pound, at least through some parts of his life – and, as he said, a royalist, a Catholic and a classicist. Well, if you're going to be a royalist, you're already looking somewhere else. And he continually looked backward rather than forward. I mean, he could look forward far enough to say the world is a shithouse right now and from this standpoint not likely to get better. But when he looked for sort of scale models of what he might like, he tended to look backwards, to look toward an aristocratic society, to look toward an aristocracy or an elitism of letters. And he looked toward a hierarchical social and a hierarchical religious system, so in that sense it seems to me he was a better spokesman for the nineteenth or the eighteenth or the thirteenth century.

But he had a great eye, and he had a great power of vision of a limited kind – or what I think of as a limited kind – and that was something of great value, I believe, because you read Eliot and you're taking the pulse of that time, the postwar, and actually you're probably taking the pulse of a lot of contemporary times too, because a lot of people haven't got much beyond that. Many of them are still prattling about the horrors of contemporary times—and of course contemporary times *are* full of horrors, but if you can't see any farther than that, that's about the end of things. And that's where I see Eliot as winding up, and Pound too for the most part.

JW: You've pointed to Hart Crane as somebody who suggested to you a whole range of language, and you've also pointed to Yeats and the early Stevens (of *Harmonium*) as people who've influenced your sound. I was wondering if you could talk a little bit more precisely about what it was about their work which attracted you, or about that sound.

McGRATH: It's not just sound exactly, it's also things like vocabulary. Ever since Wordsworth wrote in the Preface to *Lyrical Ballads* about "the real language of men," which is a notion that Coleridge later dismantled, the tendency has been to find the language of poetry in a middle-class speech.

JW: Is that what you call the middle range?

McGRATH: Yeah. Aristotle divided language into three levels: the high style, the middle style and the mean. [Laughs.] And the ideal for Aristotle—and he was sort of proto-bourgeois in some ways—was a style that was clear without being mean. The mean might be the clearest, but to be clear without being mean was his primary notion; and people went on prattling about these three divisions of style for centuries after that. There was very little change. A few odds and ends turned up in the criticism of the middle ages, but for the most part that theory, in whole or in part, went into the poets of the Renaissance, at least the English Renaissance. Shakespeare, of course, broke all those rules, and of course Shakespeare is the ultimate language-user in English. Well, it was from Crane I had the sense of, I suppose, two things: 1) a kind of metaphor that I had only encountered in the French surrealists, before I read Crane, or 'round about the same time (some of Crane's imagery is as irrational and powerful as some of the surrealists' images); 2) his language was not limited to the middle style or to a class language. Nobody can avoid it altogether, because it's sort of the center of things. But in Crane you have slang and various patois or jargons, or whatever you

194

want, of ethnic groups. That's one level. And it goes way on up to things in the high style. This is one of the things that Crane did; so did the Harmonium Man, especially in his earlier work. It became thinned out as time went on, maybe beginning with "The Man with the Blue Guitar." Yeats, well, it's hard to say.

Certainly with Crane it was also partly sound [that attracted me]. A big line. Sometimes it was only an iambic line, but it seemed to bulge in lots of ways.

JW: Was it something specific? You've pointed out *The Bridge* as being more important to you than his other work.

McGRATH: I don't say it's the most important of Crane's poems to me—maybe the *Voyages* were—but in *The Bridge*, Crane was trying to jump out of his own time and into something else. The hell of it is he didn't have the—he couldn't quite see where he was going, and his guide was Whitman, who was a terrible guide, because Whitman went on getting farther and farther away from American reality in his poetry the longer he lived, creating this grand myth of "these states," which did not exist—never has, never will. I would like to think of Whitman as a revolutionary in more than his poetic method, his subject matter, a whole series of other things, but he's not a revolutionary in any kind of political terms, even though there are places in his poems where you can see the sympathy he had with revolutionary aspirations in Europe (like his poem "To a Foil'd European Revolutionnaire," for instance).

But that was there; he never seemed to see it here, except in his prose. There he could see the same thing that's on television now—the liars, the cheats and the frauds. The post-Civil War was a time when great fortunes were made, and naturally—selling sick mules and worn-out blankets and guns that wouldn't fire and everything else to the Union troops—fortunes were founded in that war. But while Whitman lived in a time that was full of all this corruption and he saw it in his prose, it never truly entered his poetry. [Twain's and Charles Dudley Warner's] *The Gilded Age* is probably a better view of it, or some of the things that Twain wrote, though Twain also, since he was always broke and in debt, was likely to temper certain things, and leave things unpublished until after his death. By and large I think both of those writers saw things better than Whitman did, or at least wrote about them more adequately. He kept adding to this great poem—and it is a great poem, no question—but he didn't get any closer, it seems to me, to the essential nature of things in these states as time went on.

195

JW: In *Letter*, the speaker calls himself a "dream champ," and you've talked about how social conditions become internalized, distilled and transformed by language, which is a dream talk.

McGRATH: I don't know—I don't think I put it that way exactly, but I think that'll do.

JW: Could you maybe explain what you mean by language being a dream talk?

McGRATH: Well, it's not dream language. It's got to rely on what's here, because language can never be abstract in the way that, perhaps, painting can, and that music is, since there's no social referent to amount to anything in music, and in some cases not much in painting either. Yeats wrote in a poem, "in dreams begin responsibilities," and Delmore Schwartz wrote a whole book using that as the title, and Christopher Caudwell has an argument that goes something like this: before a thing can be realized, come into being, it has to be seen as possible. And so he sees all of the arts, which were once one thing, in the matrix of magic and ceremony—he sees all of art as coming from there, based on the idea that what it originally tried to do, and still tries to do in many ways, is help a desired state come into being. It can point to the enemies, it can speak of a process in which this might happen, it could speak of the goals, it can offer exemplum, exempla.

JW: Collect people for the harvest . . .

McGRATH: Exactly. So in that sense language, while it's based on the world, comes out of this social pool. Otherwise, we would never understand each other.

JW: In the beginning was the Word . . .

McGRATH: "In the beginning was the Word, and the Word was with God, and the Word was God"—so we're told in the Bible. But I think in the beginning was the word, and with the word the world was born, because before we could even think of a world we had to have a word for the world, or a tree, or a this or a that.

JW: One of your lines is "In the beginning was the world."

McGRATH: Well, the world is here—that's a given—but before it can be realized in social terms, the word has to make its intervention.

JW: You've said that language socializes the unknown, and that we'll have to be understood in language, and with that in mind I'd like to move into the Hopi *kachina* as a metaphor. You've said that in *Letter* the Hopi *kachina* dance is a kind of central metaphor; you've identified the poem as an act of consciousness-raising. And I was wondering if you find any kind of discrepancy between what I think is like the public discourse of the Hopi *kachina* dance, which involves a collective/communal inter-action, and your poem, which is a highly idiosyncratic personal vision. In Part Three, you've even left blank lines which the reader is asked to fill in—

McGRATH: Those are mostly jokes.

JW: —and you've identified that, in a kind of parodic way, as a key to the poem.

McGRATH: [Laughs.] Well, that is truly a joke, that part.

JW: But I was wondering how you conceive of an audience interacting with the poem, when the language that you use and the story you tell are in flux between the collective or representative life and what also is unique in the individual's life.

McGRATH: Well, I don't know. I'm not sure I'm zeroed in on that question. I don't quite know how it relates to the kachina.

JW: Well, in a sense the *kachina* dance is a dance in which the entire community interacts, and whose gestures are universal gestures, so the language of the dance is well-known and is passed down.

McGRATH: I guess the shortest answer would be this: I'm trying to invent a new kachina and a new set of symbolic gestures. That's too simple, I suppose; but the poem is based on real things. It's based on a seeing of life—it's my own seeing, it's my own vision (other people would see it differently), but I *see* this, and in effect I'm saying, "Now you know this much, now the next thing you have to do is so on and so on."

That's never spelled out in so many words, but it's always within the poem. Somewhere I say in a prose note that the poem is engaged in showing the materials and offering clues for a revolutionary transformation, so that the poem in a small way is engaged in making the kachina for the fifth world. And I think that is a project we should all get ourselves involved in doing. In one sense I'm laying out the materials and saying, "Now—since you see this—what should be done?" And it seems to me that these things might be done. Of course the poem is not specific about what these things are. It goes on to take a look at the world in wider terms, that is in the section that deals with the various heavens, and so on; and the future heaven is left pretty well open. The narrator's blindfolded, but he can see a little bit out of the corner of one eye. [Laughs.]

JW: In that sense it's not really a utopian work, but rather pre-utopian.

McGRATH: Well, in some ways; but you can't even say that, I don't believe. It's not utopian. The poem doesn't do what utopians do, that is, imagine a perfect future world. I don't believe in perfect future worlds. But it looks (in the heavens part anyways, and various other places in different ways) at the evils and the corruptions and the errors or whatever of the past societies that we've lived in, it tries to isolate what were some of the enemies or prime enemies of those hells, and then goes on to project something else which has *some* utopian look to it. But the speaker can't see much, and he's told by his guide that what he cannot see his son will be able to see. I don't know, maybe I was too hopeful. [Laughs.]

JW: I'd like to talk a bit about the title of the poem, *Letter to an Imaginary Friend*. Confucian doctrine states that it's up to the poet/sage to apply the corrective where it would be most effective, and he looked towards the top members of society, the upper class. I was wondering who you envision your readers to be, and who is the imaginary friend.

McGRATH: Well, a lot of my real friends have asked me, "Don't you have enough friends, that you need an imaginary one?" But what I was thinking of was people I do not know, will never know—I'm not going to live long enough, or be around enough—whose consciousness might be expanded (to use the old term), and whose desire might be sharpened, and whose will might be honed a little bit.

JW: I thought maybe it indicated a kind of skepticism about the existence of an audience . . .

McGRATH: There may be that in it too, but it's a hopeful poem, even though there's a lot in it that isn't very hopeful, and in general, I'm sort of a pessimistic/hopeful type. I guess in terms of a plane, it would have hope on one side and despair on the other.

Nostalgia and the Real Past

JW: You've written that "nostalgia is decayed dynamite." I was wondering if you could talk about some of the inherent dangers of nostalgia—it seems to have a potential that's been undermined or somehow neutralized.

McGRATH: When I was in the hospital in Cooperstown, New York, I used to get up around three in the morning, and walk around and see the headwaters of the Susquehanna flowing out of the Glimmerglass, which is Cooper's river [see *Letter*, Part Three, p. 36]. Now, Cooper is a nice case in point—he started out by writing fairly realistically in, say, *The Pioneers*, or the one where the guy dies inside the buffalo, do you know? How many names did he have?

JW: The Deerslayer, the Pathfinder . . .

McGRATH: Yeah, and a few others. But in any case those are the main ones—he dies in Indiana or Illinois in a blizzard, after he kills a buffalo, guts it and crawls inside—which makes sense, but I think he's still there when spring comes.

JW: Well, Twain does a real number on Cooper.

McGRATH: Yeah. Then as time went on he wrote the books, as it were, backwards; and the farther he went the more romantic they would be—that's what I mean by nostalgia, when the past becomes sugarcoated and you begin to live in it as if it were more real than the present. Everybody has a tendency to one degree or another to look back on the good old days, and of course it's a fact that there were good things there for most of us, as there were good things later, and maybe there'll be good things in the future.

JW: You seem to struggle with this yourself in *Letter*.

199

McGRATH: I know it would be very easy for me, for instance, to do something like this: to look back and say, *these* were the great revolutionary days, alas they're gone, too bad, forget about it — essentially the kind of thing which to some degree Eliot did — I don't want that, no. But there are heroes in the past, and one of the things about working-class revolution is that our heroes from the past get destroyed by the system. For instance, May Day came and is gone, and May Day is an American holiday, I mean it was established here by the Haymarket martyrs, and not the day itself, but the event is what did it, the struggle for the eight-hour day. Where the hell was there even a single half-inch of print in any of the newspapers about the people who died there? — Spies, or Parsons, the really great one? Nothing, no one ever heard of them. The eight-hour day itself is a thing of the past, now — fought for like crazy when people were working twelve and sixteen hours a day (which I did myself when I was a kid) — and now half of the workers are fighting to work ten- and twelve-hour days because they can't make a living on eight hours a day, which could be done then, and the woman of the house didn't have to work. [Laughs.] Isn't that something? Everybody works — men, women and children — and they're still broke! It's true, there's a little more ease now, that's true. But in any case — I know there are heroic people and things back there, but there's also betrayal, and failures of nerve, and failures of will, and all that. I know that, and some of that is in the poem too.

JW: The speaker of the poem even suspects himself at times, and stops himself very dramatically from moving forward in that direction.

McGRATH: Well, you know [laughs], it's easy to say, "I did everything I could," but if you really think so, you have to ask, "*Did I?* Could I have done more? Should I do? What can I do now?" All these things which ought to be a part, I think — they really are a part — of the existence of a revolutionary — there are no answers to those things, none, until death. [Laughs.] Then you've done what you've could. Probably if you could die on the barricades, like in Portugal — which was sort of a hope that I had when I went there . . . It seemed that the revolution might go forward, and I really wanted to be in one before I died; and I was not crippled at that time. Anyway, it didn't happen, it got sold out.

JW: Is that what's behind the conflation in place in the poem between Lisbon, Portugal, and Lisbon, North Dakota?

McGRATH: Yeah. Because of the two names I put them together, even though the little town I went to in that midnight mass was Sheldon, which is sort of my birthplace, though I wasn't born there—I was born outside of there, but we lived around that place most of the time. I was actually born near a town called Fingal—I think you're probably the only person in the world who knows this now besides me, and I think that's where I was born. It's a great Irish name, Fingal. I'm not dead certain of it, but I was born certainly out in the country and not in any town.

JW: You once said in response to the question—"What does the young writer need?"—"The essential experience of his time, whatever it may be." Do you think it's changed since you were a young writer yourself?

McGRATH: No, I don't. I probably put that badly, but the essential experience that anybody can have in any time is something that will open his eyes to what the hell society is like, the fact that it's a class society, and finally, like the old song says, "Which side are you on?" And he's got to make some kind of choice—it might not be a total choice—but he's got to make *some* kind of choice or he's putting a blanket over his head—it's always a hard choice.

JW: I remember that great moment, in Part One, of the strike in the fields, where your uncle gets in a fight with Cal, and the sympathy and friendship that your father has for Cal, and that first experience of laborer/boss conflict, that also involves family conflict, which must be very painful . . .

McGRATH: Sure, it was. My uncle was my mother's brother, and he was the apple of the family eye, and he was somebody who was thought of as being incapable of doing any wrong. Of course he was a fathead, but families sometimes don't see that so clearly. Later on it became more clear [laughs], but, I don't know, he is somebody who at that time was very thick-headed, and I don't know if his brains ever got thinned out as he went along. But that's the way he was then, and it was certainly difficult for my father, because my mother had been brought up to think that her brother was a kind of a paragon; and my father, because he had been out to be a lumberjack, and this, that and the other, there was always, I suppose—although I wasn't truly aware of it at the time—I think there must have been a certain kind of looking askance at him, especially because of his associations with people, and the people he hired and his politics. Not that he was a wild-eyed revolutionary, but he had brought back some things from the woods, some of them Wobbly things. And I remember, I think it was in 1940, he voted Communist [laughs]—probably the only farmer out there who did. He was a marvelous man, and he did more to teach me something about writing and poetry than anybody else in my life. My mother was great, too, but in a different kind of way.

Religion

McGRATH: I was raised as a Catholic. I was some kind of believer when I made my first communion at seven. Not a fervent one, I think, but I didn't have anything to put in opposition, I just had a sense that something had to be wrong in a universe when a god that was defined by the Baltimore Catechism—I think that's what we had—as all-knowing, all-powerful and all-loving, could allow the horrors of the world. I guess I probably put it to myself something like this: that it was hard to believe in a god that I couldn't think of as being better than I was—I think that's the real crux. By the time that I was confirmed, and I was confirmed at about thirteen, I was an atheist, but I wasn't a professing one *in my family* because I didn't want to hurt my mother. My father, I don't know exactly where he was at, but he was not—I suppose he was a skeptic who went to church because my mother did, and he loved her a great deal, and so did all of us. I think only one of us remained a Catholic in the family, but I was the first one on the outside of it. Nevertheless I was very, very much influenced by the liturgy of the church. I thought it was very, very beautiful, and, I don't know, it's a thing that's remained with me in a lot of ways.

We can't avoid things like love and death; we can't avoid things like departures, loneliness, renewals of one kind or another—all these things are not religious in any sense, they're a part of the fact that we're human beings. All those things were dealt with thousands and thousands of years before any kind of religion existed, and certainly far, far, far before religion was institutionalized. And while sometimes I might have used religious imagery, because it's a kind of symbolism that I was aware of practically with my first breath, I think the poem certainly distances itself from religion, especially Catholicism, very strongly. As you say, it parodies things, makes a joke out of God, the gods—I don't believe in any of that. I'm an atheist—I was an atheist when I was thirteen and I'll be an atheist when I die. And I am militantly anti-religious, anti-organized-religion. Most of it I think is a total fraud, and graft, and everything under the sun that you can imagine that's bad, outside of upper-class politics. Christ!—religion has been as much a source of war as anything else.

JW: But there are certain aspects of the ceremony that have been appropriated because they appeal to you in some sense.

McGRATH: Well, I don't know, probably so, but I can't think offhand where I haven't put some distance between myself and the religious shenanigans—certainly in the mass. There may be some places where it's possible to make that confusion. But I'm not religious in any conventional sense of that word. I believe that there is a part of us that separates itself, or becomes aware of itself as being separate from bodily needs and desires. Now I'm not putting down bodily needs and desires: they're there and they have a right to be there and they belong. But what I mean is that the body could be content—it doesn't need too much to be content: it needs food, clothing, shelter, and it needs sex; but then there are things beyond that. So in that sense I'm not a materialist, in the sense that I believe that *getting things* is of any value at all—I don't.

JW: Well, while Catholicism is being held in a critical light, Christmas as a season, and the Christ child, are being used as a metaphor as strong as the Hopi kachina stuff . . .

McGRATH: Yeah. Not to make a pun, it's a great hope, in a way. But again and again, it's seen that Christ is not what the Christians see him as. He's the Galilean water-walker, the gandy-dancer, as Cal sees him. Now, as a "holy man" (and I think there are)—that vocabulary owns you once you start using it, but I would agree within the limits of somebody else's language that Christ is a "holy man" in the way that Buddha is a "holy man," and Marx was a "holy man," and Lenin was a "holy man," and there are other holy men—Che was a "holy man." I believe that anybody who wants to stretch the limits of human existence, and who wants to ameliorate the lot of human beings, if you want to call him "holy," that's fine with me, I don't give a damn—I wouldn't. I would say he was a benefactor; a helper would probably be the best term, which is an Indian word for your totemic aid, or whatever it happens to be. That's the way I see these people, but they are around today, here; and now and again we come across such a person.

Politics and the State

JW: I was wondering what kind of distinctions you draw between the American Communist Party and the Soviet party.

McGRATH: I wouldn't even want to make a comparison, because they're in totally different situations. The Bolsheviks were one of the most heroic revolutionary organizations that has ever existed. There are others probably—it must've been true in China, and it especially must have been true in Vietnam. But, in general, there's a vast, vast difference between a party that has come into power, or some kind of power, and a party which has not. And also it depends where any party is located—I mean here it's possible to be a member of the Communist party and not be in jail or be hauled off by an assassination squad—that's not possible in El Salvador, or it's not possible in Guatemala; it wasn't possible in almost any country you can name, including China—read *Man's Fate*.

Well, once a party is in power a whole lot of things happen that they have not forseen. One of the things is that nationalism enters, not because they want to bring it in, but because they have a power base somewhere, and that power base is probably under attack. The Soviet Union has been under the gun since it came into being, was attacked almost immediately after the revolution—by various White Guard aristocratic outfits operating in what became the Soviet Union, by France, by England, by Germany, by America, by, I think, Japan, and who knows how many others involved in trying to do in the revolution. And they picked up a lot of paranoia out of that, and probably with good reason—now they're under the gun with the bomb, in my opinion, not dropped on Hiroshima, on Nagasaki, but on Moscow and Leningrad: I mean, this is a way of saying, "Look, friends." And because it was a city full of "slants, slopes, gooks and Japs," what the hell, expendable, right? I saw the other night some of the stuff that was going on when I was overseas, about what the Japanese were like. You look at it now, it's just unbelievable—the kind of fictions that were created, the kind of monsters that were made out of the Japanese, and after the Japanese, it was true of Korea, it was true of Vietnam, it's true goddamn near anywhere, because, after all, WE are the greatest nation that ever was. [Laughs.] That's a line from Sandburg, the only one I remember—I put it in a poem the other day.

204

JW: What do you think of countries like Poland and Czechoslovakia, where—

McGRATH: They're places where the power has come into the hands of the working class by way of the Communist parties; or in both of those countries, the ruling organization is Communist/Socialist—sometimes peasant groups that existed. United fronts of one kind or another. And it's true the CP is generally the power in those, because they were the main resistance leaders, and also because the Soviets came in and gave them an assist in the end, but in most cases they have legitimate rights. But the thing is, it's like Nicaragua—I was there a few months back, in January—well, here's the situation: they've got these sons-of-bitches on the borders, so they have to have say 65,000 people, men under arms in Nicaragua, and women under arms, to prevent the Contras from coming in. They don't really regard the Contras as any problem—somebody I saw on television asked the Vice President of Honduras what will happen when they unleash the Contras, and the guy, he practically died laughing—he said, if they ever go in that will be the end of them. Our problem is we have these X thousands of armed thugs here—what's going to happen to them if they don't? If they go in that'll be the end of the bastards—so it isn't that which is the problem. What the problem is, is that it was the poorest country in Central and South America—the first thing we did was to pull the rug out from under them. First there was some money—we thought we could manage them— then that was taken away. Then they're embargoed . . .

JW: Well, what do you think of the—

McGRATH: So what I think is this: they're all deformed, to one degree or another, by the fact that they don't live in a free world. U.S. imperialism won't *let* Nicaragua—*or* Cuba, or any other revolutionary socialist-communist country—be free, if U.S. imperialism can prevent it—not now and not in the past and not *ever*. If they lived in a free world, it would, I think, be totally different. But they don't, and they won't for some time to come. So the struggle is still going on there; some people would like to do what appears to be the simple way, lay down the law—others don't, so that struggle is going to go on. The struggle doesn't stop, it goes on after the revolution—it isn't something that just stops—and that's the way it is. And all these countries were poor or backward countries—China; the Soviet Union, which is now an advanced country in just about any kind of terms you want to lay out, had practically nothing to begin with, didn't even have tractors for its farms—and now they're selling to farmers in Louisiana.

But in all cases it's not at all what—the expectation was, the revolution would sweep all over the world, in one wave, as it were, and then there would be cooperation between the advanced countries and the backward countries. That's never come about—it's coming about on a limited scale now, in Eastern Europe, and to some degree in other parts of the world, but it's deformed, and it will be deformed because—I don't think anybody has lost sight of where it wants to go, but it's a hell of lot harder to get there than anybody thought it would be.

Letter

JW: I have some very specific questions about specific things in the poem: what is "gopher light"? [From: "A flickering of gopher light. The Indian graves . . . / And then the river."—Part One, p. 4]

McGRATH: Our farm was on a coulee, and the late afternoon, quite late, the sun would hit the eastern slope, and all the gophers would come out to salute the last of the sun and they would be everywhere, so that's why. It's probably a bad choice, because nobody probably would know that, but I suppose you could say it's the color of the gopher too, as far as that goes, because it's very slant-west light.

JW: There's a line that keeps coming back: "Out of imperfect confusion, to argue a purer chaos," and I was wondering if that was a quote from somewhere.

McGRATH: No, it isn't a quote—as far as I know it's mine. But I think when I first used it I put it in quotes, as I've done sometimes with lines that are my own, suggesting that somebody is my adviser or my helper. We live in an imperfect confusion, and if we can get back to the purer chaos of revolution we might make something.

JW: You write, "I am a journey toward a distant wound"—and at one point you write, "I am a journey toward a distant and perfect wound." And I was wondering what the distinction is.

McGRATH: Well, I think I first wrote it, "toward a distant wound," meaning that I was probably going to end my life in a sadder state than I was in at that time. Later I thought, "No, that can't be—the perfect wound would be the wound of death, and if I live my life right, it will be perfect, a good death, in Catholic terms."

206

JW: In the beginning of Part Four, you say in block letters: "NOW MOVE ALL THE SYMBOLS THREE LEAPS TO THE LEFT!"

McGRATH: *You* know that! [Laughs.] You know what that means! It means: really change the way you're looking at things.

JW: There's a recurrence throughout the poem of the river. At one point you say: "The river is dry, it's finally, completely bearable," and you're always encouraging those who are not free to step free of the stone, that you'll take them over the river.

McGRATH: Well, there's a lot of things there. The first usage of it [that you state] refers to being near a place I lived—I wrote a poem, which later became incorporated in the long poem, but it was called "Return to Marsh Street," which is the place where the poem began. And that was freeway-ized, but one of the things I remembered out of it was the time when somebody had opened the floodgates up the line and some kids were playing in the Los Angeles River, which normally is about this wide [small hand gesture], and is paved. And down comes this rush of water, and children were close to being swept away and drowned. Some neighbors saw this, someone called cops, fire departments, and the rest of us were trying to put ropes on the kids, and finally they did get a rope out, and then we all took hold and dragged them back. "The river is finally dry" is that flood, which was gone—the river which was normally dry was dry again.

The whole place, which had been a magical place for me, the place where the poem started, where I go back to look at what used to be the gardens—all that is under the concrete now, so the river is dry, and water is life-giving, and so forth, and I've always loved running water, and I always hoped to have a little shack on a river. When I got to the place where I could retire I would have one, live there part of the year, get an old van for the warmer climes in the winter. Well, of course I had this operation, and that undid all my life, but if you read in *Movie** the section called "Return to Marsh Street" you'll see it framed. And "over the river"—well, rivers are often boundaries, and there are rivers in hell—and you know when Theseus went to hell, for his friend, to look for his friend's wife, he sat down in a stone chair, and in effect was frozen into stone. [Laughs.] So the poem says "slip your foot free of the stone," and in this poem and other poems I've referred to pieces of granite or

*The Movie at the End of the World

207

rock in which the form of the hero is sleeping, waiting to be released. In Part Four the first circle is underground and there are a number of oblique references to Theseus and to Orestes. It's been part of my own mythology for a while, and I'm liberated there—that's one place where Tomasito enters the poem, really enters the poem.

JW: Is this DNA?

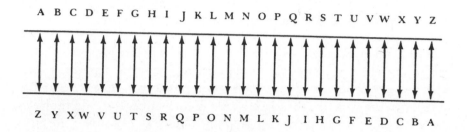

McGRATH: Yeah. [Laughs.] There was a whole two-page schematic, which I wanted to put in here, which a girl had done for me at that time, a very brilliant woman. I had it Xeroxed, and the Xeroxes came out very, very badly, and by that time she was somewhere else for the summer, and I had lost the originals, so I couldn't include it, but it was something I wanted to include—I thought it would add to the texture. [Laughs.] You're very good, because I don't think most people get it, and the ogams of Ogma—you know there's the ogam alphabet, very old Celtic alphabet—invented by the god Ogma [laughs], so there's a reference to that also.

JW: I was wondering what the "AUM!/AUN!" stuff is.

McGRATH: Well, "AUM!" is the mystical releasing syllable, right? And one of Neruda's later books was called *AUN*. Which can mean "still," "maybe," "although," "just the same." I put them together, and then there's the reference to Bill O'Daly's ranchito, the Neruda-O'Daly ranchito. Bill O'Daly translated the Neruda book. But you're probably the only person in the world besides me who knows it, and Bill of course—Neruda, I can't say, he may be watching all of this. [Laughs.]

JW: The poem ends "Explicit Carmen," the song has ended—are you happy with the way your song has ended?

McGRATH: I'm happy with it, yes. I would dread it if something more came along—I used to think I'd write something that journalists call "sidebars" but I would never interrupt the poem again with anything else, though there are many things that I wrote along the way thinking, "This must belong in the poem." I could tell by the sound and, oftentimes, line quality, and maybe even in terms of some the images, that it probably belonged in the poem, but I didn't know where, and when I was writing Part One, that was the way the whole of Part One went—I started here, and I'm writing, and then something comes along and I write it down. I don't know where it goes, but I was confident that it belonged somewhere and that I'd find out. And so I went on and, lo and behold, I found the place. So Part One, maybe more than most, was written sort of all at once—beginnings, middles and ends—at the same time. There were ones that were separate and that I never used in the poem, but I thought that they had probably belonged there. Are we done?

JW: One more question. It's about the six-beat line, with an emphasis on cadence.

McGRATH: Oh God, that's such a long answer . . .

JW: I was wondering how that line emerged as the line that seemed to you to be the most expressive of the experience portrayed.

McGRATH: I don't know exactly how it did. Well, I became aware that I had written a lot of poems in which six-beat lines occur, and more and more it seemed like the line I should use, and in the beginning of the poem there were a lot of six-beat lines that had been broken and brought back to the margin and so on—I stopped doing that. If they were broken, I took them as part of the line. Where did that originate? I can give you some idea. One of the sources would be Blake's Prophetic Books. Another source, believe it or not, would be Robert Bridges's A Testament of Beauty. It's a poem nobody reads now. He experimented with a whole lot of things, and while he seems a very tame poet in many ways, he was very experimental in a somewhat quiet kind of way. And maybe the line goes as far back as reading Virgil.

JW: Well, what is it about the line that was so attractive? What did it allow you to do?

McGRATH: One of the things that was attractive about it was that, if you count hard beats (I'm not "scanning" or anything like that, and I know that "hard beat" begs the question, because what does that mean?—but to me it means something, and that's all I was interested in) it allows me to put six beats in a line, and let almost any number of syllables gather themselves as they will, more or less—subject to my governance—and that seemed to me to give me a kind of maximum strength and variety.

JW: I guess it also allows you to vary the line to meet emotional pitches.

McGRATH: Oh, sure, it allowed me to do that, to write very slow lines or rapid lines, or even to break the line, if I felt like doing that for purposes of meaning or emphasis, but I'm not writing so that the line itself was a unit—I wanted the line to be defined, but I wanted it to be a part of a larger, what I call a cadence, and I don't know exactly what that means, it's not a very definitive word, but it's something analogous perhaps to a musical phrasing of things—so that's essentially where I think the line came from, and essentially what I think is its value. I've been able, since I wrote the poem, and during the time I was writing it, to use it as the line in a lot of other poems that are much more lyrical, and it's become a way in which lines often appear now when a line comes into my head. O.K.?

JW: O.K.

McGRATH: I'm totally exhausted now.

Remembering Tom McGrath

Roland Flint

On June 28, 1989, I was driving home to Park River, North Dakota, for a high-school reunion, and at about mid-afternoon I stopped in Minneapolis. I had planned this stop mostly to visit Tom McGrath, who had been in and out of the hospital for a number of weeks.

Tom didn't seem to notice—or recognize—me at first, and his ex-wife, Eugenia, said, Here is Roland Flint who's come to see you, or some such. Then Tom did seem to know me, but I don't remember that we shook hands or even tried to. He was obviously very sick, emaciated, pale, and small; even his big hands looked diminished, though at the same time disproportionately large for the wasted look of the rest of him. When I told him I had just come from visiting mutual friends in Wisconsin, who had sent love and greetings, though he didn't reply, he seemed to register it, nodding a thanks. I mentioned that the last time I had seen him in this town he was also in the hospital and that I was getting tired of it, and he said the only clear thing I was to hear from him: "Me too."

When Tom abruptly closed his eyes and began snoring, Eugenia suggested that we leave the room. In the visitor's lounge, she told me that a few weeks previously Tom, who was living alone, had fallen and hurt himself; that he had fallen before and was most frail; and that he was unable to care for himself. Some of this I already knew. Tom had been scheduled to lead a seminar and give a reading the previous February at the Folger Shakespeare Library in Washington, but he wasn't up to it, we were told, because he had recently fallen and hurt his hip. (He had asked that Reed Whittemore and I fill in for him, and we did.)

The next morning at about 10:30 I returned to Tom's hospital room. I thought he had declined badly overnight. He was still asleep or, probably more exactly, semiconscious; he was talking, but incoherently, raving really, his eyes closed, only now and then a clear word or phrase emerging from the jumble of sounds. He seemed in terrible distress. I called a nurse and she gave him an injection, and almost immediately Tom subsided into relative peacefulness, except that occasionally he still pulled at his restraints, as if to get at the annoying tubes hooked into him.

I couldn't help but feel a pang of sorrowing admiration that even this, whatever it was to be, Tom was doing, as Phil Levine says, the hard way: like that nine-year-old in *Letter* who, half dead from substituting as a grown-up field hand, refuses an honorable return to childhood; like that ten-year-old revolutionary waiting at the bridge to kill the banker who foreclosed on the McGrath place; and, later, like the poet himself, fighting a world of social abuse while ignoring massive critical neglect. Who has gone more profoundly his own way? — especially in his eccentric long letter to a friend who can only be imagined, one invited by the poem to approach in filial gratitude, recalcitrance, mutual outrage, and joy. Writing *Letter* was also doing it the hard way, because McGrath knew it to be true, on its own stubborn terms — compelled by the mysterious specifications of his personal contract: those of his talent, and his calling, both poetic and social.

If there is a path to writing the poem of one's age, maybe McGrath's career shows the way. What did Robert Fitzgerald say about *Homage to Mistress Bradstreet?* That Berryman "bided his time and made the poem of his generation." Of Berryman's work, Fitzgerald's statement fits the *Dreamsongs* better. (Remember that Berryman always referred to them as one long poem.) And if we change "generation" to "age" it also fits McGrath and his *Letter.* These were the thoughts trying to shape themselves to me, as I stood at McGrath's bedside, and later as I drove home.

But before I left his room, I wrote Tom a longish note, and then his brother Martin and Martin's wife, Marion, came in. We talked, and both repeated something I had heard Tom say a few years before, that he would rather be dead than to be long in this condition. They both seemed to think he was dying, and his brother — a younger, larger lookalike of the healthy Tom, with the same intelligence of focus — was especially touching in his wonder at Tom's having said only a month before that what he was writing then was among the best work he had ever done.

Martin and his wife were very friendly and seemed glad I had come, though they were obviously used to the attention and regard paid Tom

212

by other writers. Martin spoke with pride of Tom's courage in having rallied recently to speak forcefully and well before the North Dakota legislature. Before coming out into the hall to say goodbye, Martin stood at Tom's side, with a tenderness at once familiar and awkward, stroking his brother's forehead, all the while telling Tom to relax and try to sleep. An aura of Tom's family poems played movingly about this scene for me: "Blues for Jimmy," the poems for Tomasito, and others, but especially those passages from parts I and III in *Letter to an Imaginary Friend*, scenes from the brothers' childhood together. I left and went on, as I've said, toward North Dakota. I drove through Minnesota and North Dakota countryside that looked like home all the way, as it would to Tom.

Tom was eighteen when I was born and, as we know from *Letter*, by then an old hand on the threshing machine. As a boy I saw some of the old tractor-pulled swathers and threshers still in use, but the conversion from horses to engines, from steam to gas, from thresher to combine was complete I think, or nearly so, by the time I reached eighteen. Even so, Tom's descriptions of work in those wheat fields near Sheldon have a rock-hard authenticity for me. Though I never worked in the fields on such a machine, I did scoop-shovel wheat from grain trucks into granaries, so I had been in the neighborhood. I gather from *Letter* that the McGraths lost their farm; many did during the depression, including the Flints. When my siblings and I were old enough to work during harvests, we did so on someone else's farm. Once or twice I even worked for the man who had eventually bought my father's farm from the bank. My father worked for him too, as his foreman.

By the age of eighteen, I was an old hand myself, having done almost every job involved in potato harvesting, from riding the planter in the spring to loading hundred-pound sacks (eight-high, labels up) in boxcars in the fall. And during the years I was so involved, potato planting and harvest went through a similar conversion to nearly complete mechanization. If I didn't start as young as Tom did, I did get in on what was then thought to be the hardest work in the potato harvest: loading bagged bushels of potatoes onto the trucks as they groaned in low or super-low down the endless sack-rows, from early morning sometimes until past midnight. During the urgency of harvest people really did work such hours. Maybe this is why I feel a special kinship when Tom refers (at least twice in *Letter*) to his solitary midnight swim after work. For me his whole description of that swim has a rightness similar to James Wright's "It is the good darkness of women's hands that touch loaves" ("Trying to Pray," in *The Branch Will Not Break*), where I see the farm wife, after dark if not after midnight, confirming by her reverie of

213

completion, in the half-conscious telling of this touch, that all is ready for the field hands' breakfast.

The other time I had seen Tom in Minneapolis, it was in the veterans' hospital. It must have been in 1983, the year after Tom had retired from Moorhead State, after a freak accident during his last winter teaching: someone had run into the back of Tom's car on an icy street. Tom said he was signaling to turn into his own driveway, that he could see the guy behind him was too close and going too fast, but that he couldn't do anything to avoid the collision. Now Tom had undergone surgery to relieve pain in his neck and a partial paralysis, but the procedure had been botched and somehow had left him in more pain than before and more impaired in his movement. He was sitting upright, but I think he could not walk very well; and, to correct the errors of the first, he was scheduled for yet another surgery. Still he was very much himself, cursing the doctors' incompetence with his usual wit and eloquence. He was also very much himself, despite his obvious discomfort, in his generous friendliness and curiosity about my writing, my family, and so on.

Now, after this more recent visit, as I drove toward Dakota, I considered that I might have seen Tom for the last time. I found myself thinking a lot about the man as I first knew him.

In the fall of 1971 I was invited to a literary festival at my alma mater, the University of North Dakota, invited to read my poems, to serve on various panels in the usual ways, and to meet with students. The afternoon I read, Thomas McGrath was in the audience, and though I don't remember clearly all the details of our meeting, when I heard he was there I did go—before I began to read—and introduced myself. I had only recently discovered his poems, through a gift from James Wright, whom I had met at the University of Minnesota. (I should say at once that Wright and I were not such pals as this may suggest: he was older, a professor and a *poet*, the first I'd known; I was a very green graduate student. In addition, I was such a fan of his that I think I embarrassed him into keeping a little extra distance. But he was friendly after a time, and kind.) One day Wright had asked me if I knew the poems of Thomas McGrath, and he'd been surprised and slightly embarrassed to hear that I didn't. "But you *must*," Wright had said, "he's a marvelous poet—and he's from *North Dakota*." Not long after that Wright had given me two of his own paperback books by McGrath from Swallow Press; both were signed. One was *Letter to an Imaginary Friend*, part I; this was signed by Robert Bly, who had written, "For Jim by proxy from old Tom McGrath The Irish Threshing Machine *RB*." The other was *New and Selected Poems* (1964); it was signed by McGrath ("for Jim Wright all best, Tom").

214

It includes (just to remind you) poems from *First Manifesto*, *The Dialectics of Love*, *To Walk a Crooked Mile*, *Longshot O'Leary's Garland of Practical Poesie*, and *Figures from a Double World*.

Tom was pleased to hear that Wright had recommended his poems so highly, and he was keenly interested when I told him of Wright's system for keeping track of his favorites in *New and Selected*. In the table of contents Wright had put asterisks, or asterisks with parenthetical exclamation points, next to the poems he admired the most. "Blues for Jimmy" had two asterisks; others, such as "The Odor of Blood" and "Remembering That Island," had but one. "The Deer in the Ditch" and others had two; some of those with asterisks and exclamation points were "John Carey's Song," "The Imperfect Warmth," and "Mottoes for a Sampler on Historical Subjects." "Ode for the American Dead in Korea" was marked with three asterisks. Later I photocopied the contents pages and sent them to Tom. I was pleased and moved to see that he seemed to regard Wright as highly as I did.

In all the years since that first meeting I saw Tom only now and then; usually on visits to my brother David in Moorhead. Tom and I would read each other a new poem or two, and he would always be serious about this in a way that seemed to validate my efforts. He would talk to me about my writing as if it were a matter of real importance, and in general he gave the impression that he saw my writing as otherwise only I did. Once he gave a reading at Georgetown and brought his son Tomasito along. They stayed in my tiny apartment and I stayed in a friend's basement, where a drain-bug got into my ear and gave me a poem. Reed Whittemore came to that reading and, self-effacing as usual, didn't introduce himself; afterward, among the many milling around Tom, getting books signed, and so on, he thanked and congratulated Tom. After a moment Tom realized who had spoken to him, and he hurried after Whittemore. They talked quietly and earnestly for several minutes. I don't remember whether I then told Tom how, some time before this, when Whittemore had been giving a reading at the Textile Museum in Washington, he had departed from his own work to speak of Tom with great admiration. If I recall correctly the gist of his remarks, it was this: Thomas McGrath was so good a poet that had he been either a Marxist *or* from North Dakota, the single eccentricity could not have kept him from being as famous as he deserved to be—Whittemore may have said as famous as Robert Lowell. But the Eastern critical establishment could not tolerate the oddball presumption of Tom's being a Marxist *and* from an amusingly rural redoubt like North Dakota. (Knowing

Whittemore, I guess he was probably more charitable—that is, smarter—than this, but so I remember it.)

Years later, when I was on the board of the Poetry Society of America, Tom's name surfaced to be put in nomination for a senior NEA grant. Almost everyone spoke with admiration of his work; David Ignatow, a past president of the board, referred to Tom's *Letter*, with obvious respect, as an epic of the Plains. There was present, however, a younger poet, a New Yorker of many public distinctions, who snorted audibly at Ignatow's reference. His response, stifled when he saw Ignatow meant it, put me in mind of what Whittemore had said at Washington. It seemed clear, then, that this poet wasn't sneering at McGrath, whom he had almost certainly not read, but at the idea of a Plains epic.

Tom McGrath was vigorous and young in those days, wiry but with heft—the impression partly of impressive shoulders and those hands. He was lean, hard, and handsome in an untended, unself-consciously rakish and go-to-hell way. He looked rather as he does on the cover of *The Movie at the End of the World*, maybe like the model revolutionary, or like what some poet describes as the best sort of leader, a soldier's general: short, tough, bandy-legged, and both feet planted firm in the guts.

What I cherish most about our first meeting is partly that James Wright was in our connection; partly it is the talk we had at a party after the reading. As I now remember it, I had read in the afternoon and McGrath, as the featured poet, had read in the evening, just preceding the party. I have an enduring impression of how modest Tom was in manner and, if I may call it this, in his personal presentation. One of Saul Bellow's characters remarks that the less secure one is, the louder he is likely to play that questionable instrument the personality. None of that in Tom. In fact, if he had spent his life on the farm near some small town like Sheldon or Park River, he might have spoken and borne himself as he did when we met. I can imagine his fitting in with the friends I was on my way to meet, including those who have stayed on the farm or in my hometown. They would be easy in his company.

You wouldn't expect that in Tom McGrath is our master in the long poem, at least since *Paterson*: an epic poem, complete with great but lightly borne learning, complete with references arcane in themselves but set down in a context that explains them without your looking them up; a text implying a writer who is a thorough classicist and social historian. You wouldn't know from his modestly colloquial chat how Tom commands a vocabulary that can send the most learned of his readers to the dictionary. You feel these big strange words are deployed, typically, in part for the music they can make, and typically also for something at once foolish (or satirical) and serious: "Happily habilimented; in paletot, dolman, sagum and chlamys; / In yashmak, in haik and huke, in tabard, redingote and wraprascal / Accoutered" (*Letter*, part III).

To meet and talk with McGrath, or even to read or hear him in interviews, you wouldn't infer that here is the poet most exuberantly in love with language in our American tongue; or that, at the same time, here is the poet with the largest vision of our age. And if he is furious (always partly McWrath to me) about the social injustices of our system, especially the cruel maldistribution of wealth, no first-rate poet in our language has praised more or asked more blessings on whatever there is left, after all, to bless and praise. He has had something more than—as in Frost's modest epitaph—a lover's quarrel with the world, but love does emerge intact.

It seems that no amount of official or bureaucratic stupidity or failure or poverty or neglect can squeeze out of him his loving hunger for the world, and for his country. And that hunger's exuberance gets into almost everything he writes: "Of the living and the dead and the flowering and laboring world we sing." In some notable way, in other words, he has had a happy life. Garrison Keillor tells me that once when he and McGrath spent an evening together—a public reading and then a party—McGrath said to him something like, I think you're a sad man who has a happy life, while I'm a happy man who has a sad life. If McGrath wasn't seeing Keillor quite as I see him, he was seeing himself as I do, and as Robert Bly does, who compares McGrath with Yeats's old men in "Lapis Lazuli": one whose eyes are insatiably avid and bemused with light, if not quite gay.

In one of his interviews, Tom says that he hopes someday others will live in the Hopi Fifth World, will achieve the ideal society, but that he wouldn't want it for himself; he goes on to say that his life has been the right one for him. One finds traces of that awareness in *Letter*, part IV: "This is the heaven I'm not allowed to see . . . / Heaven of Transformation. . . ." Of course, if the ideal exists already, the quest of the poem is moot; and for McGrath the poet, the artist, the quest itself may *be* that fifth world, transformation in trying to transform, in making. No matter how serious McGrath the social thinker and revolutionary, more serious—called to a higher contract—is McGrath the poet.

At that party in the evening after we met we had, as I say, the first of those genially and fraternally exclusive talks between writers that we were to have now and then over the years. I told him I had been suddenly nervous, when getting ready to read, to realize that, though many of my poems were somehow about North Dakota, I would be reading them for the first time to an audience mostly of North Dakotans. (I didn't tell him how my stomach turned over when I was told *he* was there.) He laughed and said, "Yeah, we've got the book on you out here."

Notes, Personal and Theoretical, on "Free" and "Traditional" Form

Thomas McGrath

I

1. "Not meter but a meter-making *argument*" (according to Emerson) makes poetry.

2. But we can't be *argued* into feeling. For that we must be *transported*.

3. "If I had the wings of an Angel / Over these prison walls I would fly . . ." so it was sung. And what sustained the heavenly airfoil? The wings of song. That is: an inherited (though degenerated) tradition going back to "primitive" times.

II

1. In such times all the arts (music, dance, poetry, drama, painting and sculpture—for the making of masks and painted bodies)—were present in magic.

2. Magic was an effort to extend the economy by coercing (or placating) the gods or spirits of the corn or the buffalo or whatever.

3. So sympathetic magic (in the buffalo hunt dance or in those for planting or harvesting) was part of the "means of production."

4. In the era of private property the primitive human collectivity is largely destroyed.

5. Land is *owned*; as a result slaves, serfs, rich men and kings appear.

6. Magic breaks up. On the one hand it becomes organized cults or religions at the service of kings and the newly invented state; on the other hand it breaks up into the several arts.

7. Where the arts become autonomous they become in part (the part that got recorded) the art of the courts and the rich. They are elaborated e.g. dance ultimately becomes ballet or "modern" dance. *Decadent*—not in moral or political terms but in terms of ontogeny and phylogeny.

8. The other road (though sometimes there were convergences) led to POP—so the popular song should be seen as a degenerate form of what was once popular i.e. of the people.

9. Occasionally from the thousands of inept and lazy rhymers and the makers of boring or vulgar music a beautiful song turns up—if it can be heard over the roar of juke boxes and suitcase radios; occasionally a religious prophet appears and is strung up or burned at the stake.

III

1. This suggests that *form* rather than freedom from form is poetry's power.

2. But, it has been argued, the "dead" forms of traditional poetry can no longer be used because they contain (in their *forms*) the echo of the enemy class.

3. It is good argument, and there *may* be some truth in it—but I think that is indeterminable. Anyway consider:

4. Consider Brecht.

5. And consider: no one (I hope) is foolish enough to think that the form of, say, a sonnet is simply 14 lines rhymed in one of the several ways.

6. That is the *external* form.

7. The *internal* form has to do with the way (ways) in which the "content" is organized.

8. I put "content" in quotes because the *real* content (a terribly thin word) of a poem is determined by and determines its form. That is true even when the form is "open" or when "free" verse is used. That is the dialectics of it.

9. Rat poison and good wine can both be put in the same bottle— though not at the same time if you want to drink from the bottle. It's true, too, that bottles are—in our time anyway—industrial products and so the truth in #2 above. Minimal, I think.

10. Again consider Brecht—or Aragon during the resistence in France—or MacDiarmid from time to time. Or—or . . . (Rhymers all, at times.)

11. Can rat poison be put in "free" verse? Who were the inventors of the form?

12. Read the first imagist anthology (and the manifesto) and think of the authors.

13. A POET SHOULD BE ABLE TO WRITE IN WHATEVER FORM THE POEM DEMANDS! (maybe?)

14. Again consider Brecht and (some) others.

IV

1. Who invented "free" verse?

2. Whitman aside (and the King James Bible) there are forms in other literatures that parallel or suggest it.

3. But, for our purposes: Pound, Eliot, (sort of) the Imagists, etc.

4. Most of the inventors were political reactionaries, even Fascists. Why should they smash up the traditional forms?

5. Because those forms—once folk-popular, then elaborated into the courtly and aristocratic—had become bourgeois: "middle class." And

221

all of the Big 3 of modernism despised the middle class: they were reactionaries, "royalists," aristocrats.

V

1. There are 3 Categories of poets:

   A. Cattlemen = aristos: Eliot; Yeats; Tate, etc. etc. etc.

   B. Sheepmen = bourgeois "democrats": most of Whitman, alas; Williams; most of Crane, alas; Ginsberg, etc. etc. etc. Open almost any little (or big) literary magazine and turn to almost any page.

   C. Outlaws = proletarian or allied Social Revolutionaries and classless crazies: Brecht; Joe Hill; Emily Dickinson; Neruda; Rimbaud; Leonel Rugama, and a few more.

2. And there are 2 Categories of people:

   A. Live-O's (Live Ones): e.g. those who come into a very poor working-class bar, waving money and possessed by a desire to buy drinks for the house, dance the buffalo back and overthrow capitalism and imperialism by force and violence.

   B. Mechanicals: computer programmers, paper-hustlers, people who say "at this point in time" instead of "now," media mediums, doctors, lawyers—all those called "dull mechanicals" by Shakespeare.

   C. "People are born Live-O's but are everywhere mechanicals," said a prophet of the French Revolution. But some do remain alive, in whole or in part. (If they are poets, that helps them.)

VI

1. But I don't think it's important who invented the form of free verse ("Vers Libre" in the hoity toity language of the early snobs of the form). [After the first night, the queen says to the king: "That was *soooper!* What is it called?" "Fucking," says the king. Then, after a moment of aristocratic "thinking," the queen asks: "Do the lower

classes do it?" "Yes," says the king. More "thinking." "Much too good for them!" says queenie.]

2. But free verse seems good enough for most of us and, for many, liberating.

3. The cynics have said since the beginning that poets use it because they are incapable of using traditional forms or because their little editorials, impressions or vignettes look better when set with irregular lines.

4. But what of many of our best poets, at home and in the world, who have turned from tight to open forms or who, like Brecht and others, may continue to use both?

5. Perhaps some poems seem to *want* a particular form?

6. In that case, disregarding #3 above, why does free verse — or at least more opened-out forms — have such wide use at present?

VII

1. #3 above cannot be disregarded — a glance at the magazines in any bookshop tells us that.

2. *But* free verse has often been used to bring new materials, attitudes and feelings into poetry. In this century it always flourishes when poets interest themselves in social-political matters, when they take sides, even tentatively or unknowingly, in the class struggle. Examples: the Thirties poetry and that of the resistance during the Vietnam war. A fair amount of this "oppositional" poetry still remains, and some that is truly revolutionary.

3. Another source of incalculable strength and value for open forms comes from the work of Blacks, Chicanos, Native Americans and other ethnic groups.

VIII

1. In #2 & #3 above we are looking at poetry with different immediate interests. What is held in common is a sense of *urgency* and *commitment*.

223

2. When a poem comes to such a poet he wants to send up a cry of outrage or solidarity and it may seem a violation to impose on this outcry a traditional form—now often seen by poets as simply academic.

3. [But here a caveat: Academics and Antiacademics have a thing in common.]

4. So the poet cries out, attempting to communicate his experiences, attitudes and feelings in impassioned speech. Sometimes this works powerfully. *Impassioned* speech creates rhythms which reinforce and modify meanings and feelings.

5. Yes. When it is truly impassioned and when the rhythms are "organic" to the matter. (A vicious fallacy? See Yvor Winters). That is to say "*when it works.*"

6. There is nothing sacred or poetic in speech rhythms as such, and we should remember that most primitive peoples—and most peoples until fairly recently—used languages for poetry (just *because* they were making poetry) which were far from the daily speech usage— "sacred" languages.

7. Even more important we must remember how easy it is to fake passion by imposing a mechanical rhythm on bad prose. We hear this all the time: the Falwellization of cliché. He who has ears will hear this at once, but true believers may accept the fake for a long time.

IX

1. I think what we seek from open forms is—with all its dangers— *immediacy.*

2. Any stanzaic rhymed form takes longer to *arrive* for the reader. The poem doesn't (generally) grow in the incremental way common to our other form. The last rhyme may rearrange the whole poem.

3. This *can* create great power, as in a shaped charge. And we should remember that the great blues makers and the English Marxist poets of the Thirties were capable of creating formal poems of great immediacy too.

224

X

1. For what it may be worth, in my own experience, a poem appears as a kind of footprint—as sharp as the one Crusoe saw or as faint as a ghost fossil in stone—but always solitary and iconic: an image, a phrase or a rhyme that is like a bit of music seeking words.

2. Once I have that "evidence" all I can do is sit and wait. Or, as the old poets said: "Court the Goddess," the muse. I've described this as a kind of magical night journey underground to find the Goddess, present the heiratic emblem that has been given to me and ask for her help. What it comes down to is waiting and attempting to tap into unconscious associational processes to get the next line or two.

3. Once I have two or three lines I begin to feel how the poem wants to be written—in open or tight form and the *shape* of the one or the other. *That is why I feel the poet should be capable of writing in either way.* Of course the poem can be *forced* to accommodate itself to either; and some poets *always* write the poem the same way. Alas. Though I'm sure it is comforting and the process creates "a style."

4. I've written sometimes one way, sometimes the other. While writing *Letter to an Imaginary Friend* in open form, I was completing *Figures of the Double World* where most of the poems are in traditional forms— even though most of these forms were opened or "rotated" a few or many degrees.

XI

1. While working on *Letter* I came to use a loose six-beat line. It appears in a lot of earlier poems but I hadn't realized the range of its possibility. So while *Letter* is open, I had a base. I didn't have to question the length of every line (and sometimes I used longer or shorter ones) but only the speed, density, "music" etc.

2. Something in us delights in seeing patterns in nature, people's lives and in the arts. The patterns need not be as unvarying as those of a particular crystal or sonnet form. Perhaps out of freedom and a chosen necessity we may create that unity of opposites from which the great patterns and great poems will come.

XII

Then there is *language*—perhaps, an even more important question. It seems clear that the middle style is not enough. We need a language that ranges from slang all the way on out. Or, to paraphrase what MacDiarmid said of the kind of poetry he wanted: language that is high, low, Jack and the whole goddamned game.

January 1986

Eight New Poems

Thomas McGrath

Look on My Works!

1

Once I was like a revolutionary party:
The delegates assemble, vote, the Line is worked out;
Then: forward!
Head and Heart have agreed: Ready!
Ready! say Imagination and Spirit.
Ready, Comrades Hands? *Ready*!
Ready! says the Comrade Body. *Let's Go!*

2

Now all's in dispute—I'm like a declining empire
Falling apart in its last days. Rebellion
In the backlands, discipline faltering at the frontiers,
The language changing and the passwords lost,
The chain of command broken, the very heartland,
An uneasy confederation, breaking up . . .
—The Goingunder of the western lands! . . .
Sundown, out there in the far deserts . . .

*   *   *

The imagination, trapped in a burning building, cries out . . .
Consciousness, furtive as the dark, invades the City,
Peers out from fallen temples, from the splendid ruins.

The Black Train

I'm still struck (as when I saw my first pasqueflower)
Now, at a single soft shoot of daffodil, arching, slow,
Through the face of the rock-like ground and on: up: through
The flinty shingle of March-blown sleet and snow
On the winter-wasted ice-bound lawns of Milwaukee Avenue.

Spring was a million adjectives: once: one noun:
All green and milky: furry as pussy-willow . . . sweet . . .
As the blood of maple. But the gleamy stealth of gold in the
        river-winding wood
Blurs quicksand or flood. And spider-silk blinds and binds.
Then mullein, purslane, milfoil, milkweed, dandelions . . .
        tiresome.

Summer wearies me . . . Endless the combers of wheat: gold:
Endless in amber distance. And the endless dance of the
        aspenleaf
Tires. No new word in the mile-long rasp and rattle: endless
Corn-gossip. The grasshopper burdens and the humblebee is no
        friend.
But I'm glad the homeless sleep warm in this landlord's season.

Autumn tires and conspires: draws forth its druggy water
Where the dreamy souls of strolling poets drown, slow,
In their little ecstasies. Troll fire seams the north woods:
Ghosts of goatsbeard false bird's nests of Queen Anne's lace
Tourists divining with goldenrod beside sluggish rivers . . .

Stern winter frowns. A stiffening mortal rigor
Sets flowerheads rolling and the crowns of summer fall.
Moral as death, a white stealth, cold, beards all the grass
That robes, on sunny thrones in its last and desperate green:
        false.
False-foxy all: the green of autumn and the gold of spring.

I've lived inland too long. It sickens me—
Land-islanded. Winter may harden. But spring unties

All icy strings. Fool's gold of summer. Treacherous trollopy
        autumn . . .
No. Enough of this comic death-dance. I long, in mortal
        longing,
For the shine and silence, the flash and wallop of the sea.

Somewhere in that sea, still, on a tide-bound salt siding,
Hunched, a black train halts, sighing and clanking, slouched,
        crafty,
Breathing like a rusty pump and waiting for bills of lading.
The telegraph office clicks its beads and abacus, ticks and
        chatters.
And the empty cars wait for the black train to head inland.

In the Confusion of Empires

Forts become castles
Castles forts . . .

It goes on:
Crenellation
Fenestration
Even ventilation.

Styles change:
Redesigned by
Gunpowder:
By greed by suffering by
Struggle . . .
Rise and fall . . .
Empires
Breasts
Yoni and lingam
Wither . . .

The wave builds
Fails
Falls away . . .

And all the while,
Men, in different costumes,
On opposite sides of the river
Feed the war horses
Of the Great King
Of the Great Khan.

Praises IV

On the Beauty and the Wonders of Women
And Some of the Problems Attendant Thereunto

I wake in the early dawn and my hand has fallen asleep,
(Bedded between her legs in the nest of her sex)
And is dreaming it is a bird—my left and dreaming hand.
And the birds begin: footnoting the long paragraphs of the
　　　　　light
That are daybreak—birds she will scold for presumption when
　　　　　she awakes.
I move my hand. She whimpers. But her own dream still holds.
I drag this dream-hand into my life . . .

　　　　　　　　　　　　　　Suddenly Spring
Fills all the house, the county—
　　　　　　　　　　　maybe the whole world—
With the odor of orchards, gardens, orange blossoms, attars,
Essences: musk, civet, ambergris, frangipani,
Emanations, effluvia, eidolons—volatile oils sweeter
Than all the perfumes of Araby assault my sense and my soul!

My god, I must be Huysmans!—I think I've invented his scent
Organ—or at least harmonium. Next thing I know I'll be
　　　　　writing
Au Rebours, sparking the Goncourts or Remy Gourmand or
　　　　　Gourmet!
And it's Guermantes all the way in this swan-like or Proustian
　　　　　light.

But it's *not* that. It's just ("just" think of it!—"just"!)—
My hand which has come from between her legs where her
　　　　　cunt and my spunk
In the dialectic of essences formed this sacred fragrance
All else sublimed away . . .
　　　　　　　　　　And now it's loose in the world!
Like the hand of a prophet!

And what will the neighbors say?
                              Oh, I hear them
Groan and laugh in their sleep and the street has both ends
        flapping
Like an oversized wig on a windy day as a most un-Lutheran
        lust
Is loosed in the glacial bedrooms of the sensible petty
        bourgeois!
They'll be coming to get us, girl! How can you sleep and
        slumber?
Fuck off, care-charmer sleep, thou son of the sable night!

But that's alarmist thought—time now for Irish cunning . . .
What can I do to save this taboo hieratic hand?
It can't, in the back garden, like a dog's bone be buried,
And it's not the kind of a thing you can take to your local
        bank—
Considering the box it came from no safety deposit system
Will hold this myrrh and frankincense—the Three Wise Men
Would arrive early this year and stick up the dismal joint!
And all the investors would come, and anyone with a loose
        dime
Would start an account—and they'd all, by god, *live* there
Eating from the giveaway pots and pans and burning the tellers
        for fuel!

What a scandal! Copulating among mortgages
And second mortgages: everyone: getting off on the scent.
And they'll call in the Federal Reserve and the National Guard
        and Oh god!—
Annuit Coeptis . . .
                      End of the world as we know it.
                                            And all for
        a hand!
Perhaps a secret account in Switzerland . . .
                                        But then the dollar
Would fall and the whole slave world would have to live on the
        yen
This hand produces without even lifting a finger.

232

It is not an easy problem to solve—what to do with this hand.
It has never been faced before by another living man . . .
Perhaps by sleight-of-hand I can charm it away?

                                    Or demount it?
Then, like a pressed flower, I could fold it up in a book.
Little five-leaf clover from the world's ten fateful fields,
Spade-handed ugly peasant appendage that she has made
        perfect . . .

Excellent! Excellent . . . But what book will I choose?
Marx's *Kapital* comes to mind . . . safe from the liberals
And all econ professors—but what of the Thought Police?
Their sacred quest for the Word . . . anything underlined?
So maybe the Bible—one of the lagered and barbwire books
All *don'ts* and *do's*, the Angel in irons, Mr. Moses Moreso.
But this hand would confound all law: theologic, economic and
        bourgeois.
And just as I insert it (where meat is forbidden) it jumps
Into Apocalypse! Turns to a burning bush and sends
Bluebirds of purest flame to aid the World Revolution!

   Envoi

Comrades, if we had more of these hands we *could* make love,
        not war.
And neighbors: more of these shennhandigans could change
        the world without arms!

Ambitions

The crow:
Coat black as an undertaker's.

His song . . .
Even darker.

He wants to be judge
Of the dead!

In Dream Time

Dear Tomasito:
We talk about dreams.
Yours always amaze me,
Though you've moved out
Beyond the castles.

As for me
I seem to spend many nights
Walking a perimeter of rotten ice
Around a bad break
Where someone less lucky
Just had a last fall.

The Migration of Cities

We love Paris:
   The domes of garlic and Gauloises
   (Where the surrealist poets are buried)
   Rising over the boulevards of hexameters . . .
   And the Parisian girls, ambassadors of perfume,
   Sauntering . . . clothed only in moonlight and nostalgia.
   —Mythic city, capital of revolutionary longing,

   The spectral barricades, built from the blood of the
               Commune
   Which remains forever . . . and the red flag of roses and
               manifestos
   Streaming in a wind of bureaucratic sulphur . . .
   We read the news in the lightning from cemeteries:
   Starshine reflected from the bones of martyrs.

And we love Florence:
   Where the cypresses of Fiesole whisper the name of Laura,
   And the bad-tempered poet: Florentine by birth but not
   By politics: or much of anything else but language
   Haunts the square where little David takes on the world
   And all the marble of darkness lies enslumbered in cthonic
               tombs.

   And further:
   Because the Arno pussyfoots toward the sea
   Under its clotheslines of bridges hung with the quaint decay
   Of cages where commerce lived its bright and blighted
   Infancy and all was for sale: Popes by the yard or the pound.
   And because Florence is a gate to the cities of the Red north!

And we love Chicago:
   Though it hog butchers the world—
   Or as much as New York leaves it. And we love
   The dense cities of Asia with their auras of inscrutable pain;
   And of the Mid-East: the cities of lace and blood
   (Each city lifting above itself its former selves:

Istanbul, Constantinople, Byzantium
Vaporizing into the irrational Islamic skies
Blue . . .
    dervishes . . .
      Koranic agonies . . .
       kismet.

And we love the cities of the south with their moonrise of
    gunfire:
Managua . . . heart city . . . horizon of hope—
Madrid of the South "as of this writing" while the world
          outside my window
Goes by in its idiot clothes, seeking a warmer climate . . .
Tegucigalpa, Guadalajara, Isla Negra
Pah-gotzin-kay, Ciudad Niño Perdido
Salvador Salvador Salvador Salvador Salvador

And I love even little forgotten Pueblo
    (In Colorado) for I saw it once: "shining between earth and
          heaven,"
    As the Compañeros and I rode out on a slow freight—
    Behind a locomotive powered by tequila and chilis—
    Toward nowhere: besotted by wild hope and tortillas.

And still I see the places and the great cities we love
(Landlocked though they may be) sailing out
On the heart-stopping sea toward the Revolutionary Country.
All we need do is cut the anchor chains,
Burn all the contracts and polluted cargo,

Set the captain and owner adrift on a raft,
Shake up the crew and the menu—
And then, the beautiful cities, proudly, under the full sail,
Will arrive at the ports which have waited for them so long:
Ports where the Red flag has secretly flown for years.

Nuclear Winter

After the first terror
        people

We were more helpful to each other—
As in a blizzard
Much comradeliness, help, even
                 laughter:
The pride of getting through tough times.

Even, months later,
When snow fell in June,
We felt a kind of pride in
              our

"Unusual weather"
And joked about the geese
Migrating south,
Quacking over the 4th of July presidential honkings.
It was, people said,
The Way it had been in the Old Days . . .

Until the hunger of the next year.
Then we came to our senses
And began to kill each other.